Gluten-Free 101
Carol Fenster

Photography by
Jason Wyche

Houghton Mifflin Harcourt
Boston • New York • 2013

Copyright © 2013 by Carol Fenster. All rights reserved.
Photography © 2013 by Jason Wyche
Cover image by Jason Wyche
Interior design by Joline Rivera
Food styling by Chelsea Zimmer
Prop styling by Kira Corbin
Published by Houghton Mifflin Harcourt

www.hmhco.com

Library of Congress Cataloging-in-Publication Data
Fenster, Carol Lee.
Gluten-free 101 / Carol Fenster; photography by Jason Wyche.
pages cm
Includes index.
ISBN 978-1-118-53912-5 (paperback); 978-0-544-18657-6 (ebk)
1. Gluten-free diet—Recipes. 2. Gluten-free diet. I. Title. II. Title: Gluten-free one o one.
RM237.86.F455 2013
641.5'63—dc23
2013025612

Printed in the United States of America
DOC 10 9 8 7 6 5 4 3 2 1

Other Books by Carol Fenster

100 Best Gluten-Free Recipes
1,000 Gluten-Free Recipes
125 Gluten-Free Vegetarian Recipes
Gluten-Free Quick and Easy
Cooking Free
Wheat-Free Recipes and Menus

Contents

Acknowledgments 》

I have many people to thank for their help with this book—both the original version and this new edition. A special thanks to my original testers: Anne Barfield, Jamie and Lisa Bridges, Julie Cary, Caroline Herdle, Debbie Lee, Chrissy Rowland, Judy Sarver, Chris Silker, Leen Spear, Anne Washburn, Betty Wass, Cecile Weed, and Sue Weilgopolan—and to their families and friends for lending their critical palates to the tasting process for nearly 10 years. I truly appreciate your contributions!

And in the past 10 years, these recipes have been reviewed, revised, and reworked thanks to input from students in my cooking classes, attendees at the trade shows where I have been an exhibitor, and the many friends and family who have gathered around the dining table in my home. I confess: Although we enjoyed each other's company over those meals, I was also gathering information about the food for this cookbook. Did it taste good? Did it look attractive on your plate? How could it be better? Notice how I deftly worked those queries into the dinner-table conversation?

To all of you, thanks so much for your help. You made this a better cookbook.

I am also deeply indebted to the following professionals who gave me their wonderfully informative and constructive feedback on this book: Shannon T. Bishop, RD; Mary Bonner; Shelley Case, RD; Helke Farin, MD; John H. Hicks, MD; Cynthia Kupper, RD; Betsy Prohaska Hicks; Janet Rinehart; Peggy Wagener; and Ann Whelan.

Special thanks go to my marvelous agent, Lisa Ekus, and her team—Sally Ekus, Sean Kimball, Corinne Fay, and Jaimee Constantine. You have been so wonderfully supportive of my work, and I cannot imagine traveling on this journey without you.

I am also extremely grateful for my superb editor, Linda Ingroia, at Houghton Mifflin Harcourt and her assistant, Molly Aronica. They make my books so much better! Thanks also to Jackie Beach and Jamie Selzer in production; Michaela Sullivan for a vibrant, enticing cover; and Joline Rivera for an engaging book design. Photographer Jason Wyche, food stylist Chelsea Zimmer, and prop stylist Kira Corbin delivered gorgeous photos of my recipes and were a joy to work with.

And finally, thanks to my wonderful family—especially my husband, Larry, for his patience, support, and encouragement. To those of you who don't know Larry, no recipe gets into my cookbooks without his approval, because he tastes everything. If he doesn't like it (and, by the way, he is not gluten-free), it doesn't go in the book. Thank you, Larry!

Preface: A Few Words from Carol ❯

"Toto, I have a feeling we're not in Kansas anymore," says Dorothy in *The Wizard of Oz*. That's how I feel about our new gluten-free world; it's not the same world I entered more than two decades ago. And it's certainly not the same as when I wrote the first edition of *Gluten-Free 101* in 2003. We have new laws, new ingredients, and new techniques that make our gluten-free food so much safer and better. Given all these changes, I had to totally rewrite this book to bring it up to date for you.

But why would I write a gluten-free cookbook in the first place? It may surprise you to learn that I am an "accidental" author. Writing cookbooks—especially gluten-free cookbooks—was not part of my life plan. But life is full of ironies.

You see, I am the daughter of a Nebraska farmer—a farmer who grew wheat. Wheat was a good thing at our house. It put food on the table and paid for my college tuition. After college, I married into a wheat-farming family. In fact, that is all that they raise on their farm in western Nebraska. Furthermore, my father-in-law is an internationally known professor emeritus of agronomy at the University of Nebraska. What is his main area of expertise? You guessed it—wheat!

After I first discovered my intolerance to the gluten protein in wheat, I thought I was the only person on the planet who had to avoid this seemingly healthy food. At least, I certainly didn't know anyone else with this life-altering situation, and back in 1988, there wasn't much information on the topic. The Internet—as we know it today—did not exist. I was in a state of denial for some time, bewildered by this unexpected turn of events that disrupted my otherwise wonderful life. Because the condition was virtually unknown, there was little concern from others, and I was often told it was "all in my head." There were virtually no gluten-free foods in stores back then, so I had to revise my entire repertoire of recipes to exclude wheat. Over time, I met more and more people who also avoided wheat and realized that my revised recipes might help others. Following the old adage about turning lemons into lemonade, the idea for a cookbook was born.

GLUTEN-FREE: NEW DIET FOR THE 21ST CENTURY

Today, 25 years later, I know that I am one of about 21 million Americans who live with what is now called non-celiac gluten sensitivity. I do not have the genes that are associated with celiac disease—an autoimmune condition that affects another 1 percent or about 3 million Americans—but I am still sickened by the gluten in wheat and related grains, so I must avoid it. That is much easier today than it was back then because the gluten-free industry has mushroomed into a multi-billion dollar industry, with large corporations introducing gluten-free products alongside the mom-and-pop entrepreneurs who founded the industry decades ago.

Growth of the industry was fueled by the passage of the Food Allergen Labeling and Consumer Protection Act (FALCPA) of 2004, which requires manufacturers to identify the eight major food allergens, including wheat, on any food manufactured after January 1, 2006. In August 2013, the FDA defined "gluten-free" as a product with "less than 20 parts per million (ppm) of gluten." There is no requirement that gluten-free foods be labeled "gluten-free," but when a manufacturer chooses to put "gluten-free" on food packaging, the item must comply with the new FDA definition.

Adopting a gluten-free lifestyle makes it imperative that we prepare much of our own food at home, not only for safety reasons but also because it is much less expensive than dining out. Beginners need simple recipes—like the dishes they grew up with—so they can eat well and stay healthy.

HOW DOES THIS VERSION DIFFER FROM THE ORIGINAL VERSION?

This new edition builds on all the new ingredients and techniques introduced since 2003 to be bigger and better in the following ways.

* More recipes: about another 30 recipes to give you more choices and more value for your money.
* More whole-grain dishes: Whole grains are essential to a healthy gluten-free diet, so there are recipes for using them in breakfast cereals, salads, soups, and main dishes to help you get three to five servings a day.
* More dried bean and lentil recipes: There are bean and lentil dishes to make sure you eat important B vitamins.
* More emphasis on time-saving recipes: one-pot, one-skillet, and slow cooker recipes.
* More time-saving techniques: such as starting bread to bake in a cold oven, which saves precious time ordinarily spent "rising" the bread.
* More recipes based on store-bought ingredients: such as a simple soup with only three (store-bought) ingredients.
* More small meals: a whole new chapter of "small-bite" meals to use as snacks, mini-meals, or as appetizers to precede the main meal.
* Menus: Many beginning cooks like to know what foods look and taste good when served together at a meal.
* More tips, hints, and ideas for beginners to make

cooking easier.
* A list of brands used in developing recipes for easier shopping.
* Icons that show whether a recipe is quick or vegetarian, plus preparation times for dishes so you know how much time to allow.
* Photos to show you what the food will look like.

Despite these new features, the book remains the same in ways that made it a best seller for 10 years.
* Nutrition information for each recipe so that you can monitor your daily intake.
* Emphasis on a wide variety of basic, comfort food dishes that we crave when starting a gluten-free diet.
* Easy-to-understand directions that simplify food preparation.
* Thorough explanation of gluten-free flours and how we use them.
* A versatile flour blend that can be used in a wide variety of dishes for greater efficiency.

A Note About the Nutrition Information
Although nutrition information is included for every recipe, this isn't a "weight-loss" cookbook. Some of the recipes, particularly the desserts, have a fair amount of calories, fat, sodium, and so on. People on a gluten-free diet have to give up a lot of their favorite foods, so this book helps you continue to enjoy those foods. But you should always strive to maintain a healthy eating plan based on a balanced diet and be sure to watch those portion sizes. You should also consider any other health issues specific to you or your family when selecting recipes and choosing ingredients.

Introduction 〉

The year was 1988. I finally knew the cause for my lifetime bout with chronic sinusitis. My physician had absolutely *delighted* me with a diagnosis. All I had to do was avoid gluten and I would be cured. No more sinus infections, no more antibiotics, and no more laryngitis. No more debilitating fatigue and brain fog.

Unfortunately, my euphoria lasted only until the next meal. As I contemplated my choices for dinner that night, I realized that this wasn't going to be so easy after all. To make matters worse, I am one of those people who "live to eat" rather than "eat to live." Food is my passion, my comfort, my joy. I had to find a way to continue eating my favorites— bagels, fresh-baked bread, pizza, cakes, and brownies—without gluten.

Thus began the journey of what my daughter-in-law calls "discourse, dishes, and discovery" about living without gluten. But I've learned a lot on this journey. Most important, I consider avoiding gluten a lifestyle rather than a diet. It affects every part of my life, yet it doesn't define me or who I am, and I don't think of it in terms of what I have to give up. It is simply how I live. I am writing this book so that you can quickly grasp and easily apply the essentials of a gluten-free lifestyle to your own life.

An Overview of This Book

I specialize in helping people live a gluten-free lifestyle by showing them how they can eat well and still avoid gluten (and dairy). You can do it, with the help of this book. I urge you to read the introductory chapters and **The Gluten-Free Kitchen** section so that you have a clear idea of how to shop for and work with the recipes in the book.

In the meantime, here is a quick overview of what this book contains.

Preface: How things have changed since the original *Gluten-Free 101* was published and how this version differs from the original version.

Introduction: An overview of the book's chapters and the **Gluten-Free Survival Guide** to help you know what store-bought foods to eat while you learn to cook the recipes in this book.

Gluten: A Real Pain in the Gut: An explanation of who can't eat gluten and where to get help. Tips for living without gluten, psychologically and emotionally.

Going against the Grain: A glossary of gluten-free flours for baking and cooking, plus other ingredients and how to use them.

The Gluten-Free Kitchen: How to read a recipe. Comprehending mysterious culinary terms. What you should know about these recipes. How to assemble and use one easy, versatile flour blend for everything. Stocking a gluten-free kitchen. Choosing helpful appliances such as bread machines. Secrets to bread machine success. **Recipes:** Breakfasts, snacks and appetizers, soups and salads, main dishes, breads, and desserts.

But in case you are newly diagnosed and aren't ready to start cooking because you need a little more time to adjust to this new way of life, check out the **Gluten-Free Survival Guide** below. It gives you a few ideas about store-bought foods that you can safely eat until you start cooking for yourself.

Gluten-Free Survival Guide ❯

For most people, finally learning that gluten is the problem is actually quite liberating. At least we know the enemy! However, I recall walking into the kitchen immediately after my diagnosis—and realizing just how many of my old favorites were off-limits. There was food in the kitchen, yet the cupboards were effectively locked. A friend once told me that she avoided breakfast for the first three months after her diagnosis because she didn't know what to eat. How sad and unnecessary! It occurred to me that a simple list like the one that follows might be very helpful for beginning cooks so that they don't have to stop eating while they are learning what and how to cook.

So, here are a few safe foods that you can readily find at your grocery store or natural foods store. Of course, always read labels on *everything*. As time goes on, you will naturally add to your list of acceptable foods and perhaps shift to cooking more of your own food using the recipes in this book—but this list gives you a list of quick options so that you will always have something to eat, even if it is cereal for dinner.

Breakfast

Cold Cereal

Brown rice crisps (Barbara's, Erewhon, General Mills)

Corn flakes (Nature's Path, Arrowhead Mills, Erewhon)

Crunchy Flax Cereal (Perky's Enjoy Life)

EnviroKidz (Nature's Path)

Nutty Rice/Corn Cereal (Pacific Grain)

Maple Buckwheat Flakes (Arrowhead Mills)

Mesa Sunrise (Nature's Path)

Ancient Grain Granola (Purely Elizabeth)

Hot Cereal

Corn grits (Bob's Red Mill)

Cream of buckwheat (Wolff/Pocono by Birkett Mills)

Creamy rice (Bob's Red Mill)

Mighty Tasty Hot Cereal (Bob's Red Mill)

Instant oatmeal (Bakery on Main, Eco-Planet)

Quinoa cereal (Cocomama)

Quinoa flakes (Ancient Harvest)

Rolled oats (Bob's Red Mill)

Eggs, bacon, ham, fruit, hash browns—prepared without gluten in sauces, dusting, flavoring, or handling. Sausage may contain wheat fillers, so read the labels.

Lunch

Cold

Lettuce salads (gluten-free salad dressings only)

Sandwiches (Canyon Bakehouse, Rudi's, or Udi's bread)

Deli meats (Boar's Head)

Pasta salads (Dr. Schär, Ener-G, or Tinkyada pasta)

Hot

Soups* (bean, tomato, Manhattan clam chowder, split pea, chili)

Enchiladas (with pure corn tortillas)

unless thickened with wheat flour

Dinner

Main Dishes

Roasted/baked/grilled meats (beef, pork, chicken, or fish)

Spaghetti sauce on pasta (Dr. Schär, Ener-G, or Tinkyada pasta)

Side Dishes

Baked potatoes

Brown rice

Steamed/roasted/grilled veggies

Desserts

Fresh fruit pudding/custard*

Baked apples

Cookies (Pamela's, Enjoy Life)

Ice cream*

Coconut macaroons*

Sorbet in meringue cups

Flourless cakes

unless prepared with wheat flour

Snacks

Cookies (Pamela's, Enjoy Life)

Crackers (Flackers, Mary's Gone Crackers, Crunchmaster, Blue Diamond, Edward & Sons)

Fruit leather

Nuts and nut butters

Hummus

Raisins and other dried fruit*

Fresh fruits and vegetables

Popcorn

Bean, corn, or lentil chips*

unless dusted or made with wheat flour

Sources of Gluten

Gluten is a protein in wheat and wheat-related grains such as barley, rye, spelt, kamut, and triticale. It occurs in most American foods in the form of wheat flour. This list shows the obvious foods in which wheat may be found. But it also includes surprising foods in which wheat lurks, like soups and salad dressings. Don't worry; this book shows you how to find or make foods without gluten.

Many products can be made with or without gluten—such as tortillas, cookies, Worcestershire sauce, beer, bread crumbs, and pasta. Read labels to make sure your brand is gluten-free.

Obvious Sources of Gluten

Bagels
Pastas
Breads
Tortillas
Cake
Waffles
Cereals
Anything made with wheat and related grains of barley, rye, spelt, kamut, and triticale. Look for gluten-free oats.
Cookies
Crackers
Muffins
Pancakes

Surprising Sources of Gluten

Beer
Malt vinegar
Bouillons
Salad dressing
Broths
Seasonings
Candy
Soup and soup mixes
Deli meats
Soy sauce
Imitation seafood
Tea (flavored, usually with barley malt)
Licorice candy

Gluten: A Real Pain in the Gut ❭

Unless you are a baker or a food scientist, you may very well go through life not knowing or caring much about gluten. That's why gluten intolerance comes as such a surprise—we didn't know gluten existed in the first place!

Nonetheless, gluten (a protein in wheat and related grains such as barley, rye, spelt, kamut, and triticale) plays a major role in several medical conditions. I will give you a brief explanation of these conditions and point you toward resources that provide more details. I cook (I don't practice medicine!), so I urge you to check out these resources so that you can get the full picture instead of just the brief snapshot I provide here.

WHEAT ALLERGIES AND INTOLERANCES

Wheat is one of the top eight food allergens. We don't know exactly which of the many proteins in wheat is the actual culprit for those with true wheat allergies, but we do know that people can be deathly allergic to it.

I know of one young man who is so allergic to wheat that if he inhales the tiny particles of flour that waft through the kitchen during baking, he experiences an anaphylactic reaction and must be treated with an epinephrine injection to "buy" him enough time to get to an emergency room. Experts think that less than 1 percent of Americans have true wheat allergies, but nonetheless, this is a very serious condition.

For others, wheat is bothersome but not necessarily life-threatening, so it is classified as more of an intolerance. These people feel better without wheat, but they may be able to eat spelt and other wheat-related grains that contain gluten in limited amounts. We don't know how many people are intolerant (rather than truly allergic) to wheat. Different people may experience various types of reactions, making this condition hard to define and difficult to study.

CELIAC DISEASE (ALSO KNOWN AS CELIAC SPRUE)

Today, most people know someone who has the autoimmune condition known as celiac disease—once called the "common disease no one's heard of"—but it is so common now that it is viewed as a public health concern. Its prevalence has risen dramatically since World War II and we are not exactly sure why (although the type of wheat we consume today versus the type eaten before World War II may be a factor—experts are still studying this possibility). It is a genetically transmitted condition in which gluten damages the small intestine's ability to absorb food nutrients. If someone in a family has it, the odds are quite high that relatives have it as well. Another form of gluten sensitivity—dermatitis herpetiformis (DH)—causes skin rashes and blister-like spots.

According to Dr. Alessio Fasano's research—conducted while he was at the Center for Celiac Research at the University of Maryland—approximately 1 in 133 people in the United States have celiac disease. Other parts of the world, such as Great Britain, Ireland, and Northern Europe, report a 1-in-300 incidence in the general population. Celiac disease is a lifelong condition requiring strict adherence to eating only gluten-free foods. The condition is diagnosed by a gastroenterologist; then dietitians and nutritionists can help patients manage this new lifestyle.

The Special Case of Oats. Persons with celiac disease must avoid all gluten grains, and oats have typically been avoided in the past. Regular oats—which do not inherently contain gluten—may be contaminated with wheat during the growing and manufacturing process and so remain off-limits. However, one of the growing and manufacturing changes since this book was originally published has resulted in pure, uncontaminated oats, which are now available from several manufacturers. Look for the gluten-free label, and don't buy any products made with oats unless the labels specifically list *gluten-free oats*. Check with your physician for guidelines about eating oats; some people don't tolerate oats, and they should be introduced gradually so that their high fiber level doesn't upset your system.

Non-Celiac Gluten Sensitivity. Recently, Dr. Fasano coined the term *non-celiac gluten sensitivity* as a label for those of us (6 to 7 percent or between 18 and 21 million Americans) who don't have celiac disease but are still sickened by gluten. I am in this category. My response to gluten was nasal congestion and stuffiness, often resulting in sinus infections that lasted up to year at a time. Then the antibiotics required to treat them were another blow to my system, and sinus surgery to correct all the damage from the infections was yet another setback. Other people have stomachaches, headaches, rashes, joint aches, fatigue, or brain fog—to name just a few symptoms. Consuming gluten may not kill those of us with gluten intolerance, but it certainly compromises the quality of our lives.

OTHER CONDITIONS, INCLUDING AUTISM

Although there is not a lot of solid research to support it, others avoid gluten as well. For example, the Web site Autism Speaks (www.autismspeaks .org) says that 1 in 88 children have autism, a neurobiological disorder that perplexes families and the medical community alike. As part of their overall treatment (not as a substitute for other treatments or as a cure), several experts advocate a gluten-free and casein-free (casein is a milk protein) diet, called the GFCF diet.

Other conditions may warrant a gluten-free diet. For example, people with food-triggered asthma or various autoimmune conditions (such as lupus or multiple sclerosis) are sometimes placed on gluten-free diets. While I am not an expert in autism or any of these other medical conditions, many people tell me that they use my recipes to avoid gluten. You should rely on the advice of your physician as to whether a gluten-free diet is appropriate for you.

Check out the list of resources at the end of this chapter to learn more about the various conditions that are addressed with a gluten-free lifestyle.

LIVING THE GLUTEN-FREE LIFESTYLE

Let me say this first . . . *I think that eating is the most profound thing we do to our bodies, each and every day.* Everything we put in our bodies contributes to our well-being, so why would you want to eat foods that are toxic to your health? It seems quite clear to me now, but back in 1988 I was not yet a believer, and I fought my diagnosis for nearly five years because I was certain that the doctor was wrong. Every day I expected a phone call with his apology for an incorrect diagnosis. I hope that you won't be a slow learner like me. But one important lesson I learned from this long journey is that giving up my favorite foods is like any other loss, involving the stages of denial, anger, and, finally, acceptance. I went through all these stages, and here is how I adjusted to this new lifestyle. Perhaps you can benefit from my experience:

First, get a reliable diagnosis. This is important so you know *exactly* what you *can* and *can't* eat. All too often, patients try to diagnose themselves and end up confused, frustrated, and unsure of what's really bothering them. Furthermore, they might unnecessarily omit very nutritious foods from their diets without adequate replacements.

If your symptoms are gastrointestinal (typically bloating, diarrhea, constipation, or gas), a gastroenterologist should test you for celiac disease. Often, patients correctly suspect food as the culprit, but *incorrectly* assume that they should see an allergist. But an allergist tests for allergies. Celiac disease is not an allergy, so the test results are often negative. This leaves the patients (and their physicians) believing that food isn't the problem, and so they resume eating the very foods they should actually avoid.

To further complicate matters, only about one-third of people with celiac disease actually experience the "typical" symptoms outlined above. Others may just experience fatigue; still others may have no symptoms at all. Some people accidentally learn that they have celiac disease when other conditions—such as anemia, osteopenia, or osteoporosis—are diagnosed.

Many such patients come to believe that they suffer from some other unknown malady, *or* they're told "it's all in your head," *or* they're accused of using a food sensitivity to "get attention." I personally heard these very things from well-meaning physicians. They are no longer my physicians because I fired them.

Vent your feelings. Honor your feelings by expressing them. Join a support group, share your thoughts, and listen to the feelings of others. It will help you put your situation in perspective and allow you to let off steam in the process.

In addition, support groups provide valuable information on how to manage a gluten-free diet—including recipes and tips on cooking, shopping, reading labels, dining out, and traveling.

If you have close friends or family members (who are willing to listen without judging), share your thoughts with them. Get their input. Ask them to support your efforts to avoid gluten. People who are with you every day need to understand *why* you can't eat your particular food culprit and where it might be lurking.

Enlist family, friends, and coworkers to form your own private support group. This is very important because family members unwittingly (or sometimes knowingly) sabotage our diet efforts (like those who give chocolates to friends or relatives who are trying to lose weight).

And don't forget that family members may initially regard your gluten intolerance as a threat to their way of life. They don't want to give up *their* favorite foods just because *you* can't have them. Be open and honest with them about your needs. Ask for their help. Learn to prepare or choose foods that don't compromise mealtime at your house. At my house, we eat gluten-free because that's the only choice I provide. My family and my guests enjoy all the usual foods, except I serve them in gluten-free versions. Another approach is to choose naturally gluten-free foods such as meats, fish, and poultry supplemented by whole grains, legumes, fruits, and vegetables—all simply prepared. Later, you can gradually add more seasonings, sauces, and so forth.

Let go of the past and latch on to your new life. You can no longer eat with abandon; you have to examine every morsel of food that goes into your mouth. Your world seems like it's tilting out of control because you think you can't have the customary birthday cake

. . . or join your friends for coffee and pastry at your favorite coffeehouse . . . or simply eat pizza with a beer at your local hangout. You can now enjoy all of these foods, but in gluten-free versions. It is OK to have feelings of anger or even guilt as you adjust to this new situation. You may even try to blame an ancestor who passed on celiac genes to you *or* your parents from whom you inherited your intolerances.

Well, get over it! Accept the facts and be grateful that all you have to do is control what you eat. That's a lot better than having a terminal illness or losing a limb or being horribly ill every day of your life with no remedy in sight. Choose to look at your cup as half full, not half empty.

It is also important to accept the fact that you can't have even a little bit of the forbidden food. It took me five years to learn this extremely important fact. With my demanding executive schedule and constant travel, I thought I could eat a little bit of wheat now and then to make my life easier. Wrong!

But eventually—after all the anger, tears, denial, and guilt—most of us accept the hard, cold facts that we can't eat certain foods. That's when we're ready to learn about choosing food that is right for our bodies. This means embracing—rather than rejecting—the opportunity to live a lifestyle that is tailored to you and your needs rather than a "one size fits all" approach that has you trying to eat like everyone else.

Don't whine, complain, or express sorrow for yourself. Most people live with some sort of limitation or disability. Dwelling on it makes you a bore. Again, remember the cup is half full. Learn to answer questions about your condition with tact, not regret. If you don't want to go into the gory details, simply tell others, "[Blank] makes me feel sick." Or "[Blank] doesn't agree with me so I don't eat it." Or simply say, "No thanks."

This means embracing—rather than rejecting— the opportunity to live a lifestyle that is tailored to you and your needs, rather than a "one size fits all" approach that has you trying to eat like everyone else.

Learn to cook or—if you don't want to cook—at least know how to choose prepared foods wisely. In the end, you're responsible for what you eat. When you cook in your own kitchen, you have control over what goes into your food and the standards under which it is prepared. Some people cook all of their own meals. Others balance meal preparation at home with some store-bought foods and dining out at carefully selected restaurants. Even though manufacturers are producing more gluten-free foods and restaurants are becoming more knowledgeable, you'll fare better if you develop some basic cooking skills. The better you get at cooking, the better your food will look and taste, and you will have fewer chances of a gluten "accident." And research shows that we consume fewer calories and less salt and fat when we prepare our own food.

Make small changes first. Of course, you have to give up gluten entirely. But rather than trying to learn how to cook (or buy) everything in one week, take small steps. Master a basic recipe first and adapt it to your lifestyle. For example, my Basic Muffin recipe (page 135) can be made into a variety of different flavors, as can the Basic Sandwich Bread (page 150).

Allow time for your palate to adjust. You perhaps never thought of this before, but we Americans expect baked goods to taste like wheat because we are accustomed to that taste. In fact, most American foods carry the distinct flavor of wheat— we just don't realize that fact until wheat is omitted. Avoiding wheat means adjusting to the newer flavors such as flours made from rice, beans, corn, sorghum, or quinoa. That process is similar to shifting from cow's milk to soy milk; one's palate gradually adjusts over time. Eventually, these new flavors will seem normal to you.

Read labels. The Food Allergen and Consumer Protection Act (FALCPA) of 2004 requires manufacturers to identify the eight major food allergens on food labels, one of which is wheat. These allergens must appear in "plain English" on the label of any food manufactured after January 1, 2006. The other gluten grains (such as barley, rye, or spelt) are not covered by this ruling but will appear in the ingredient list so that you can detect them. In August 2013, the FDA defined "gluten-free" as a product with "less than 20 parts per million (ppm) of gluten." There is no requirement that gluten-free foods be labeled "gluten-free," but when a manufacturer chooses to put "gluten-free" on food packaging, the item must comply with the new FDA definition.

In the meantime, several associations certify gluten-free products with a logo on the package that indicates their safety. These associations include the Gluten-Free Certification Organization (www.gfco.org), the National Foundation for Celiac Awareness (www.celiaccentral.org), and the Celiac Sprue Association (www.csaceliacs.org). However, many manufacturers do their own testing and offer gluten-free foods that have not been certified by these organizations yet are still safely gluten-free. So, again, read the labels.

Be prepared by planning ahead. Keep your own kitchen stocked with the right ingredients so that you can put together a meal at a moment's notice (see The Gluten-Free Kitchen, page 30).

Keep a bag of snacks (dried fruit, nuts, crackers, jerky, trail mix, and so forth) on hand for when you're at work, traveling, running errands, at a doctor's appointment, or at the kids' soccer games. Stick this bag in the glove box of your car or in your purse or briefcase. When you're hungry, munch on your safe foods rather than giving in to temptation.

Stand up for your rights. Whether you're a schoolchild, a teenager, or an adult, you have a right to expect your food and the conditions under which it is served to be safe. This means that you have a right to query the restaurant about its menu or your child's school about its lunch program. And check out Section 504 of the Rehabilitation Act of 1973, a federal civil rights statue that prohibits discrimination on the basis of a disability in an educational program or institution. Also, see the Individuals with Disabilities Education Act (IDEA) to learn more about your rights.

Where to Get Help

There are many different approaches to living without gluten. My advice is to read as much as possible about the physical aspects of avoiding gluten—but also about the psychological, sociological, and emotional issues that we all face when the doctor says "no gluten." Here are some excellent places to start:

National Associations

Several nonprofit associations provide a wealth of information on the gluten-free lifestyle, including newsletters, magazines, and Web sites. Many hold conferences and also sponsor support groups in many cities, so check to see if one is in your area.

- Celiac Disease Foundation (*www.celiac.org*)
- Celiac Sprue Association (*www.csaceliacs.org*)
- Gluten Intolerance Group (*www.gluten.net*)
- National Foundation for Celiac Awareness (*www.celiaccentral.org*)

Magazines

These are lovely, full-color magazines available by subscription. Some are also found on magazine stands.

- *Easy Eats* (*www.easyeats.com*)
- *Delight Gluten-Free* (*www.delightglutenfree.com*)
- *Gluten-Free Living* (*www.glutenfreeliving.com*)
- *Journal of Gluten Sensitivity* (*www.celiac.com*)
- *Living Without* (*www.livingwithout.com*)
- *Simply Gluten-Free* (*www.simplyglutenfree.com*)

Universities and Medical Centers

Many universities and medical centers have established research centers that conduct research, diagnose patients, hold conferences, and offer a wealth of information on their Web sites.

- Celiac Center at Harvard University–Beth Israel *www.bidmc.harvard.edu/celiaccenter*
- Celiac Center at Paoli Hospital *www.mainlinehealth.org/paoliceliac*
- Celiac Disease Center, Columbia University *www.celiacdiseasecenter.columbia.edu*
- Celiac Disease Clinic, Mayo Clinic *www.mayoclinic.org*
- Center for Celiac Research *www.celiaccenter.org*
- Jefferson Celiac Center *www.jeffersonhospital.org/departments-and-services/celiac-center.aspx*
- University of Chicago Celiac Disease Center *www.celiacdisease.net*
- William K. Warren Medical Research Center for Celiac Disease, University of California at San Diego *http://celiaccenter.ucsd.edu*

An excellent book that will help you understand the nutritional aspects of the gluten-free diet is *Gluten-Free Diet: A Comprehensive Resource Guide*, by Shelley Case, RD (Case Nutrition Consulting, 2013). Also visit *www.glutenfreediet.ca*.

Going against the Grain: Flours for Gluten-Free Baking ❱

Life was certainly simpler when we only needed wheat flour for baking. But I think we gluten-free folks have a lot more variety in our diets because of the many gluten-free flours available to us. I use the same basic flour blend for most of the baking recipes in this book, but I love to add other flours to boost the nutrient content of my baked goods, and I appreciate the way various gluten-free flours bring unique flavors to our food. You may be curious about a wider variety of flours, so here is a basic description of the various flours on the market, in alphabetical order, and how to use them. Some are available in both whole form (grains, nuts, legumes, or seeds) and flour form.

Almond: Whether called almond meal (ground almonds with skins on) or almond flour (ground almonds without skins), the two are usually used interchangeably in baking. You can grind your own almond flour from blanched almond slivers, using a small coffee grinder. It has a high fat content, so refrigerate and use it within 2 months. Grind it as finely as possible for the best texture in baking— but not too much or it turns into almond butter. Not surprisingly, it tastes like almonds.

Amaranth: Cultivated as a sacred food by the Aztecs for centuries, amaranth is a seed related to spinach and chard. Cortés forbade its cultivation, so amaranth all but disappeared from the culinary horizon. Today, it is sold as flour and whole seeds at natural foods stores.

Amaranth's extremely small seeds are hard to manage, but the flour handles just like other flours. It slightly lengthens baking time and tends to brown a little faster than other flours, but adds important protein, calcium, and amino acids—especially lysine—lacking in many common grains.

Described as "woody," "grassy," or "nutty," the flavor of amaranth is stronger than rice flour, but not as strong as quinoa.

Arrowroot: A neutral-flavored starchy flour from the arrowroot plant grown in the West Indies, arrowroot is useful in thickening dishes without making them cloudy. It also can be substituted one-to-one for tapioca flour/starch or cornstarch in baking, where it lightens the crumb and aids in binding the ingredients.

Because of its shine, arrowroot flour is best used as a thickener for fruit dishes or in dishes where its gloss gives the appearance of fat (even when there is none).

Be sure to purchase arrowroot in the baking aisle of your local health food store, where it is considerably cheaper than the little jars in the supermarket spice racks.

Barley: Although you see this ingredient listed on wheat-free products (often as barley flour or barley malt), it technically is a member of the wheat family and as such it contains gluten. Wheat-allergic persons and celiacs *should not* eat barley in any form, and barley is not used in this cookbook.

Bean flours: There are many varieties of bean flour: black, pinto, navy, garbanzo (also called chickpea), and white. All add protein and fiber to baking, and their resistant starch produces baked goods with good texture and a longer shelf life. Each has a slightly different taste and color, but all add a distinctive "beany" flavor to baked goods. Dry beans are too hard to grind into flour at home; they require professional milling.

Most bean flours are sold as single flours, but one blend that is commonly used in gluten-free baking is the blend of garbanzo and fava beans (either called garfava or garbanzo/fava bean flour). It has a very high protein and fiber content, but it lends a pleasing texture to baked goods. All beans are found in some grocery stores and natural foods stores, but bean flours are mostly found in natural foods stores.

Buckwheat: Despite its name, buckwheat is not really wheat. Instead, it is a seed related to rhubarb. Buckwheat flour is milled from groats (kernels) and graded as light, medium, or dark depending on the amount of remaining hulls. Typically, the darker the flour (like the kind used in buckwheat pancakes), the higher the lysine content and the stronger the flavor—which some find overpowering.

For baking, I favor lighter, unroasted buckwheat, which has a milder flavor. If you can't find unroasted buckwheat flour, grind unroasted groats or cream of buckwheat cereal (from Bob's Red Mill or Birkett Mills) in a blender or coffee grinder until it reaches the texture of flour.

Chestnut: Ground from whole chestnuts, this light tan flour is usually available at natural foods stores or online. Chestnut flour lends a silky texture and nutty flavor to baked goods. It is not the same as water chestnut flour, which is quite starchy. Also called marrons, chestnuts are lower in fat than other nuts. Chestnut flour should be used in combination with other flours (up to 25 percent of

the blend) in baking. It is commonly used in holiday baking but is appropriate year-round because of the superior results it yields. It is available in natural foods stores or online.

Chia and Salba: Both are members of the mint family, but chia looks like poppy seeds, while salba is lighter, with a smoother, rounder seed. Both are high in protein and fiber and can be ground into flour with your coffee grinder or tossed into smoothies, mixed with batters for bread or muffins, or stirred into cereals or yogurt. They are crunchy when chewed and have a mild, nutty flavor. They are also stirred into water and used as an egg replacer for binding in baking, but they don't possess the leavening power of eggs.

Coconut Flour: Coconut flour is ground from coconut meat and has high levels of protein and fiber. It works best when used as a very small portion of the flour in baking or in recipes that are specifically designed for it. Recipes made with coconut flour typically require much more liquid than other flours, so the ratio of liquid ingredients to dry ingredients needs to be adjusted.

Corn Flour and Cornmeal: Milled from whole corn kernels, the major difference between corn flour and cornmeal lies in particle size. Use corn flour (the finer particles) in breads, desserts, pancakes, waffles, and homemade tortillas. Use cornmeal (coarser particles) for breading, corn bread, muffins, and polenta, where the larger particles lend crunch and texture. Coarse cornmeal is also known as grits and can be yellow or white.

Corn flour lends a distinct yet mild corn flavor to baked goods. If you can't find corn flour, grind cornmeal in your coffee grinder until it reaches the consistency of flour. Don't confuse corn flour with cornstarch (the latter is sometimes called "corn flour" in the United Kingdom).

Cornstarch: Highly refined corn with little nutritive value, cornstarch lightens baked goods and is an indispensable part of some flour blends. It is snow white and virtually flavorless and can be used interchangeably with potato starch in baking, but it produces a slightly crispier product than potato starch. It is used to coat meats and vegetables before frying.

As a thickener, cornstarch is second only to wheat flour. It may even be more desirable because it produces a smoother, more transparent texture and holds its thickening power better. However, for some savory dishes such as soups or gravy, this shininess isn't appropriate, and potato starch or sweet rice flour will produce a more natural-looking result.

Expandex: This is the brand name for modified tapioca starch, a flour that improves the rise and texture of baked goods and lengthens the shelf life of baked goods—all without altering the flavor or color. It has many unique properties, so follow directions for its use. See *Tapioca* for more discussion on Expandex.

Flaxseeds and Flaxseed Meal: Flaxseeds are high in fiber and omega-3 fatty acids. They are a delicious way to add nutrients to gluten-free baked goods. You can buy flax meal already ground—or buy your own flaxseeds and grind them as you need them in a little coffee grinder. Use flax meal in baking, smoothies, cereals, and side dishes. Flax meal contains oil, so you may need to reduce the amount of fat or oil in your recipe.

Mesquite: This sweet-tasting, light brown flour is ground from the pods of the mesquite tree and is high in protein and fiber. It is currently available as flour in selected specialty stores or online. It lends a slight cinnamon flavor to baked goods.

Millet: This flour lends a light yellow tint to baked goods and produces a light, dry crumb with a smooth, thin crust. Very high in protein—due to its high alkalinity and lysine—it is one of the easier grains to digest and makes a nutritious hot breakfast cereal in its whole-grain form. Purchase millet flour and millet grains in small amounts and always refrigerate it, because it can quickly become bitter and rancid. Or, just buy whole millet grains and grind them into flour with your coffee grinder as you need them.

Oats: Once forbidden for those with gluten sensitivities, oats are inherently gluten-free but have been off-limits because of cross-contamination in fields and manufacturing plants. But six companies in North America now offer gluten-free oats in several forms: bran, rolled, steel-cut, flour, quick-cooking, and whole groats. These gluten-free oats are grown in specially isolated fields without contact with gluten grains and are processed and packaged in facilities that are dedicated to gluten-free products. Baked goods made with oats are especially soft and moist, with a cake-like crumb. Rolled oats, whole groats, and steel-cut oats make hearty breakfast cereal. Check with your physician before eating gluten-free oats, since not everyone tolerates oats to the same degree and newly diagnosed persons should introduce them gradually if they are unaccustomed to high-fiber grains.

Pecan: Ground from pecans, this is sometimes

called meal and sometimes called flour. Pecan meal is often used in flourless cakes, accompanied by several eggs for leavening. Due to the skins, pecan meal lends a slight nutty taste, adds an interesting texture, and slightly darkens the crumb of baked goods. Pecans have a fairly high fat content and can turn rancid quickly, so refrigerate or freeze. Or, buy whole pecans and grind in a food processor as needed.

Potato Flour: Made from whole potatoes that have been cooked and then ground, this heavy flour is seldom used in large quantities for baking. In small quantities, it balances flour blends by adding weight, body, and "chewiness" in items such as cookies and yeast breads. Like tapioca flour/starch, it hardens the crust of baked goods. Off-white in color, potato flour has a much stronger taste than potato starch. Buy small amounts and use quickly. Since the flavor deteriorates quickly, refrigerate or freeze in an airtight container for up to 2 months.

Potato Starch: Unlike potato flour, potato starch is made from only the starch of potatoes (not the whole potato), so it produces a fine, pure white powder that lightens baked goods. Because it may clump during storage, whisk before using.

Potato starch is rarely used alone in baking, but typically blended with other flours and can be used one-to-one in place of cornstarch. It contains little or no protein or fat and can be used to thicken soups and stews.

Quinoa and Kañiwa: Quinoa is an ancient grain (really a seed related to lamb's quarter, spinach, and beets) originally grown high in the Andes of Peru. It produces a delicate, cake-like crumb in baking but brings a distinct flavor as well. Originally light tan in color, the seeds are now available in red or black varieties and make excellent cereal, side dishes, or soups. Like other soft grains and seeds, you can grind them into flour with a coffee grinder.

Unlike most imported quinoa, domestically grown quinoa isn't always rinsed of its saponin, a natural insect repellent that tastes bitter to humans, though it is harmless. So, rinse the grains at least three times or until the water runs clear. If you're grinding your own flour, be sure to rinse and then dry the kernels first. If you are not sure whether the quinoa has been pre-rinsed, then be sure to rinse it.

Kañiwa (also called baby quinoa) is related to quinoa, but the seeds are smaller and don't cook up as fluffy as quinoa. Its flavor is nutty and has none of the saponin bitterness found in some unrinsed quinoas. Use it as hot cereal, side dishes, and added to batter to improve the protein, fiber, calcium, and iron levels of baked goods.

Rice (Brown or White): Perhaps the most common of wheat flour substitutes, rice flours lend a light color, but somewhat sandy texture, to baked goods. The flavor of rice is neutral, and rice is one of the least allergenic foods on earth, making it a natural choice to replace wheat.

Both brown and white rice flour are milled from rice kernels. White rice flour has more of the exterior layers milled away than brown rice flour, so the latter is more nutritious. But these "layers" are available as rice polish or rice bran (see below). White rice flour produces grittier baked goods than brown rice flour; however, this grittiness is excellent for dipping meats and vegetables to achieve a crispier coating in frying. Whole brown rice makes excellent breakfast cereal and side dishes.

Rice Bran: This is the outside layer of the rice kernel that is removed to make brown rice. It contains the bran and part of the rice germ. Dark in color, it adds fiber and protein to baked goods. Add to breads or muffins for increased fiber content. It is available at natural foods stores or online.

Rice Polish: This is the portion of the brown rice kernel removed in the process of making white rice. It contains part of the rice germ and bran. High in fiber, it is light in color (unlike rice bran, which is darker in color). It is available at natural foods stores or online.

Sorghum: The flour made from this nutritious, high-protein grain tastes similar to wheat. An ancient grain popular in Africa and Egypt, and sometimes called milo, it is light tan in color, not gritty, and produces baked goods with a pleasing texture. Sorghum is the fifth most important cereal crop grown in the world. Early varieties were grown only for cattle feed (as on the Nebraska farm where I was raised), but today's versions are grown as food sorghum. Faintly sweet and somewhat dry, sorghum flour can also be used to coat vegetables and meats before frying. The whole grains make excellent side dishes and can be used instead of bulgur in grain salads, or in place of pearled barley in soups and stews. Sorghum flour is available in grocery stores and natural foods stores, while the whole grains are available online.

Soy: Soy flour is made from soybeans and brings wonderful qualities to gluten-free baking—including a moist, fine crumb and a smooth, hard crust. It works especially well in baked goods containing nuts, fruit, or chocolate, but it carries a strong flavor.

Spelt: This sweet, nutty grain produces flour that is often used in place of wheat flour. However, gluten-intolerant people *must not* use this flour because it contains gluten. You'll find many cookbooks with recipes for using spelt, but it is not used in this cookbook.

Sweet Potato: Ground from sweet potatoes, which are one of the least allergenic foods on earth, this flour is a good choice for persons with multiple sensitivities. It has a slightly sweet taste and produces baked goods with a pleasing texture. Its yellowy orange color is visible in light-colored baked goods, so use it in chocolate or darkly colored baked items such as spice cakes for best results. Its faint sweetness will affect gravies and savory sauces, so it is best reserved for sweeter items. It is available in specialty stores or online.

Sweet Rice: Also called sticky rice, this flour is made from a particular kind of rice called glutinous rice (although it contains no wheat gluten). This bland, starchy flour has stronger binding qualities than other rice flours. Manufacturers recommend using it in muffins, breads, and cakes. My experience suggests using it as a small part (perhaps 25 to 30 percent) of the total flour blend.

Sweet rice flour works particularly well in items that require a great deal of elasticity and pliability, such as piecrusts. Sweet rice flour really shines as a thickener in savory dishes because it produces a creamy sauce and inhibits separation of the sauce when chilled or frozen. Sweet or sticky rice is also available in whole-grain form and makes appealing side dishes, breakfast cereals, and desserts such as puddings. There are also various colors of sticky rice available such as black or purple rice. It is available in natural foods stores and online.

Tapioca: Also called tapioca starch or manioc, this neutral-flavored, pure white starch is made from the cassava plant, which is cultivated in South America and Florida. Some experts distinguish between tapioca flour and tapioca starch; however, most of the tapioca found in natural foods stores is labeled as tapioca flour (such as Bob's Red Mill) and—whether it is labeled starch or flour—the two perform virtually the same and the terms are used interchangeably.

Tapioca flour lightens gluten-free baked goods, lends some chew to baked goods, and encourages browning with a crispy crust. Used in a similar manner to arrowroot, it usually makes up 25 to 30 percent of the total flour blend. It is widely available in grocery stores and natural foods stores.

Tapioca flour does not have the same baking qualities as Expandex, the brand name for modified tapioca starch, which is available in selected stores and online. (Check *www.expandexglutenfree.com* for availability.) Expandex makes baked goods rise higher and have a more wheat-like crumb, and it extends their shelf life—without altering the color or flavor of the food. I typically replace $\frac{1}{4}$ to $\frac{1}{3}$ cup of the gluten-free flour blend with Expandex in breads, muffins, and quick breads.

Teff: Grown in Ethiopia for centuries, this tiny grain wasn't introduced to the United States until the 1980s. It is so small that it takes 150 grains to equal one kernel of wheat, although it is not related to wheat at all.

Teff produces a sweet, nutty, almost malt-flavored flour that works especially well in cookies, cakes, and quick breads. Like other gluten-free yet highly nutritious grains—such as quinoa or amaranth—teff should be combined with other flours for success in baking.

The teff flour you will find in natural foods stores is darker and most likely grown in Caldwell, Idaho. There is also an ivory (light-colored) version as well. The grains are so small you won't be able to grind the flour yourself. Teff is available in natural foods stores and online.

Walnut: Ground from whole walnuts, this is sometimes called meal and sometimes called flour. It is hard to find in stores, so you may need to grind whole walnuts in a food processor. Walnut meal is often used in flourless cakes, accompanied by several eggs for leavening. Due to the skins, walnuts lend a slightly nutty taste, add an interesting texture, and slightly darken the crumb of baked goods. Walnuts have a fairly high fat content and can turn rancid quickly, so refrigerate or freeze. Or buy whole walnuts and grind in a food processor as needed.

Wild Rice: Wild rice is not actually rice at all, but a seed. It is richer in protein, minerals, and B vitamins and higher in carbohydrates than wheat. Wild rice flour lends a rich, nutty flavor to baked goods, and—as with all gluten-free flours—it needs to be blended with other flours for best results—making up perhaps 25 to 30 percent of the total blend of flours.

It is hard to find wild rice flour, but you can grind the rice into flour using a small coffee grinder. Whole wild rice makes excellent side dishes and soups. Wild rice is available in grocery stores, specialty stores, and natural foods stores.

SUBSTITUTES FOR WHEAT FLOUR AS A THICKENER

Many of us learned to cook using wheat flour as a thickener in gravies, soups, and sauces. Other starches and flours can thicken certain foods, but each alternative has certain traits that we should know about. Use the following information to choose among them; my favorites are cornstarch for dessert sauces and sweet rice flour for gravies and savory sauces.

In place of **1 tablespoon of wheat flour**, use the following:

Ingredient/Amount	Traits	Suggested Uses
Agar (Kanten) 1½ teaspoons	Follow package directions. Colorless, flavorless. Sets at room temperature. Gels acidic liquids. Thin sauces need less agar.	Puddings, pie fillings, gelatin desserts, ice cream, glazes, cheese. Holds moisture and improves texture in pastry products.
Arrowroot 1½ teaspoons	Mix with cold water before using. Thickens at lower temperature than wheat flour or cornstarch; better for eggs or sauces that shouldn't be boiled. Add during last 5 minutes of cooking. Serve right away after thickening. Clear, shiny, and semisoft when cool. Don't overcook or sauce will thin somewhat.	Any food requiring clear, shiny sauce, but good for egg or starch dishes where high heat is undesirable. Gives appearance of oil even when none used.
Bean Flour (Chickpea/ Garbanzo, or White) 1 tablespoon	Produces yellowish, rich-looking sauces. Slight beany taste.	Soups, stews, gravies.
Cornstarch 1½ teaspoons	Mix with cold liquid just before use; stop stirring after boiling starts. Transparent, shiny sauces with slight starchy flavor. Thicker and rigid when cool.	Puddings, pie fillings, fruit sauces, soups. Gives appearance of oil even when none used.
Gelatin Powder (unflavored) 1½ teaspoons	Dissolve in cold water. Then heat until clear before using.	Cheesecakes, gelatin salads, puddings, aspics. Won't gel acidic fruit such as pineapple.
Guar Gum 1½ teaspoons	Mix with liquid before use. High fiber can act as laxative.	Especially good for rice flour recipes.
Kudzu (kuzu) Powder 1½ teaspoons	Dissolve in cold water before using. Odorless, tasteless. Makes transparent, smooth sauces with soft consistency.	Puddings, pie fillings, and gelled preparations. May need experimentation for exact amount to use.

Ingredient/Amount	Traits	Suggested Uses
Potato Starch **1½ teaspoons**	Mix with cold liquid before using. Makes smooth, but not transparent, sauces with soft consistency.	Soups, stews, gravies.
Rice Flour (brown or white) **1 tablespoon**	Mix with cold water before using. Makes coarse, grainy gravies and sauces. Consistency is the same hot or cold.	Soups, stews, gravies.
Sweet Rice Flour **1 tablespoon**	Excellent thickening agent; resembles wheat-thickened sauces in color and texture.	Cream soups; sauces such as white sauce.
Tapioca Flour **1½ tablespoons**	Mix with cold water before using. Add during last 5 minutes of cooking to avoid rubbery consistency. Makes transparent, shiny sauces. Thick, soft gel when cool.	Soups, stews, gravies, potato dishes.
Quick-Cooking Tapioca **(pre-cooked)** **2 teaspoons**	Mix with fruit for pies, cobblers, crisps. Let stand for 15 minutes before baking.	Fruit pies, cobblers, tapioca pudding.
Xanthan Gum **1 teaspoon**	First, mix with dry ingredients or oil until blended, then add to recipe.	Puddings, salad dressings, gravies.

A FRAMEWORK FOR GLUTEN-FREE FLOURS & STARCHES

One of the hardest things for beginners to understand is that gluten-free baking requires a blend of flours. No single flour performs like wheat, so we blend flours to maximize their individual performance traits. People often ask me how I know which flours to use—I agree that it can be confusing.

My formula for flour blends is part art and part science, developed over many years of gluten-free experiments. I have formulated some general principles about how to categorize these flours based on their performance traits and how to blend them for maximum effectiveness. I use these principles as a guide when I develop recipes. While our understanding of gluten-free flours is still emerging—and other experts use different flour blends based on different approaches—this simple framework has served me well—and the many cooks I have advised over the years. In this chart, the symbol "~" means "about or roughly," and percentages are rounded.

Step 1	Step 2	Step 3	Step 4 (Optional)
Start with protein flours ~35%	**Add starches (see A, B, and C below for the performance traits of each category)**	**Whisk together.** **Store in dark, dry place.**	**When baking, add the following as ~10–20% of flour blend**
Almond Millet Bean Pecan Brown rice Oat (gluten-free) Buckwheat Chestnut Sorghum Coconut Walnut Hazelnut White rice	**A. ~35%** Arrowroot Cornstarch Potato starch Sweet rice flour **B. ~30%** Tapioca flour/tapioca starch **C. ~10–15%** Modified tapioca starch (Expandex): to replace some of the flour blend	Use flour blend when recipe calls for gluten-free flour blend.	Amaranth flour or grains Chia seeds Corn flour or cornmeal Flax meal (whole or ground) Mesquite flour Oats (gluten-free; quick/rolled/flour) Potato flour Quinoa flour or cereal Rice bran or rice polish Salba seeds Soy flour Teff flour or grains
What these flours do . . . Flavor Texture Stability of crumb	**What these flours do . . .** **A.** Lighter color; airier, softer crumb **B.** Browns and crisps crust; better mouthfeel and "chew" **C.** Higher rise, better crumb, longer shelf life		**What these flours do . . .** Add fiber, nutrients, flavor, color, and visual interest

Following this line of thinking, I assembled the following flour blend to be used in a wide variety of baked goods. I chose sorghum flour because it provides protein for structure and stability, potato starch (or cornstarch) because it lends lightness and airiness, and tapioca flour because it browns and crisps the crust, while also providing "chew" to the crumb. For lighter-colored baked goods—such as the Basic Vanilla Bundt Cake (page 193)—I sometimes replace sorghum flour with the same amount of brown rice flour. I whisk these flours together, store them, and measure just as I would measure wheat flour.

Carol's Gluten-Free Flour Blend

1½ cups sorghum flour or brown rice flour (35%)
1½ cups potato starch or cornstarch (35%)
 1 cup tapioca flour (30%)

Whisk together until thoroughly blended and store, tightly covered, in a dark, dry place.

How I Use This Flour Blend The blend is quite versatile, so I use it in a wide variety of breads, cakes, and cookies, but you can also tailor it to what you are baking. With most recipes, I use the flour blend constructed in Steps 1, 2, and 3 of the recipe as is, and do not add any other flours.

In other recipes, I start out with this blend but then add additional flours to reach my goal. If I want more lightness, as perhaps in a sandwich bread, I would start with the sorghum blend, but add more potato starch for a lighter, fluffier loaf. If I wanted an even higher rise with a better crumb and longer shelf life, I might replace the flour blend with ¼ cup to ½ cup Expandex (modified tapioca starch) using a one-to-one ratio. For recipes where I want more suppleness and elasticity in the dough—

perhaps for a piecrust—I construct the recipe to include sweet rice flour for greater pliability in rolling and shaping the dough.

For other recipes in which I want a heartier bread, I continue on to Step 4 of the framework, where I begin with my flour blend but add rice bran, flax meal, or whole-grain teff (or other whole grains) to boost the bread's fiber and protein content, not to mention lending a marvelous whole-grain nutty flavor. Of course, whenever you add whole grains or whole-grain flours to a recipe, the total amount of dry ingredients will have to be balanced with an appropriate amount of liquids to achieve the right texture in the bread dough. Some experimentation will be needed. Hopefully, this explanation gives you some idea of how I assemble recipes to take advantage of the different traits inherent in gluten-free flours.

How You Use This Flour Blend The goal of this book is to streamline things as much as possible, so mix up a batch of this flour blend and store it on your pantry shelf or in your refrigerator, and it will be ready when you are. You only have to measure once, just like you did when baking with wheat flour. To learn more about each gluten-free flour, see list of gluten-free flours, pages 18–23.

Commonly used gluten-free baking ingredients include (left to right in bowls): tapioca flour, brown rice flour, potato starch, and sorghum flour (in bag). See page 18 for how these flours affect the flavor, appearance, texture, and shelf life of foods. In the measuring spoons, xanthan gum (left) and guar gum (right) enable a better rise in baked goods. See page 41 for how to use gums.

Storage of Gluten-Free Flours and Flour Blends | I prefer to store flours in large, wide-mouthed glass jars or food storage containers rather than plastic bags. You can find them in housewares and storage stores. The wide openings allow me to measure the flour directly over the top of the container, scraping the excess right back into the container.

I also recommend refrigeration or freezing of flours and grains or seeds if you don't use them up quickly, because their oils can turn rancid. Bring them to room temperature before baking so the chill doesn't hamper the leavening action. If you choose not to refrigerate or freeze your grains or flours, store them, tightly covered, in a dark, dry place. To my knowledge, no one has conducted research on exactly how long these grains and seeds can be stored. I have had brown rice flour and amaranth flour turn rancid when not refrigerated, undoubtedly due to the higher oil content in whole grains.

My formula for flour blends is part art and part science, developed over many years of gluten-free experiments.

The Gluten-Free Kitchen ❯

Some people are naturally comfortable in the kitchen. Others avoid the kitchen as much as possible and are bewildered at the thought of preparing their own gluten-free food . . . with unfamiliar ingredients and unusual techniques, no less. Despite all the new gluten-free ready-made foods on the market, it is much less expensive to prepare your own food at home. Plus, you have greater control over what you eat and the standards under which it is prepared—and your home-prepared food will most likely contain fewer calories and less salt and fat.

I was fortunate to have a mother who cooked *all* of our meals, and that gave me the opportunity to observe her in the kitchen, although I don't remember any overt attempts on her part to teach me how to cook. Nor did my maternal grandmother—who raised 12 children and cooked all of her family's meals—take me under her culinary wing. With 40 grandchildren, she didn't have a lot of one-on-one time to offer. My aunts were excellent cooks, but I don't recall cooking with them either. Luckily, by the time I married, I knew enough basics to cook all of our own meals and I was comfortable in the kitchen. This experience provided a solid foundation for cooking gluten-free meals, but I readily admit that I had to learn how to bake all over again.

Remember, both experts and novices alike can learn to be excellent gluten-free cooks. It takes a little patience and lots of practice, but the reward is food that you know is safe and just right for your body. This chapter will ensure your success in the kitchen, so let's start with the basics.

THE BASICS

These tips may seem extraordinarily simple, but sometimes it is the littlest things that make the difference between success and failure in the kitchen. So read through these tips before you start using the recipes in this book and you will be on your way!

Using the Recipe

- First, read the recipe completely to make sure you have all the ingredients you need, along with the right pans and utensils. This may sound overly simple, but you would be surprised at how many people call me when they're in the middle of preparing a recipe, saying, *"Help . . . I'm baking a [cake, bread, etc.] and just realized I don't have a [ingredient/utensil/pan]. What should I do?"* Planning ahead is critical to success. It's called *mise en place*, or having everything in its place before you begin.

- Follow the recipe as directed. This means *exactly* as directed. I have already made the ingredient substitutions for you. Don't make any other changes. After you make the recipe for the first time, then you can try substitutes. It is better to start with a gluten-free recipe that is tried and true than it is to try to adapt your own recipes to be gluten-free—at least until you become familiar with gluten-free food preparation.

LEARN THESE CULINARY TERMS

For some, being diagnosed as gluten intolerant simply means spending more time in the familiar environment of our own kitchen. For others, it is a whole new adventure in kitchens we hardly recognize and one where many culinary terms might as well be written in a foreign language. Here's some help with those bewildering terms.

Blend: Thoroughly combine two or more ingredients.

Boil: Heat until bubbles rise continuously and break the surface.

Chill: Refrigerate food until cold.

Combine: Stir ingredients together until thoroughly blended.

Cream: Mix fat and sugar together until soft and smooth.

Dredge: Coat or cover food lightly with flour or sugar.

Fold: Combine ingredients lightly with two motions. The first motion cuts vertically through a mixture with a spatula; the second motion slides the spatula across the bottom of the bowl and up the side of the bowl. Gently repeat these motions until the ingredients are blended.

Melt: Heat to a liquid state (but cool before using, unless the recipe says otherwise).

Mix: Combine two or more ingredients until evenly distributed.

Preheat: Heat to a desired temperature before baking.

Puree: Blend in a blender or food processor to a smooth consistency.

Room temperature: Usually 75°F to 85°F (although some homes may be cooler, especially in winter).

Sauté: Cook and stir in a small bit of oil over high heat.

Simmer: Cook slowly in liquid at just below the boiling point.

Sift: Shake in a sifter to mix together and incorporate air.

Whisk: Beat with a wire whisk until blended and smooth.

For additional help with culinary terms, see *Cookwise* by Shirley O. Corriher (William Morrow).

Assemble Everything Beforehand

- Gather all the utensils and bowls you will need. I place all the ingredients on one side of the countertop and, after I use them, I transfer them to the other side of the counter. This way, interruptions such as phone calls, kids, pets, or other distractions won't make me forget the xanthan gum—or add the salt twice.

Measure Correctly

- Before measuring flour, stir it with a whisk to aerate it. As flour sits over time, it tends to settle and become more compacted and heavy, so whisking is important. Lightly spoon it into a dry measuring cup and level the mound of flour with a knife. Don't shake or tap the cup and don't force the flour down into the cup. Not following these tips can yield up to 20 percent more flour than you need and is one of the chief causes of baking failures. To see my demonstration on measuring flour, go to Videos at *www.glutenfree101.com.*
- Use liquid measuring cups to measure liquids.

How do you know which cups are for liquids? They usually have a pour spout, are made of clear plastic or glass so you can see through them, and the gradations don't go all the way to the top as they do with dry measuring cups. Never use dry measuring cups to measure liquids. This can yield more liquid than is necessary and possibly ruin a recipe.

- Use real measuring spoons—not spoons from the silverware drawer. Make sure measuring spoons are a standard size from a reputable manufacturer.

Use Your Oven Correctly

- Preheat the oven for at least 15 to 20 minutes to make sure it reaches the specified temperature. Some ovens take even longer, while some newer ovens have quicker preheat times. Unless the recipe says otherwise (as in my yeast bread recipes that have a cold-oven start), be sure to preheat the oven so that it reaches the right temperature *before* you start baking. None of this book's recipes use a convection oven.

- Use the oven temperature specified in the recipe. And use an oven thermometer to be sure your oven is actually heating to the *right* temperature. Some ovens need to be recalibrated if they are not baking at the specified temperature (check with an oven thermometer, available in the baking aisle of your grocery store). And not all ovens produce the same results, so there can be variations across the same recipes baked in different ovens.

- Use the middle oven rack unless directed otherwise. Place the baking pan in the center of the rack so the heated air can circulate freely around it. However, some foods—like pizza crusts and piecrusts—brown better on the bottom when baked on the lowest rack, so follow the recipe's instructions.

- Start checking doneness a few minutes before the time specified in the recipe, especially the first time you make a dish. There are so many variables that can affect the baking time (oven temperature variations, pan size, ingredients, temperature of ingredients, humidity, ambient temperature, and so on). If your baking time differs from that in the recipe, make a note on the recipe margins so you know what to do next time.

- Cool baked goods in the pan for 10 to 15 minutes. Then loosen them by running a sharp knife along the edge of the pan and transfer them to a wire rack to cool. To avoid sogginess, don't leave baked goods in the pan longer than 15 minutes, because moisture builds up inside the pan as the baked item cools.

Choose the Right Pans and Utensils

- Following the recipe means using the right utensil. If the recipe says "whisk," then you should use a wire or ceramic whisk, not a spatula or spoon. If it says to use a food processor to mix the dough, it will blend more quickly and more thoroughly than with an electric mixer because a food processor distributes liquid more quickly and evenly—making a smoother, more consistent dough.

- Pan size is important. If you use a 7x11-inch pan instead of an 8-inch square pan for baking, the same amount of batter is distributed over a larger area. As a result, it will probably bake in a shorter period of time, it won't rise as high, and it might burn more quickly. If you have metal, nonstick baking pans in 8-inch (round and square), 9-inch (round and square), 5x9-

inch, 7x11-inch, and 9x13-inch sizes, you're well prepared for both baking and cooking. I also like mini pans (3x5-inch or 4x6-inch sizes) for making little loaves of quick bread. Make sure your pie pans are nonstick 9-inch. Choose nonstick muffin pans in standard size (12 muffins), jumbo (6 muffins), and mini (24 muffins) and you will be ready to bake any size muffin or cupcake.

- In addition to pan size, the composition of the pan is critical in baking. For breads and cakes, I prefer nonstick pans (gray, not black) because they brown the crust better, which promotes a better rise. Gray is preferred to black because black promotes too much browning and can cause burning. Glass, ceramic, and shiny aluminum don't promote browning as well so are not good for baking items like breads and cakes that must brown somewhat. Flexible silicone baking forms do not brown well, so don't use them. For cookies—which are smaller and bake more quickly—I prefer the shiny aluminum baking sheets in 9x13-inch or 13x18-inch (half-sheet) sizes to avoid overbrowning the cookie bottoms.

- For cooking, I prefer heavy-bottomed pots with thick walls and tight-fitting lids. These pots may cost a bit more than the thinner versions, but they are well worth the investment since you will use them frequently. Additionally, you should have a Dutch oven or large soup pot, a large roasting pan (11x15-inch) for turkeys and beef roasts, and small and medium skillets in 8-inch and 10-inch sizes (nonstick, if possible). A 12-inch cast-iron skillet is nice to have, as is a 2-quart casserole dish and 4- or 6-ounce ramekins for baking individual-serving dishes such as Cherry-Almond Clafouti (page 214).

- Knives are often sold in large sets, yet all you really need are a chef's knife (8-inch), a serrated knife or electric knife (for cutting gluten-free bread), and a paring knife for small jobs.

Invest in Time-Saving Appliances

Our grandmothers did without them, but they make your life much easier, so it is worth investing in these time-saving appliances:

- blender for smoothies or pureeing food such as soups
- electric stand mixer (for heavy doughs) and handheld electric mixer (for small jobs)
- food processor (larger sizes are preferable), such as 11- or 14-cup, for chopping vegetables, making bread crumbs and cookie crumbs, and blending dough.
- bread machine (see the bread primer on page 43 for help in choosing and using a bread machine); but if you are more comfortable making bread by hand, you won't need one.
- panini machine, if you love panini sandwiches (pressed and grilled sandwiches), although a heavy-duty skillet or grill pan and a heavy object (like a cast-iron skillet) can be used instead.

WHAT YOU SHOULD KNOW ABOUT THE RECIPES IN THIS BOOK

Here are a few things to remember when using these recipes:

- If an ingredient is preceded by the word "gluten-free," that means you should look for a gluten-free version, since it is also available in gluten-containing versions. To see what brand(s) I used, see Brands Used in Testing Recipes (page 227). These brands are specific to the United States; you may find other gluten-free brands in other countries or regions.
- Eggs are large; each should be 3 to 4 tablespoons in volume.

- Sugar is granulated white—not brown, raw, or turbinado sugar unless otherwise specified.
- Yeast is active dry yeast, not instant yeast unless specified in the recipe. Typically, I use active dry yeast and add vinegar or lemon juice as the acid that boosts the yeast's performance. So, don't use instant yeast (which already contains acid) in this book, unless the recipe specifies it.
- Milk of choice can be any dairy-free milk beverage you choose; I used 1 percent milk. Dairy substitutes are offered for all cow's milk ingredients, including buttermilk, cheese, cream cheese, nonfat dry milk powder, sour cream, sweetened condensed milk, and yogurt. (See Dairy Substitutes below for more on dairy products.)
- Serving sizes may be smaller than you expect—and a serving isn't necessarily enough to satisfy your hunger. In this era of supersized meals, most people eat more than one standard serving at any one meal. The serving sizes in this book are the standard sizes defined by the American Dietetic Association.
- Nutritional content of recipes is analyzed with MasterCook Deluxe Version 9.0. Calories are rounded to the nearest 5 calories, using 1 percent milk and the Gluten-Free Flour Blend on page 27. When an ingredient has a possible substitute (for example, butter or buttery spread), the nutrient calculations are performed with the ingredient that is listed first—in this case, butter.

DAIRY SUBSTITUTES

All of the recipes in this cookbook are naturally dairy-free or suggest substitutions for dairy products. If you are not dairy sensitive, then use the cow's milk or traditional version of the product. Lactose-free cow's milk products may be used if you can tolerate them. If you are among the 30 to 50 million Americans who can't tolerate cow's milk, then use the brand I used or a gluten-free, dairy-free version that you are familiar with. To see which brands I used, look in Brands Used in Testing Recipes (page 227).

Here is what you should know about dairy substitutes:

Butter: Substitutes for butter are usually called buttery spreads and come in bars or tubs. They have a texture and flavor similar to butter and perform a lot like real butter in baking and cooking. Do not use any butters or buttery spreads labeled as diet, low-calorie, whipped, or spreadable in baking because they may contain more water, and that can upset the balance between dry and liquid ingredients. I am often asked if coconut oil can be used in place of butter in baking. The answer is yes, but be sure to measure it and use it as a solid (it melts at room temperature) so that it is as close to butter in volume and texture as possible when it is mixed into batter or dough. However, unlike the buttery spreads, coconut oil has no buttery flavor. There is a new coconut spread by Earth Balance that can also be used in baking, and it lends a slight buttery flavor.

Cow's milk: There are many gluten-free milk "beverages" (as they are called, but it's easier to call them "milk"), but each has its own unique flavor and performance traits. None of them taste just like cow's milk, so your palate will need to adjust to the new flavor(s). You can choose gluten-free milks made from almond, coconut, hazelnut, hemp, rice, soy, and sunflower. Some are darker in color with stronger flavors (such as hazelnut), while others are white and mild in flavor (such as coconut). I try to use milks that are fortified (especially with calcium) and have a high protein content to provide as much nutrition as possible. Generally speaking, if a recipe calls for milk, it will turn out better with a high-protein rather than a low-protein milk substitute, but that outcome can vary by recipe. Try a variety of milks to see which ones you prefer, but in the end, you should use the milk that you and your family like.

Cheese: There are many cheese alternatives available, so try them all to see which ones you prefer. They are generally available in cheddar and mozzarella flavors—usually in shredded form—but Daiya offers wedges in several flavors. None melt quite like traditional cheeses, but Daiya's tapioca-based version comes the closest. It stays freshest when frozen, but bring it to room temperature before using for best results.

Cream cheese: Cream cheese alternatives are slightly darker in color than traditional versions but will produce dishes that are very similar in flavor and appearance. They contain more gums and stabilizers that make them a bit firmer than traditional cream cheese, and this can slightly affect the consistency of dips and cheesecakes.

Kefir: Kefir is cultured milk, similar to buttermilk. The only gluten-free, dairy-free version is cultured coconut milk by So Delicious. Use it in place of buttermilk, but it is quite thick, so dilute it using this formula: For every 1 cup of buttermilk in a recipe, use ¾ cup kefir and ¼ cup water so that its consistency is more like real buttermilk.

Nonfat dry milk powder: This is milk that has been dehydrated. It is very dense and powdery and is found in natural foods stores, usually labeled as nonfat dry milk powder. It is not the same as that sold by Carnation, the granulated milk product most often found in grocery stores. Because of nonfat milk powder's density, it has a higher protein and sugar content, and these traits make for better yeast breads than Carnation. The same amount of Better Than Milk soy powder is an excellent dairy-free substitute for nonfat dry milk powder.

Sour cream: Dairy-free versions taste and look very similar to traditional versions and can be used on a one-to-one basis. They make excellent toppings for savory foods—such as baked potatoes—but can also successfully be used in baking.

Sweetened condensed milk: See the sidebar Homemade Sweetened Condensed Milk (page 192) to make your own, dairy-free version. The recipe makes the same amount as a can of the store-bought version.

Yogurt: When recipes call for yogurt, be sure to use plain yogurt—especially in savory recipes—unless the recipe says otherwise. The plain yogurts that are usually found in natural foods stores are made from coconut or soy, but they often contain more sugar than those made from cow's milk. If you can find plain, unsweetened soy yogurt by WholeSoy or Wildwood, use it. The texture of nondairy yogurt varies by brand; generally, coconut yogurt is more watery while soy yogurt (especially WholeSoy or Wildwood) has a texture most similar to cow's milk yogurt.

EGGS

Although many people avoid eggs (for allergy reasons or vegan diets), the recipes in this cookbook are meant to be made with eggs. Eggs perform many important functions, especially in baking. They lighten baked items and help them rise (for example, popovers and cream puffs are leavened entirely by eggs, with no additional baking powder or baking soda). They also act as binders to hold ingredients together, and they add critical moisture in baking. It is possible to bake without eggs, but it is best to use a cookbook with recipes that are specially designed for this purpose.

SALT

Salt is an essential component of our diet, not the least because it makes food taste good. Here are a couple of issues regarding salt that you should know about:

1. Butter should be unsalted. Experts believe that unsalted butter tastes fresher and allows you to control the amount of salt in your food because the amount of salt added to butter varies across brands. However, the buttery spreads (such as Earth Balance) used as a substitute for butter contain salt. So here is how I handled this issue: The amount of salt recommended in my recipes is based on salted buttery spread rather than on unsalted butter. If you use unsalted butter, your dish may require more salt, but I designed the recipes this way because it is always easier to add more salt than to take it out.

In baking, if you make my recipes with buttery spread, use the amount of salt specified in the recipe (unless you are on a salt-restricted diet, in which case follow your own guidelines). But if you use unsalted butter or canola oil (which contains no salt), prepare the recipe with the specified amount of salt and decide if it needs more when you taste the finished product. You can always add more salt (try $\frac{1}{4}$ teaspoon to start) the next time you make the recipe and see how you like it. Again, it is always easier to add more salt than to remove it.

2. For other non-baking dishes, taste the dish before adding the final seasonings, such as salt and pepper. Some experts say a recipe should specify the exact amount of salt and pepper. Others recommend saying "salt and pepper to taste." My advice is to season your food in stages as you cook it, not all at once at the end. This means that for certain dishes, you should taste before adding that final recommended amount of salt and pepper. Soups and stews are a good example. Depending on the broth type (homemade, low-sodium, full-strength), the saltiness of your soup or stew could vary a great deal. You can always add more salt, but it is very difficult to tone down an oversalted dish.

STOCKING THE GLUTEN-FREE KITCHEN

Part of the challenge of preparing your own meals is keeping the basics on hand so that you don't waste precious time with last-minute trips to the store. Keep these ingredients in your pantry so you are always prepared.

Pantry Essentials: Baking Ingredients

Ingredient	Use
Flours: sorghum, brown and white rice, cornmeal, potato starch, cornstarch, tapioca, and sweet rice are staples. Buy these flours as needed: almond, amaranth, arrowroot, buckwheat, chestnut, chickpea, garbanzo/fava bean, mesquite, quinoa, teff, white bean.	Flours for baking; thickens sauces, gravies, puddings
Butter, shortening, margarine, cooking oil	Adds fat to baked goods; grease baking pans
Chocolate: natural and Dutch-processed cocoa, plus chocolate chips	Use in baked goods and cooking
Coconut (shredded and flaked)	Baked goods, granola, frostings, garnishes
Cooking spray	Prevents food from sticking to pan
Dairy products: milk, eggs, sour cream, yogurt, cream cheese	Baking, cooking
Herbs and spices	Basil, cinnamon, chili powder, coriander, cumin, curry powder, dill, fennel seeds, oregano, crushed red pepper, rosemary, tarragon, thyme
Leavening: yeast (active dry and instant/rapid-rise), baking powder, baking soda, cream of tartar	Leavens baked goods
Dry milk powder (nonfat)	Adds protein and sugar to improve texture of yeast bread. Dairy-free version is soy-based Better Than Milk
Sugar (brown, granulated, powdered)	Sweetens foods
Vanilla extract (pure, not artificial)	Baked goods, beverages, granola
Vinegar	Acidifies milk into buttermilk; food for yeast in breads
Xanthan gum, guar gum	Prevents crumbling in baked goods; thickens sauces and salad dressings

Pantry Essentials: Canned and Dry Goods

Non-perishable items like these can be kept on your pantry shelf until opened, then perishable liquids should be refrigerated.

Ingredient	Use
Beans and legumes, canned and dry: black, cannellini, chickpea/garbanzo, kidney, pinto, split pea	Casseroles, side dishes, soups/stews, dips such as hummus
Chicken broth (gluten-free, low-sodium)	Casseroles, liquid for cooking beans or rice
Condiments: mayonnaise, mustard (Dijon, coarse-grain, and yellow), soy sauce, hoisin, hot sauce, Worcestershire sauce (gluten-free)	Casseroles, sauces, side dishes
Marinara (spaghetti) sauce (gluten-free)	Pasta, main dishes, pizza
Mushrooms (canned and dried)	Casseroles, soups, stews, entrées
Oats: quick-cooking, rolled, and steel-cut oats (gluten-free)	Breakfast, bars/cookies, stretcher for meatballs/meat loaf
Olives	Pizza, salads, sauces, pasta
Pasta: elbow, fettuccine, penne, spaghetti, spiral (gluten-free)	Casseroles, pasta main dishes, pasta salads
Polenta: quick, regular, and pre-formed in tubes	Side dishes, or base for marinara sauce, or under entrée such as shrimp or sausage, or dusted with cheese
Quinoa flakes and whole-grain quinoa	Breakfast cereal, side dishes, whole-grain salads
Rice (brown)	Breakfast cereal, side dishes, whole-grain salads
Roasted red peppers (jarred)	Pizza, salads, soup, on crostini
Salsa (canned or jarred)	Southwestern food topper; also on baked potatoes and in soups, dips, side dishes
Taco shells	Tacos, appetizers
Tomatoes (peeled whole tomatoes—fire-roasted boosts flavor—are most versatile, but also sun-dried, tomato juice, tomato paste)	Casseroles, stews, soups
Tuna (canned or packets)	Sandwiches, salads, pasta

Pantry Essentials: Refrigerated and Frozen Essentials

These items are perishable and should be purchased as you need them.

Ingredient	Use
Refrigerate once opened	
Capers	Casseroles, sauces, pasta
Tomato paste (can or tube)	Broth, sauces
Perishables (should be refrigerated)	
Bacon, deli meat	Breakfast, soups/stews, casseroles
Bread (bagels, quick, sandwich, tortillas)	Sandwiches, wraps, bread crumbs
Butter, buttermilk, cream cheese, milk, sour cream, yogurt	Drinking, eating, baked goods
Cheese (cheddar, mozzarella, Parmesan)	Cooking, snacking
Eggs	Baked goods, egg dishes
Fish (cod, salmon, shrimp)	Soups/stews, casseroles
Fruits/vegetables (apples, berries, blueberries, broccoli, corn, green beans, lemons, limes, oranges, peas, raspberries, spinach, strawberries)	Snacking, baking, cooking
Nuts/seeds (almonds, pecans, pumpkin seeds, sunflower seeds, walnuts)	Baked goods, snacks, granola

CONVERTING YOUR OWN RECIPES TO BE GLUTEN-FREE

One of the most frequent questions at my cooking classes is, "How can I make my own recipes gluten-free?" We all have favorite dishes that hold fond memories for us, and it is only natural that we want to continue eating them.

I usually recommend that new gluten-free cooks start out making recipes from gluten-free cookbooks before modifying their own recipes. That way, you can see what the dough or batter should look like and get a feel for how gluten-free cooking differs from the way you formerly cooked. I also recommend that you find a recipe in a gluten-free cookbook that resembles yours and then use your own spices and flavorings to make the dish taste like your version.

When I first started baking gluten-free food—when white rice flour was all we could buy—my approach was to reduce the total flour amount by 10 to 15 percent in order to compensate for the very dense nature of white rice flour. So, for a recipe that used 1 cup of white rice flour blend, I would use 1 cup minus 2 tablespoons. I added xanthan gum (using the guidelines that follow) and three-quarters of the liquid. I then checked the consistency of the batter or dough and then added the remaining liquid, if needed, in small amounts. I always kept notes on what I did so that I could replicate these results the next time.

Today, when I use my own Gluten-Free Flour Blend (page 27), which is lighter than those white rice flour blends, I assume that the flour blend will replace wheat flour on a one-to-one basis. Of course, that depends on the recipe, and I don't know if this is true until I prepare the recipe. Then I look at the batter or dough to see whether it is too wet or too dry and add more flour blend or liquids accordingly. Remember, gluten-free batter and dough is typically wetter and stickier than wheat-based versions. I write down what I do in the margins of the recipe so that I know what to do the next time. And I add xanthan gum or guar gum to all baked goods using the chart below. In some recipes, both gums are used because they have a natural synergy that makes for a better texture.

SAFETY AND CLEANLINESS IN THE GLUTEN-FREE KITCHEN

Some families ban all gluten from their kitchens to assure a safe environment for food preparation. But this may not be realistic for your family if you store and prepare gluten-containing food in the same kitchen out of necessity or as a matter of principle. Some family members won't give up gluten, or they believe that a totally gluten-free kitchen shelters the gluten-free person from the realities he or she is bound to confront outside the home.

The biggest issue in home kitchens (as in restaurants) is cross-contact, sometimes called cross-contamination. This is when gluten-free food touches food containing gluten. For example, gluten-free bread toasted in the same toaster where regular bread has been toasted can come into contact with bread crumbs left behind. Using the same utensil to spread peanut butter can transfer gluten particles to gluten-free bread. Airborne particles of wheat flour can settle on gluten-free food.

To avoid cross-contamination when preparing gluten-free food at home, follow these guidelines:
- Use separate utensils, cutting boards, and serving bowls so food with gluten doesn't touch gluten-free food. Cutting boards with deep crevices can harbor gluten particles.

How Much Xanthan Gum or Guar Gum?

Gums are a critical component of successful gluten-free baking and cooking. They act as emulsifiers and stabilizers and create an environment in which the leavening can do its job. My recipes tell you how to use them, but if you are converting your own recipes to be gluten-free, then you will need to know how much xanthan gum or guar gum to use. Here is a handy chart for that purpose.

Where?	How Much?	Tips for Success
Salad dressings	Xanthan: $\frac{1}{8}$–$\frac{1}{4}$ teaspoon per cup of liquid Guar: $\frac{1}{4}$–$\frac{3}{8}$ teaspoon per cup of liquid	Mix with dry ingredients first (such as salt, pepper, sugar), then add liquids.
Cookies	Xanthan: $\frac{1}{4}$ teaspoon per cup of flour Guar: $\frac{3}{8}$ teaspoon per cup of flour	Mix with dry ingredients first.
Pancakes, waffles	Xanthan: $\frac{1}{4}$ teaspoon per cup of flour Guar: $\frac{3}{8}$ teaspoon per cup of flour	Mix with dry ingredients first.
Cakes	Xanthan: $\frac{1}{2}$ teaspoon per cup of flour Guar: $\frac{3}{4}$ teaspoon per cup of flour	Mix with dry ingredients first.
Muffins, quick breads	Xanthan: $\frac{3}{4}$ teaspoon per cup of flour Guar: 1 teaspoon per cup of flour	Mix with dry ingredients first.
Bread	Xanthan: 1–$1\frac{1}{2}$ teaspoons per cup of flour Guar: $1\frac{1}{2}$–$2\frac{1}{4}$ teaspoons per cup of flour	Mix with dry ingredients first.
Pizza	Xanthan: 2 teaspoons per cup of flour Guar: 3 teaspoons per cup of flour	Mix with dry ingredients first.
Sauce thickener	Xanthan: 1 teaspoon in place of each tablespoon of original thickener (such as wheat flour or cornstarch) Guar gum: $1\frac{1}{2}$ teaspoons in place of each tablespoon of original thickener	Mix with dry ingredients first (such as salt, spices), then add liquids.

A Note about Xanthan Gum and Guar Gum You buy them as dry goods, but be careful when working with them and storing them. Once they get wet, they become gummy and can stick to everything. It's simple enough to clean up, but inconvenient. Be careful when opening or measuring from the packages because they fly into the air, and clean the area right away if there's any spillage.

- Clearly label the foods and the storage areas in the pantry and refrigerator so everyone knows which food is gluten-free.
- Use separate appliances if there is any possibility that gluten can become lodged in them. For example, a second toaster is a good idea, or use the white plastic sleeves (called toast-it bags) that protect gluten-free bread from touching anything else but allow it to toast beautifully in a shared toaster. Also, cast-iron skillets often retain gluten residue, so keep one especially for gluten-free food. Make sure your bread machine, panini machine, or any other appliance (such as waffle irons) doesn't have any crevices where crumbs can become trapped, or use a different machine just for gluten-free bread.
- Use squeeze bottles for condiments such as ketchup, mayonnaise, and mustard rather than dipping knives or spoons into them and increasing the risk of cross-contamination.
- Don't bake with gluten flours at the same time you are baking with gluten-free foods. Airborne particles of wheat flour can settle on gluten-free food, utensils, appliances, and bowls. If you're not paying careful attention, you might accidentally transmit gluten to your gluten-free food.
- After baking with wheat flour, wipe down all countertops, appliances, and any other surfaces that could harbor gluten particles.
- Wash hands before handling or preparing gluten-free food. Not only is this a good sanitary practice, but it also removes the possibility that your hands might transfer traces of gluten to the gluten-free food.

MAKING THE MOST OF YOUR KITCHEN TIME

People often tell me, "I would like to cook, but I don't have time!" We are all strapped for time, but here are a few simple guidelines to help you make the most of your time in the kitchen.

Master the Idea of "Planned-Overs"

Learning to cook means using your time wisely in the kitchen. Some families avoid leftovers like the plague, while smart cooks know that using them in new and different ways not only disguises the fact that they are leftovers, but also saves time and reduces waste. In fact, these clever cooks *intentionally* create leftovers—but call them planned-overs because they have definite plans for using them again. Some people call it bulk-cooking, too; here is how it works:

Plan Ahead by Cooking Ahead

Set aside a block of time—perhaps a weekend or a weeknight that's free—when you can do some serious cooking for future meals by assembling the entreés ahead of time and freezing them. (The Marinated Flank Steak with Herbs on page 102 is a good example.) You may even double or triple a recipe, freezing enough for a later meal to serve your entire family and the remainder in individual serving-size portions. I do this with chili—freezing enough for a family meal in one container, and dividing the remaining chili into single servings and freezing them, flattened, in freezer bags. Easily defrosted in the microwave oven, they are a real time-saver for a quick meal.

Cook Today, Make Many Meals for the Week

This principle applies to cooking larger items, knowing you'll subdivide them into future meals for use later that week or to go into the freezer for a later time. I have a routine that automatically determines subsequent meals. For example, if I roast a whole chicken, I know that a couple of days later we'll have chicken potpie or some other kind of chicken casserole. The chicken bones immediately go into the stockpot to make chicken broth, which usually simmers during dinner. Later that evening, after the broth has simmered, it goes into the refrigerator in 2-cup containers to cool. The next day, I skim off any unwanted fat, label the containers, and freeze them. Some cooks freeze the broth in muffin pans and store the frozen "muffins" in a freezer bag.

If I have any leftover broth after filling all of my containers, I whip up a quick chicken noodle soup or simply drink the broth as a healthy snack. If there is any leftover chicken meat, it goes into a sandwich. Nothing goes to waste. As you can see, that single roasted chicken determined several meals for later that week. If that sounds like too much chicken in one week, just freeze the cooked chicken for later use.

I employ a similar technique for pork tenderloin, one of my favorite cuts of meat. We enjoy a meal of pork tenderloin (perhaps the Pan-Roasted Pork Tenderloin with Honey-Mustard Pan Sauce on page 107), then refrigerate the leftover portions. Later in the week, I dice the pork and use it for pork and green chile stew—an easy slow cooker meal that takes little time to prepare and cooks while I'm gone for the day.

Save Time by Cooking or Preparing More Than You Need; Use the Rest Later

Always prepare more than you need, if you're sure you can use the excess later. For example, you might brown 2 pounds of beef cubes, using 1 pound for dinner tonight and the second pound later that week or freezing them for later in the month. If a recipe calls for ½ pound of browned ground beef,

brown the whole pound and freeze the unused portion. It is such a time-saver on a busy night to pull a batch of browned ground beef from the freezer and quickly thaw it in the microwave for that night's meal. Think about the dishes your family likes and ways in which you can streamline that process with these tips. You will save a great deal of time, and food preparation will be much easier.

A BASIC PRIMER ON GLUTEN-FREE YEAST BREAD

Of all the foods we miss when gluten is off-limits, bread is at the top of the list for most people. It certainly was for me. And the class I am most often asked to teach at cooking schools focuses on the question "How can I make good bread in my own kitchen?" So, I compiled all of my tips on the following pages so that you can bake bread successfully at home.

There are two ways to bake yeast bread: by hand in a conventional oven or in a bread machine. If you want to bake yeast bread by hand, then this section should help ensure success each and every time. If you prefer to use a bread machine, that information is here as well. Even though there are wonderful gluten-free breads on the market, it is tremendously satisfying to make your own bread— and much cheaper, too.

Baking Bread by Hand in a Conventional Oven

Ready, Set . . . Planning Ahead for Success!
1 Have all ingredients at room temperature; check the yeast expiration date.

2 Have all ingredients measured and on one side of the work space before beginning. As you add each ingredient, place it on the opposite side of the work space so you know it was added. This prevents you from adding the salt twice, or forgetting the xanthan gum.

3 Use standard measuring utensils; measure correctly:
   a. Run a whisk through the flour a few times to aerate it
   b. Spoon the flour lightly into a dry measuring cup (don't pack the flour down)
   c. Level the flour with the straight edge of a knife (To see me demonstrate how to measure flour, go to Videos at *www.glutenfree101.com.*)

4 Use the proper type and size of pan. Nonstick pans (gray, not black) conduct heat and brown the bread better than glass or shiny aluminum. Browning is important in providing structure so that the bread can rise properly. Generously grease the pan (and dust with brown rice flour, if desired). A 4x8-inch pan is used for 1-pound loaves; a 5x9-inch pan is used for 1½-pound loaves. Small pans work better than large pans because the heated air can reach the center of the loaf more easily.

5 Use your favorite bread recipe. To boost fiber and nutrition, add oat bran*, rice bran or rice polish, hemp seed, flax meal, and almond or pecan meal. Start slowly; add 1 to 2 tablespoons per loaf, increasing to ¼ cup later as your body adjusts to the fiber. If you add more than ¼ cup of high-fiber grains, you may need to increase the liquid in the recipe accordingly.

6 Check the oven temperature with an oven thermometer. If your oven does not bake at the specified temperature, have it calibrated.

Check with your physician before eating gluten-free oats.

Go! . . . Mixing It Up!

1 Dissolve the yeast in warm (110°F) liquid. If your area doesn't have good-tasting water, then filtered water is a better choice. Use a heavy-duty stand mixer with a regular beater, not the dough hook, because the dough hook doesn't mix the gluten-free dough thoroughly.

2 Once blended, beat the dough for 30 to 60 seconds to incorporate air and set the xanthan gum. The dough will slightly thicken and the tracks of the beater will be more visible as this happens.

3 For the proper consistency, bread dough should fall gracefully off the beater in globs, rather than cling firmly or fall from the beater in sheets. It should look like fluffy frosting or stiff cake batter. If you have to pry the dough from the beater, it is too stiff and needs more liquid. If it runs off the beater in a thin stream or sheet, it is too wet and needs more flour.

4 Smooth the dough in the pan with a wet spatula for a smoother crust and even rising. The smoother and more uniform the dough, the more attractive the loaf of bread will be.

5 Cover the dough loosely with a foil tent that is lightly oiled so that it won't stick to the dough. Let the dough rise at room temperature (75°F to 85°F). Place in an enclosed area (such as the oven or microwave) to avoid drafts and drying out (see the sidebar Where to Let Bread Rise, page 46).

6 Dough should rise no higher than the top of the pan. If it rises higher than that, it is more likely to fall because oven-spring will cause the dough to rise even higher while baking and the loaf isn't strong enough to support itself.

Baking . . . The Heat Is On!

1 For most loaf breads, place the oven rack in the lower third of the oven: not the bottom rack, but one notch lower than the middle rack. Preheat the oven to the temperature specified in the recipe. Bake for the specified amount of time, but remember that ovens differ and yours may take less time or more time to achieve a properly baked loaf than the recipe indicates. It is better to bake bread for a longer period of time at a lower temperature than it is to bake it for a shorter period of time at a higher temperature.

2 For a crisper crust on French bread and baguettes, place bread in a cold oven and then turn the oven on to the desired temperature. It will rise as the oven heats. This also works especially well for bagels and breadsticks, but it will not work with full-size loaves such as 4x8-inch or 5x9-inch—or if your oven preheats with the broiler only or has a fast preheat setting.

3 Lay a sheet of aluminum foil over the dough after 15 minutes of baking to avoid overbrowning. Don't open the door again because this allows heat to escape and slows down the baking process.

4 A properly baked loaf registers an internal temperature of 200°F to 205°F when tested with an instant-read thermometer. Don't underbake—this is one of the chief causes of fallen bread. The crust may look nicely browned, but the dough may not be fully cooked.

5 Smaller baking pans, such as 4x8-inch or 4x6-inch, or French loaf or baguette pans, work better because the dough bakes more quickly and evenly. Use parchment paper to prevent leakage if your pans are perforated.

Storing Gluten-Free Bread

Gluten-free bread is best eaten on the same day it is baked. However, even the most zealous bread eaters cannot consume a whole loaf in one day. If the bread will be consumed within 2 days, store it (tightly wrapped to avoid drying out) at room temperature. Gluten-free bread can be refrigerated, tightly wrapped, for up to a week but will get stiffer due to the starch's reaction to the cold. To make the bread more pliable after chilling, rewarm it very gently on Low power in the microwave for 10 seconds. Never reheat gluten-free bread on High power. It irreparably alters the starches to make the bread hard as a rock when it cools. Gluten-free bread can be frozen for up to 1 month. It is best to slice the bread beforehand so that you can easily remove a slice at a time. Some people insert pieces of waxed paper or parchment paper between the slices before freezing for easier removal. Frozen bread can thaw (tightly wrapped) at room temperature or be gently rewarmed on Low power in the microwave oven in 10-second intervals. Refrigerated or frozen bread can also be toasted, which is an excellent way to regenerate bread that is slightly stale or hard.

Where to Let Bread Rise

People who live in cold climates (such as Denver, where I live) have to be creative when choosing a location to let bread rise, since homes can be chilly in winter. I have experimented with many different locations. My current favorite is my warming oven, which has a setting for bread rising. It is enclosed, so I don't have to cover the bread to avoid drying out while it rises. My other favorite location is my microwave, where I bring a Pyrex measuring cup of water to a boil on High. Leaving the cup of water in the oven, I place my bread inside (no need to cover it since the microwave is enclosed and the bread won't dry out), and the bread happily rises in this warm, moist environment. The disadvantage is that you can't use your microwave during this time.

Other favorite locations include the top of a clothes dryer that is running or on a granite countertop that has been warmed by the sun shining on it. I have also placed the bread pan on an electric heating pad and slipped a large dry-cleaning bag around everything to create a little hothouse. Many people like to use their ovens, turning on the oven light to create gentle warmth. Don't turn on your oven, however, because that inevitably produces too much heat, which dries out the crust and hampers the bread's rise. Some newer ovens have a bread-proofing feature so that you can let the bread rise at a proper temperature inside the oven; if your oven has this feature, by all means use it. But you can't bake anything in the oven during this time.

Avoid locations that are warmer than 85°F because the bread will rise too quickly and have a weaker cell struture, making it more likely to fall.

Make-Ahead Yeast Bread Dough

A method that makes the most of your time in the kitchen is to make yeast bread dough ahead of time, refrigerate it (tightly covered), and bake it up to 3 days later. Here's how it is done: Make the bread dough as directed in your recipe, but use cold rather than warm liquids to avoid stimulating the yeast, and then refrigerate, tightly covered. The dough is ready to bake when you are, is easier to shape and handle while it is cold, and has a more complex flavor due to the enzyme activity that occurs while it chills. Another benefit is a better texture, with more irregular holes and a crumb that more closely resembles wheat-based bread. I use this method often with French bread/baguettes and pizza, making the dough the night before and baking it the next day. The dough may take just slightly longer to start rising, since it starts out cold, but the convenience is well worth it.

6 After baking, cool the bread in the pan on a wire rack for 10 minutes. Then run a sharp knife around the edge of the bread to loosen it and transfer it to the wire rack to cool completely. The wire rack allows air to circulate completely around the bread. Resist the urge to slice the bread right after it comes out of the oven. It is still baking, so don't disturb it. Cutting hot bread too soon releases precious steam that would otherwise remain in the loaf to keep it moist.

7 When thoroughly cooled, slice with a serrated or electric knife. If you plan to eat all of the bread within 2 days, store it on the countertop, tightly wrapped (see the sidebar Storing Gluten-Free Bread).

8 See Bread 101—a step-by-step guide for baking gluten-free bread by hand at www.glutenfree101. com. Click on Videos, then on Bread 101.

9 Although they are commonly used in restaurants and commercial bakeries, convection ovens are not recommended for the bread recipes in this book. Convection ovens tend to bake a bit hotter because their fans circulate hot air around the dough. This causes the dough to dry out, cook too fast, and not have a chance to rise properly.

Baking Bread in a Bread Machine

If you are not an experienced baker, then a bread machine may be your salvation, because it eliminates some of the guesswork. You don't have to be physically present to monitor the rising and baking times as you do when making bread by hand.

However, there are some downsides to bread machines—as I have learned from owning five of them. Most are pre-programmed for gluten breads, which need two risings. Gluten-free bread needs only one rise, so that second rise adds unnecessary time. One way around this is to buy a machine that is programmable, but you must decide each cycle's length and that can depend on the recipe.

In addition, the paddles make indentations on the underside of the loaf that mar the appearance of some of the bread slices, and the baking pan or bucket might be a cylinder rather than the traditional loaf shape. Bread baked in a bread machine rarely produces a "dome" or nicely rounded top (as it does with an oven-baked loaf).

Finally, we can't take advantage of some of the bread machine's time-saving aspects such as programming our breads to bake overnight, because most gluten-free breads usually require eggs, which should not sit unrefrigerated in the machine.

Nonetheless, despite all these disadvantages, some people prefer bread machines. If you are one of them, here are some tips for that perfect loaf.

FEATURES TO CONSIDER WHEN CHOOSING A BREAD MACHINE

Bucket or Pan Size: Some people prefer to bake smaller loaves (such as 1 pound) and have fresh bread frequently by baking more often. Others prefer to bake larger loaves ($1\frac{1}{2}$ to 2 pounds) because they have larger families or like to bake large quantities for freezing. I personally think that the smaller, 1-pound loaves turn out better than the larger 2-pound loaves.

Cycles: Ideally, your bread machine has an option for one rise, perhaps called a short or rapid cycle. However, your bread machine may have two cycles.

Don't despair. There are ways to handle this (see How to Use Your Bread Machine).

Paddles: Generally, larger paddles are better. However, there are ways to handle this, too. (See How to Use Your Bread Machine).

Size: Be sure to use the right size recipe for your machine, or vice versa. Some cooks unknowingly use a $1\frac{1}{2}$- to 2-pound recipe in a 1-pound bread machine. The dough overflows, causing a mess inside the bread machine.

Shape: Some machines produce loaves that are cylindrical (round); others are square. Still others are loaf shaped. I find all three shapes acceptable; however, buy the loaf shape if your family is committed to conventional loaf-shaped sandwiches.

Price: The price of bread machines has dropped considerably since I purchased my first one in 1994. You can get a good machine for well under $100, although the popular Zojirushi may be more expensive, depending on where you buy it.

HOW TO USE YOUR BREAD MACHINE

We gluten-free bakers are a creative bunch, so here are some tricks of the trade from my own experiences as well as tips from many of you.

Preparing and Adding Ingredients

- Measure carefully, using standard cups and spoons (no teaspoons from the silverware drawer).
- Have all ingredients at room temperature, unless your bread machine instructions advise otherwise.
- Blend the liquid ingredients together thoroughly, using a wire whisk or electric mixer (egg membranes must be completely broken up).
- Follow your machine instructions when adding ingredients (liquids first and dry ingredients next, or vice versa). There is tremendous variation across different brands, so follow the instructions. If your brand has a gluten-free bread recipe in the instruction booklet, use it instead of your recipe. After using five different brands of bread machines, I believe that the secret to success is matching the right recipe with the right machine. Some recipes work beautifully with some bread machines, while others don't, so experimentation is ongoing.
- Grease the bucket/pan with shortening or lightly coat with cooking spray for easy release and cleaning.

Selecting the Cycle/Program/Setting

- Some machines have settings for the crust color, such as normal, light, or dark. You may have to make bread twice—the same recipe on two different settings—to see which works best. I prefer the Normal setting.
- If you'd rather not have your bread go through two rises and you don't want the paddle marks (and you can't program your machine), determine when the second rise begins from your machine's instruction booklet. Set a timer so you can be ready when the second rise starts. For example, in the Welbilt example below, I would set the timer for 50 minutes because that's when the first rise begins.
- Start the machine empty, and about 10 minutes before the 50 minutes is up, thoroughly mix all the bread ingredients together. Put the dough into the bucket/pan (but don't use the paddle)

and when the timer rings, listen for the bread machine beep (or watch the LCD or LED window display) and insert the bucket/pan at the right moment. With this method, you won't have paddle marks in your loaf.

- To program your machine, adapt the cycle information below. It's from my 1-pound Welbilt and a modification of recommendations from Red Star Yeast. The third column is for a Zojirushi BBC-V20 on Home Made setting. You may have to modify your machine cycle to other lengths, but at least you have a reference point now. All machines are different and manufacturers are continually updating their models, so these instructions may need modifying and it may take several attempts to get the loaf you want. Again, follow your instruction manual for the best results.

Cycles for Bread Machines

Welbilt (1 lb)	Red Star Yeast	Zojirushi (1 lb)
Warm: 20 minutes*	Warm: 20 minutes*	Preheat: 20 minutes*
Knead: 10 minutes	Knead: 20 minutes	Knead: 25 minutes
Rest: 5 minutes	First rise: none	First rise: none
Knead: 15 minutes	Second rise: 70 minutes	Second rise: 35 minutes
First rise: 25 minutes	Bake: 60 minutes	Bake: 60 minutes
Second rise: 54 minutes	Total: 2 hours 50 minutes	Total: 2 hours 20 minutes
Bake: 40 minutes		
Total: 2 hours 49 minutes		

*Some machines don't do this.

- Another way to eliminate the second rise is available on my Welbilt ABMY2K2 Baker's Select machine (which is an older model). After the first rise, stop the machine and cancel the cycle by pressing the STOP key until it beeps. Set the machine to the BAKE setting and press the START key. (But, like the technique above, you have to be there to do this—thus reducing the convenience of bread machines in the first place.)
- Rising time can vary considerably, depending on the altitude, humidity, and type of flours used. So, you may need to alter these rising times in the table above to suit your particular situation.

During Mixing and Baking

- Use a spatula to scrape down the bucket sides during the first mixing.
- Listen for beeps that signal when to add mix-ins (raisins, nuts, and so forth).
- Don't raise the lid if your machine says not to—on some of my machines, it cancels the cycle entirely. If this happens, quickly transfer the dough to a greased pan and finish rising the bread, then bake in a conventional oven at 375°F.
- Unless your recipe says otherwise, choose a Normal or Medium setting. One of the common problems is underbaking, rather than overbaking, the bread. So don't be afraid to extend the baking time if you can program the cycles.
- Watch the dough through the window the first few times you use a bread machine. Learn to recognize the right appearance and texture at each stage. Take notes if you adjust the recipe (like adding more flour blend or more liquid) so you know what to do next time.
- Many gluten-free bakers mistakenly think that very soft bread dough doesn't look right. Actually, gluten-free bread dough (whether making bread by hand or with a bread machine) should be fairly soft and drop gracefully in globs from a spatula, rather than having to pry the dough from it.
- Once you've learned how the dough should look, you can modify it by adding more water or flour blend during the mixing stage. Generally, there should be soft lines on the top of the dough indicating the path or tracks of the paddles.

After Baking

- Some machines will keep your bread warm after baking. Others do not. For best results, don't leave bread in the machine too long or the moisture buildup will soften the crust.

- If the crust isn't crisp enough or the bread seems underdone (even though the cycles are completed), transfer the loaf to a baking sheet and bake another 10 to 15 minutes in a preheated conventional oven or until it reaches the desired level of doneness.
- To test for doneness, insert an instant-read thermometer in the middle or thickest part of the loaf. It should read 200°F to 205°F.
- Use the manufacturer's toll-free customer service department to let them know if you have problems or questions. Sometimes bread machines are defective, although that is rare.
- One final thought: Buying appliances such as a bread machine may seem expensive, but if you're a dedicated bread machine user, then you'll use it for a long, long time. So you're really investing in your health and your future. Would you rather spend more money on physician's visits, prescription drugs, and lost productivity at work—or spend a little more money on appliances to make your kitchen time as productive as possible and have good, safe food?

Troubleshooting the Problem Loaf from a Bread Machine

Sometimes things don't go as planned when baking bread. Following are some common problems and their recommended solutions.

Problem	Solution for the Next Time You Bake
Cratered (hollowed) top	Too much liquid. Add flour, 1 tablespoon at a time.
Mushroom top	Too much yeast. Reduce by ½ teaspoon and try again.
Gnarly, rough top	Not enough liquid; dough is too stiff. Add liquid, 1 tablespoon at a time. Another tablespoon of sugar may help, or try using more cornstarch in the flour blend. Or replace ¼ cup of the flour blend with Expandex (modified tapioca starch).
Unbaked, doughy inside	Adjust the cycle to bake longer, or finish baking in a conventional preheated oven, or bake loaves in several smaller pans rather than one large pan.

Breakfast & Brunch 》

Nutrition experts say that breakfast is the most important meal of the day. It is certainly my favorite meal of the day. In fact, one of my final thoughts before drifting off to sleep at night is, "What's for breakfast?" There is something really special about the beginning of each day; it's another opportunity to start anew and get things right with the world, so I always want my breakfast to be as healthy as possible.

My favorite is some type of whole grain (usually creamy, hearty hot cereal such as gluten-free oatmeal), but on weekends it might be scrambled eggs or French toast. I love to host brunch with casseroles like Quiche Lorraine or an Egg & Sausage Brunch Casserole. Whatever your preference, this chapter has all the basics—even a healthy smoothie!

Q	V
Quick	Vegetarian

Pancakes, Waffles

Pancakes
Buckwheat Pancakes (Blini)
French Toast
Waffles

Breads

Savory Breakfast Pizza
Sweet Breakfast Pizza

Cakes

Cinnamon Coffee Cake
  Cranberry-Orange Coffee Cake
  Lemon–Poppy Seed Coffee Cake

Casseroles, Quiches

Egg & Sausage Brunch Casserole
Quiche Lorraine
No-Crust Ham Quiche

Grains

Granola
Whole Grains for Breakfast

Miscellaneous

Breakfast Smoothie

Pancakes

What is more American than pancakes for breakfast? I usually reserve pancakes for weekends when there is more time, but you can also make this batter the night before, refrigerate in the blender or a jar, and just shake it up the next morning before cooking. If the batter is too thick, add 1 tablespoon of milk at a time to restore the right consistency. A squeeze of lemon juice also revives the leavening if it seems to have lost its mojo overnight. For even lighter pancakes, sift the dry ingredients together before blending.

1 cup Gluten-Free Flour Blend (page 27)
2 teaspoons sugar
2 teaspoons baking powder
½ teaspoon baking soda
¼ teaspoon salt
1 large egg
⅓ to ½ cup milk of choice
1 tablespoon canola oil, plus more for frying

Q, V
Makes 8 (4-inch) pancakes
Preparation time: 5 minutes
Cooking time: 5 to 8 minutes per pancake

Per serving (2 pancakes):
180 calories; 4g protein; 5g total fat; 1g fiber; 32g carbohydrates; 55mg cholesterol; 560mg sodium

1 In a blender, blend all ingredients together until smooth (use ⅓ cup milk to start). Let the batter stand while preheating the skillet or griddle to medium heat.

2 Lightly oil the hot skillet. Fry a test pancake using a scant ¼ cup batter. Adjust the batter if necessary by adding the remaining milk—a tablespoon at a time—if it seems too thick. Adjust the heat under the skillet or griddle if it is too high or too low. Fry until the tops are bubbly, 3 to 5 minutes. Turn and cook until the pancakes are golden brown, 2 to 3 minutes longer. Serve immediately.

Buckwheat Pancakes (Blini)

Buckwheat pancakes are sometimes called blini, and people who like them also like the flavor of buckwheat, which is stronger than that of many gluten-free flours. Sifting the dry ingredients after measuring will make these pancakes lighter.

Q, V

Makes 8
(4-inch)
pancakes
**Preparation
time:** 5 minutes
Cooking time:
5 to 8 minutes
per pancake

¾   cup Gluten-Free Flour Blend (page 27)
¼   cup buckwheat flour
2½ teaspoons sugar
2   teaspoons baking powder
½   teaspoon baking soda
¼   teaspoon salt
1   large egg
⅓ to ½ cup milk of choice
1   tablespoon canola oil, plus more for
      frying

**Per serving
(2 pancakes):**
180 calories;
4g protein;
5g total fat;
2g fiber;
30g
carbohydrates;
48mg
cholesterol;
493mg sodium

1 In a blender, blend all ingredients together until smooth (use ⅓ cup milk to start). Let the batter stand while preheating the skillet or griddle to medium heat.

2 Lightly oil the hot skillet. Fry a test pancake using a scant ¼ cup batter. Adjust the batter if necessary by adding the remaining milk—a tablespoon at a time—if it seems too thick. Cook until the tops are bubbly, 3 to 5 minutes. Turn; cook until golden brown, 2 to 3 minutes longer.

French Toast

I love to make French toast on weekends, when I can savor each bite . . . along with a strong cup of coffee. You can use any topping you like (see suggestions below). In summer, I often use seasonal chopped fruit, such as peaches, plums, or nectarines tossed with a little sugar. For special occasions, kids (and adults who eat like kids!) love it topped with chocolate-hazelnut spread.

3 large eggs
½ cup milk of choice
½ teaspoon pure vanilla extract
⅛ teaspoon ground cinnamon
⅛ teaspoon salt
    Canola oil, butter, or buttery spread, for
      frying
8 slices gluten-free sandwich bread or
    1-inch slices gluten-free French bread
    Toppings of choice, such as maple
      syrup, jam, jelly, powdered sugar, or
      chocolate-hazelnut spread

Q, V
Makes 8 slices
Preparation time: 5 minutes
Cooking time: 3 to 5 minutes per slice

1 In a wide shallow bowl or pie plate, whisk together the eggs, milk, vanilla, cinnamon, and salt until all of the egg membrane is thoroughly broken up.

2 Heat a light coating of oil in a large heavy skillet or griddle on medium heat. Dip both sides of the bread slices into the egg mixture, shake off excess, and fry until well browned on both sides, 3 to 5 minutes.

3 Serve warm with toppings of choice.

Per slice:
100 calories;
5g protein;
3g total fat;
1g fiber;
13g carbohydrates;
70mg cholesterol;
196mg sodium

Waffles

Don't you just love a crisp waffle for breakfast, buttered and drizzled with maple syrup? Or dressed up with yogurt and ripe, fresh fruit? Me, too! Be sure to prepare your waffle iron (regular or Belgian) following the manufacturer's directions, since brands may differ. The dimensions and number of waffles will also vary depending on the size of your particular appliance.

Q, V

Makes 4 (8-inch) waffles

Preparation time: 5 minutes

Cooking time: 4 to 6 minutes per waffle

2   cups Gluten-Free Flour Blend (page 27)
¾   cup milk of choice
4   teaspoons baking powder
2   teaspoons sugar
1   teaspoon baking soda
½   teaspoon salt
2   large eggs, beaten
¼   cup canola oil

Per waffle:
415 calories;
7g protein;
17g total fat;
2g fiber;
62g carbohydrates;
95mg cholesterol;
1120mg sodium

1 In a medium bowl, whisk all of the ingredients together until well blended. Heat the waffle iron according to the manufacturer's directions.

2 Pour one-quarter of the batter (or the manufacturer's recommended amount) onto the heated waffle iron. Close and bake until the steaming stops and the waffle is deeply browned, 4 to 6 minutes depending on your appliance. Repeat with remaining batter. Serve immediately.

Savory Breakfast Pizza

Pizza doesn't have to be eaten at lunch or dinner or be "Italian," for that matter. Why not try it for breakfast? This version is simply a gluten-free pizza crust with eggs, bacon, and cheese as the topping. Make the pizza the night before and cut it into 6 serving slices, then refrigerate. Microwave a slice on Low power the next morning and you have gluten-free fast food! If you're interested in a sweet breakfast pizza, see the next recipe.

Makes 6 slices
Preparation time: 15 minutes
Baking time: 30 to 35 minutes

Crust

- 1 tablespoon active dry yeast
- 1 teaspoon sugar
- ¾ cup warm (110°F) milk of choice
- ⅔ cup brown rice flour, plus more for sprinkling
- ½ cup tapioca flour
- 1½ teaspoons xanthan gum
- ½ teaspoon salt
- ½ teaspoon dried oregano
- 1 tablespoon olive oil
- 1½ teaspoons cider vinegar

Savory Topping

- 1¼ cups shredded mozzarella or cheddar cheese (or a combination) or cheese alternative
- 3 large eggs, cooked (scrambled) with ¼ teaspoon salt and ⅛ teaspoon freshly ground black pepper
- 3 tablespoons finely chopped green onions or 1 tablespoon dried minced onions
- 3 cooked, crumbled bacon slices or ⅓ cup cooked, crumbled sausage or finely diced Canadian bacon
- 2 plum tomatoes, finely chopped

Per slice:
270 calories;
13g protein;
12g total fat;
2g fiber;
28g carbohydrates;
133mg cholesterol;
378mg sodium

1 Make the crust: Arrange oven racks in the bottom and middle of the oven. Preheat the oven to 425°F. Grease (use shortening or butter, not oil or cooking spray) a 12-inch nonstick pizza pan (gray, not black). Dissolve the yeast and sugar in the warm milk for 5 minutes. In a food processor, blend all of the crust ingredients, including the yeast mixture, until the dough forms a ball. The dough will be quite soft.

2 Put the dough on the pizza pan. Liberally sprinkle rice flour on the dough; then press the dough into a 12-inch circle on the pan with your hands, continuing to dust the dough with flour to prevent sticking to your hands. At first, it will seem as though there is not enough dough to cover the pan, but don't worry—it is just the right amount. Make the edges thicker to contain the toppings, taking care to make the dough as smooth as possible. The smoother you can shape the dough, especially around the edges, the prettier the crust.

3 Bake the crust on the bottom rack for 10 minutes to brown the bottom. Remove from the oven. Sprinkle the crust with ½ cup of the cheese to serve as a base for the toppings. Chop the scrambled eggs into little pieces and arrange on the cheese, along with the green onions, bacon, and tomatoes. Sprinkle evenly with the remaining cheese.

4 Bake on the middle rack until the cheese is nicely browned, 20 to 25 minutes. Cool for 10 minutes on a wire rack, then cut into 6 slices.

Sweet Breakfast Pizza

Pizza doesn't have to be savory or topped with meat to be delicious; try this sweet breakfast version for a delightful change of pace.

Crust

- 1 tablespoon active dry yeast
- 2 teaspoons sugar
- ¾ cup warm (110°F) milk of choice
- ⅔ cup brown rice flour, plus more for sprinkling
- ½ cup tapioca flour
- 1½ teaspoons xanthan gum
- ½ teaspoon salt
- ½ teaspoon ground cinnamon
- 1 tablespoon olive oil
- 1 teaspoon cider vinegar

Sweet Topping

- 2 tablespoons sugar
- 1 tablespoon cornstarch
- ¼ teaspoon ground cinnamon
- ¼ teaspoon salt
- ½ cup orange juice
- 1½ cups dried fruit (such as apricots, blueberries, cherries, cranberries, or a mix)
- ½ cup sliced almonds
  Dusting of powdered sugar, for garnish

V
Makes 6 slices
Preparation time: 10 minutes
Baking time: 30 to 35 minutes

Per slice:
485 calories;
6g protein;
10g total fat;
3g fiber;
99g carbohydrates;
1mg cholesterol;
198mg sodium

1 Make the crust: Arrange oven racks in the bottom and middle positions of the oven. Preheat the oven to 425°F. Grease (use shortening or butter, not oil or cooking spray) a 12-inch nonstick pizza pan (gray, not black). Dissolve the yeast and sugar in the warm milk for 5 minutes. In a food processor, blend all of the crust ingredients, including the yeast mixture, until the dough forms a ball. The dough will be quite soft.

2 Put the dough on the pizza pan. Liberally sprinkle rice flour on the dough; then press the dough into a 12-inch circle on the pan with your hands, continuing to dust the dough with flour to prevent sticking to your hands. Make the edges thicker to contain the toppings. The smoother you can shape the dough, especially around the edges, the prettier the crust. Set aside while making the topping.

3 Make the topping: In a small heavy saucepan, whisk together the sugar, cornstarch, cinnamon, and salt until thoroughly blended. Place over medium heat, add the orange juice, and cook, stirring constantly, until the mixture thickens. Remove from the heat. Stir in the dried fruit; set aside to cool slightly while the crust prebakes.

4 Bake the crust on the bottom rack for 10 minutes to brown the bottom. Remove from the oven. Spread the topping evenly on the crust and sprinkle with the almonds.

5 Bake on the middle rack until the crust is nicely browned, about 20 minutes. Remove from the oven and cool for 10 minutes on a wire rack. Dust with powdered sugar just before cutting into 6 slices. Serve slightly warm.

Cinnamon Coffee Cake

This moist cake is perfect for weekend brunches, and it is sweet enough to also serve as a dessert. It is a perfect brunch complement to savory dishes such as eggs and bacon.

V

Makes 10 servings
Preparation time: 10 minutes
Baking time: 30 to 35 minutes

Per slice:
270 calories;
3g protein;
11g total fat;
1g fiber;
42g carbohydrates;
44mg cholesterol;
248mg sodium

Cake
- ¾ cup sugar
- 2 large eggs
- ⅓ cup canola oil
- 1 teaspoon pure vanilla extract
- 1½ cups Gluten-Free Flour Blend (page 27)
- 1 teaspoon xanthan gum
- ½ teaspoon ground cinnamon
- ½ teaspoon baking powder
- ½ teaspoon baking soda
- ½ teaspoon salt
- ⅔ cup buttermilk or buttermilk substitute (see Buttermilk Substitutes, page 148)

Cinnamon Crumb Topping
- ¼ cup packed brown sugar
- 2 tablespoons cold butter or buttery spread
- ½ teaspoon ground cinnamon
- ⅓ cup Gluten-Free Flour Blend (page 27)

1 Place a rack in the middle of the oven. Preheat the oven to 350°F. Generously grease a 7x11-inch nonstick pan (gray, not black).

2 Make the cake: In a large bowl, beat the sugar, eggs, oil, and vanilla with an electric mixer on low speed until well blended, about 1 minute.

3 In a medium bowl, whisk together the flour blend, xanthan gum, cinnamon, baking powder, baking soda, and salt.

4 On low speed, beat the flour mixture into the egg mixture, alternating with the buttermilk, beginning and ending with the flour mixture. Spread the batter evenly in the pan.

5 Make the topping: In a small bowl, use a fork to mash together the brown sugar, butter, cinnamon, and flour blend until it is crumbly. Sprinkle evenly over the batter.

6 Bake until the top is golden brown and a toothpick inserted into the center comes out clean, 30 to 35 minutes. Cool the cake in the pan on a wire rack for 30 minutes before cutting. Serve slightly warm.

Cranberry-Orange Coffee Cake
Add 1 tablespoon grated orange zest and 1 cup dried cranberries to the batter; omit the cinnamon in the cake batter. Proceed as directed.
Per slice: 270 calories; 3g protein; 11g total fat; 2g fiber; 42g carbohydrates; 44mg cholesterol; 247mg sodium

Lemon–Poppy Seed Coffee Cake
Add 1½ tablespoons poppy seeds and 1 tablespoon grated lemon zest to the batter. Proceed as directed.
Per slice: 275 calories; 3g protein; 11g total fat; 1g fiber; 42g carbohydrates; 44mg cholesterol; 247mg sodium

Egg & Sausage Brunch Casserole

This dish—sometimes called a strata—is perfect for entertaining guests or for a lazy weekend brunch for your family. Assemble it the night before, freeing you to focus on the meal's other dishes that may need your last-minute attention. This dish is a wonderful way to showcase seasonal vegetables, so feel free to vary it with your own style (see below).

10 slices (about 6 cups) gluten-free sandwich bread

1 (4-ounce) can sliced mushrooms, drained

2 (6-ounce) links gluten-free Italian sausage, browned and diced or crumbled

2 cups grated mozzarella cheese or cheese alternative (6 ounces)

2 cups fresh asparagus, cut into ½-inch pieces, or green peas

½ cup finely diced yellow onion

6 large eggs

3 cups milk of choice

2 garlic cloves, minced

1 teaspoon dried Italian seasoning

½ teaspoon salt

¼ teaspoon freshly ground black pepper

2 tablespoons Parmesan cheese or soy Parmesan

¼ cup chopped fresh parsley, for garnish

V

Makes 8 servings
Preparation time: 20 minutes
Chilling time: 1 hour to overnight
Baking time: 1 hour

Per serving:
335 calories;
19g protein;
18g total fat;
2g fiber;
24g carbohydrates;
180mg cholesterol;
659mg sodium

1 Grease a 9x13-inch glass or ceramic baking dish for a custardy bottom or a nonstick pan (gray, not black) for a browned, crispier bottom. Cut the bread into ¾-inch cubes and place in a large bowl. Add the mushrooms, sausage, and 1½ cups of the mozzarella. Add the asparagus and onion and stir together with a spatula. Spread evenly in the baking dish.

2 In a medium bowl, whisk together the eggs, milk, garlic, Italian seasoning, salt, and pepper until thoroughly blended and then pour the mixture evenly over the bread. With a spatula, press on the bread cubes to flatten a bit and make sure they are immersed in the liquid. Refrigerate, tightly covered, for at least 1 hour to let the bread soak up the liquids, up to overnight.

3 Place a rack in the middle of the oven. Preheat the oven to 350°F. Uncover the casserole and bake for 45 minutes. Sprinkle with the Parmesan and the remaining ½ cup mozzarella and continue baking until the cheese is melted and browned, about 10 more minutes. Remove the casserole from the oven and let stand for 10 minutes, then cut and serve, garnished with the parsley.

Varying a Basic Casserole

This recipe just begs for tinkering. Next time, try Mexican-style with chorizo instead of Italian sausage, dried oregano instead of Italian seasoning, and corn instead of asparagus. Another time, go Southern-style with ham instead of Italian sausage, ½ teaspoon Cajun seasoning instead of Italian seasoning, and chopped kale, chopped okra, or baby spinach instead of asparagus. The recipe can go Greek, with ground lamb instead of Italian sausage, oregano instead of Italian seasoning, and eggplant or zucchini instead of asparagus, plus a handful of feta for an authentic Greek touch.

Quiche Lorraine

Quiche is perfect for Sunday brunch, but it is also appropriate for luncheons and even dinner. The wee bit of sugar and nutmeg in the filling makes the flavors pop. Pair this quiche with a crisp tossed salad or fresh fruit.

Makes 6 servings

Prep time: 15 minutes

Cooking time: 50 to 55 minutes

Per serving: 360 calories; 13g protein; 23g total fat; 1g fiber; 23g carbohydrates; 155mg cholesterol; 508mg sodium

1 gluten-free store-bought 9-inch piecrust or homemade piecrust (page 208), unbaked
4 bacon slices
4 ounces Swiss cheese or cheese alternative, diced or shredded (1 cup)
½ cup finely diced yellow onion
1 tablespoon cornstarch

¾ cup half-and-half or whole milk or milk of choice
4 large eggs
½ teaspoon salt
¼ teaspoon sugar
⅛ teaspoon ground nutmeg
¼ teaspoon freshly ground black pepper

1 Arrange racks in the bottom and middle positions of the oven. Preheat the oven to 375°F. Place the piecrust on a rimmed baking sheet for easier handling.

2 In a heavy skillet, fry the bacon over medium heat until crisp, drain on a paper towel, and finely chop. Sprinkle the bacon and the cheese in the bottom of the crust. Discard all but 1 tablespoon of bacon grease from the skillet and fry the onion in it over medium heat until golden and translucent, 3 to 5 minutes. Arrange the onion over the cheese.

3 In a medium bowl, whisk the cornstarch into ¼ cup of the half-and-half until smooth, and then add the rest of the half-and-half. Whisk in the eggs until smooth and then whisk in the salt, sugar, nutmeg, and pepper until well blended. Pour over the cheese.

4 Bake the quiche on the bottom rack of the oven for 15 minutes, then shift it to the middle rack. Continue baking until a knife inserted in the center comes out clean, another 35 to 40 minutes. Lay strips of aluminum foil over the piecrust edge if it browns too quickly. Remove from the oven and let stand for 10 minutes on a wire rack before cutting into 6 slices. Serve warm.

Adding Vegetables to Quiche Lorraine

Quiche Lorraine is delicious as is, but it's also a great dish to get more vegetables into your diet. When I tested this recipe, I used ½ cup chopped asparagus, spinach, or broccoli. But my favorite was dried tomatoes, which not only add flavor but interesting color as well. Adding vegetables is a great way to use up leftover cooked vegetables.

❪ For easier handling, roll piecrust dough between two sheets of heavy-duty plastic wrap, anchored by a wet paper towel underneath to prevent slipping.

No-Crust Ham Quiche

It is absolutely amazing how this recipe miraculously turns into a quiche that is perfect for dinner, lunch, or brunch—yet you don't have to make a pastry crust, as you do with the previous recipe for Quiche Lorraine. You can use your favorite cheese alternative, but the flavor won't be as strong as real Swiss cheese. I like to serve this to my egg-free guests.

Makes 6 servings
Preparation time: 10 minutes
Baking time: 30 to 40 minutes

1 cup finely diced ham
1 cup shredded Swiss or Gruyère cheese or cheese alternative
1¾ cups milk of choice
¾ cup Gluten-Free Flour Blend (page 27)
¼ cup dried minced onions
¼ cup butter or buttery spread, melted
2 tablespoons grated Parmesan cheese or soy Parmesan
¼ teaspoon beau monde seasoning
⅛ teaspoon ground nutmeg

Per serving:
265 calories;
12g protein;
16g total fat;
1g fiber;
19g carbohydrates;
53mg cholesterol;
527mg sodium

1 Preheat the oven to 400°F. Lightly grease a 9-inch glass pie plate and sprinkle the ham and cheese evenly on the bottom. Whisk together all of the remaining ingredients until smooth and pour over the ham and cheese.

2 Bake until the top is golden brown, 30 to 40 minutes. Cool on a wire rack for 5 minutes before cutting into 6 slices. Serve hot.

Granola

This not-too-sweet recipe fits nicely in a fairly thin layer on a 10x15-inch rimmed baking sheet. For more sweetness, increase the honey or brown sugar by a tablespoon each time until you reach your desired level. Vary the dried fruit as you wish—try dried cherries, blueberries, peaches, or bananas—and feel free to use more or less of various kinds of nuts. In other words, make this your own!

2 cups gluten-free rolled oats*
½ cup flaked coconut
¼ cup sunflower seeds
¼ cup pumpkin seeds
¼ cup slivered almonds
½ teaspoon ground cinnamon
¼ teaspoon salt
¼ cup hot (120°F) water

¼ cup honey or maple syrup
¼ cup packed brown sugar
2 tablespoons canola oil
2 teaspoons pure vanilla extract
¼ cup golden raisins
¼ cup dried sweetened cranberries
¼ cup chopped dried apricots

1 Place a rack in the middle of the oven. Preheat the oven to 300°F. Line a 10x15-inch rimmed baking sheet (not nonstick) with parchment paper.

2 In a large mixing bowl, stir together the first seven ingredients (rolled oats through salt) until thoroughly blended.

3 In a measuring cup, whisk together the hot water, honey, brown sugar, oil, and vanilla until smooth. With a spatula, toss this mixture with the oat mixture until thoroughly coated and then spread it evenly in the pan.

4 Bake until the granola is lightly browned, stirring every 10 minutes to promote even browning, 20 to 30 minutes. For darker granola, bake in additional 5-minute increments, stirring each time. Watch carefully to avoid burning. Remove from the oven and cool completely. Add the dried fruit. Store in an airtight container in a dark, dry place.

V

Makes 8 servings of 1½ cup each
Preparation time: 10 minutes
Baking time: 20 minutes or more

Per serving:
250 calories;
6g protein;
10g total fat;
4g fiber;
38g carbohydrates;
0mg cholesterol;
84mg sodium

❨ *Check with your physician before eating gluten-free oats.

Whole Grains for Breakfast

The Whole Grains Council recommends that we eat three to five daily servings of whole grains because they are an essential and very nutritious component of a healthy diet. Although whole grains can be found in cold cereals, a hearty stick-to-your ribs hot cereal for breakfast is an absolute necessity for many of us.

Just because you don't eat wheat doesn't mean you can't have hot cereal. There are many gluten-free grains (some are seeds, but we often call them all grains for easy reference because they can be used in similar ways). Listed below are many grains that are delicious when topped with sugar, cinnamon, honey, maple syrup, brown sugar, fresh fruit, jam, jelly, or nuts. All grains are vegetarian as long they are prepared with water or vegetable broth.

The following table gives you basic guidelines on how to cook them. Use salt as you wish. Serves 4.

Grain/Seed (1 cup)	Water or Broth	Approximate Cooking Time
Amaranth	2 cups	20 to 25 minutes
Brown rice	2½ cups	50 to 55 minutes
Buckwheat	2 cups	15 to 20 minutes
Corn grits (polenta)	4 cups	10 to 15 minutes
Kañiwa (baby quinoa)	2 cups	15 to 20 minutes
Millet whole grains	4 cups	35 to 40 minutes
Millet grits/meal	3 cups	10 to 15 minutes
Oat groats**	3 cups	40 to 45 minutes
Oats (steel-cut)**	4 cups	10 to 15 minutes
Quinoa	2 cups	15 to 20 minutes
Sorghum*	2 cups	45 to 60 minutes
Teff	3 cups	10 to 15 minutes
Wild rice	4 cups	40 minutes

*Soak whole sorghum grains in water overnight. Drain thoroughly, then cook as directed above.

**Check with your physician before eating gluten-free oats.

For detailed information on the nutrient content of these whole grains, see *The Gluten-Free Diet: A Comprehensive Resource Guide*, by Shelley Case, RD (Case Nutrition Counseling, Inc., 2013).

Breakfast Smoothie

You can pack (sneak) a ton of nutrients into a simple little smoothie. Here is my super-easy recipe for two servings. You can replace the spinach or kale with other vegetables such as celery, carrots, or whatever you like . . . just pack it with whole, nutritious foods. Smoothies are not just for breakfast, either: A famous resort serves healthy afternoon smoothies to bridge the gap between lunch and dinner. Great idea!

1   cup berries (blueberries, strawberries,
      or raspberries), fresh or frozen
½   cup (about a handful) fresh spinach or
      kale
1   small ripe banana
½   cup plain, low-fat yogurt or kefir
¼   cup protein powder (or amount
      suggested by manufacturer)
½   cup milk of choice
1   teaspoon honey, maple syrup, or
      agave nectar (optional)
1   or 2 ice cubes (if fruit isn't frozen)

Place all of the ingredients in a blender and blend until very smooth. Pour into glasses and serve immediately.

Q, V
Makes 2 smoothies (1 cup each)
Preparation time: 5 minutes

Per serving:
235 calories; 14g protein; 5g total fat; 6g fiber; 37g carbohydrates; 6mg cholesterol; 93mg sodium

Protein Powder

There are many nutritious protein powders available today, such as pea, soy, rice, hemp (and whey, if you tolerate dairy). Read the labels carefully to choose one that is right for you. My own smoothies include a wide variety of powders, rotating through my favorites of hemp, pea, and rice, but I also stir the protein powder into yogurt, breakfast cereal, or puddings whenever they can use a healthy protein boost.

Small Bites 》

Despite today's supersized food portions, sometimes all you want is "just a bite" instead of a multi-course meal. Maybe it's an appetizer for guests or a light meal that can be eaten quickly, or perhaps you just want to graze. Whatever the reason or occasion, the simple, small dishes in this chapter are sure to satisfy with their vibrant flavors.

Many of the recipes have a "bread" aspect to them, since bread is what we miss most on a gluten-free diet. So, several recipes are made with some version of bread (sandwich bread or French bread), flour tortillas, breadsticks, or polenta—all lending a "bread-like" substance to these small but mighty plates. Of course, soups, salads, and vegetables make excellent small meals, so check out the Soups & Salads chapter on page 82 for additional recipes that can easily be made in smaller portions.

Q	V
Quick	**Vegetarian**

Warm Olives

This is one of the easiest recipes you'll ever make. I prefer to use pitted olives so my guests don't have to dispose of olive pits, but use whatever you have on hand. You can also vary the herbs. This is equally good with fresh rosemary or fresh dill.

- 2 cups olives of your choice, well drained
- 2 whole sprigs fresh oregano or ½ teaspoon dried
- 1 (3-inch) strip lemon zest
- 1 garlic clove, halved
- ¼ teaspoon crushed red pepper
- 2 tablespoons extra-virgin olive oil

1 Place a rack in the middle of the oven. Preheat the oven to 350°F.

2 Combine all of the ingredients on a sheet of heavy-duty aluminum foil (or use a doubled sheet of regular foil). Fold up the edges of the foil to create a pocket and place on a small baking sheet.

3 Warm the olives in the oven until they become fragrant, 15 to 20 minutes. Remove from the oven and serve warm in a bowl.

Q, V
Makes 8 servings (about ¼ cup each)
Preparation time: 20 minutes

Per serving:
70 calories;
1g protein;
7g total fat;
1g fiber;
2g carbohydrates;
0mg cholesterol;
295mg sodium

Chicken Salad Wraps

Chicken salad sandwiches are delicious, but they are more contemporary when made with flour tortillas to create homemade wraps. There are several brands of gluten-free flour tortillas on the market, but my favorite is Rudi's (available in plain, spinach, and fiesta flavors); they are quite pliable and make terrific wraps.

Q

Makes 4 wraps
Preparation time: 15 minutes

1½ cups finely diced cooked chicken (about
8 ounces or 2 small chicken breast halves)
½ cup light mayonnaise or salad dressing spread
1 cup finely diced celery (about 2 stalks)
¼ cup finely diced white onion
¼ cup sweet pickle relish
2 tablespoons chopped fresh herbs, such as chives, dill, tarragon, and/or thyme
¼ teaspoon celery salt
¼ cup slivered almonds
Salt and freshly ground black pepper, to taste

4 gluten-free flour tortilla wraps
4 small lettuce leaves

Per wrap:
580 calories;
24g protein;
31g total fat;
4g fiber;
52g carbohydrates;
74mg cholesterol;
796mg sodium

1 In a medium bowl, stir together the chicken, mayonnaise, celery, onion, pickle relish, herbs, celery salt, and almonds until blended. Or whirl the ingredients in a food processor until well blended for a more shredded consistency. Taste and add salt and pepper, if desired.

2 Soften the tortillas (see How to Soften Gluten-Free Flour Tortillas below). For each wrap, spread one-quarter of the chicken salad (about ½ cup) down the middle of the tortilla. Top with a lettuce leaf. Gently roll one side of the tortilla toward the center and finish rolling into a loose roll to create a wrap. Place seam side down on a serving plate, using a toothpick to keep the wrap rolled, if necessary. Repeat with the remaining tortillas, and serve immediately.

How to Soften Gluten-Free Flour Tortillas

Store-bought gluten-free flour tortillas might not be pliable enough to roll into a wrap without breaking, especially when refrigerated, frozen, or slightly stale. However, they can be made pliable if you steam each tortilla on a splatter guard (a flat, handled screen that keeps bacon from splattering while frying) set over a skillet of simmering water for 5 to 10 seconds. They will soften very quickly, so watch carefully and remove from the heat before they get soggy. If you are steaming several tortillas at a time, place the steamed tortillas between sheets of parchment paper so they stay warm and soft while steaming the remaining tortillas. They are best when served immediately after steaming.

Lettuce Wraps

Lettuce wraps are very popular in Asian restaurants but are also super easy to make at home. They are most often served as appetizers, but they are hearty enough to be a meal if you increase the servings to 4 wraps per person and serve other side dishes such as steamed rice or vegetables. Using store-bought slaw shaves considerable time from this recipe.

Q

Makes 12 wraps (6 appetizer servings or 3 entrée servings)

Preparation time: 15 minutes

Per wrap:
60 calories;
5g protein;
3g total fat;
2g fiber;
3g carbohydrates;
12mg cholesterol;
231mg sodium

1 tablespoon peanut oil or canola oil
8 ounces lean ground pork or turkey
½ small red bell pepper, diced
1 cup cabbage-carrot slaw (or ½ cup shredded cabbage and ½ cup shredded carrot)
½ cup chopped fresh cilantro
3 green onions (white parts only), thinly sliced
1 garlic clove, minced (or more to taste)
2 tablespoons gluten-free soy sauce
2 tablespoons gluten-free hoisin sauce

1 tablespoon Thai Kitchen sweet red chili sauce, or to taste
1 tablespoon minced fresh ginger
2 teaspoons rice wine vinegar (seasoned or unseasoned)
2 teaspoons gluten-free fish sauce
1 teaspoon toasted sesame oil
½ teaspoon sugar
½ cup finely diced English (hothouse) seedless cucumber
12 Boston or Bibb lettuce leaves, washed and patted dry

1 In a large heavy skillet, heat the peanut oil and cook the pork over medium heat until deeply browned and cooked through, 5 to 7 minutes. Transfer the pork to a paper towel–lined plate to drain.

2 In the same skillet, add the bell pepper, slaw, 6 tablespoons of the cilantro, the green onions, garlic, soy sauce, hoisin sauce, sweet red chili sauce, ginger, vinegar, fish sauce, sesame oil, and sugar. Cook over medium heat, stirring constantly, until the cabbage begins to wilt, 3 to 5 minutes. Add the cucumbers and browned pork and heat to serving temperature. Transfer the mixture to a serving plate and garnish with the remaining 2 tablespoons cilantro.

3 Arrange the lettuce leaves on a serving platter. Spoon the pork mixture into the hollow of each lettuce leaf, roll up the lettuce, and serve.

Basic Polenta in the Microwave

Most polentas require standing over the stovetop while stirring the polenta (also known as corn grits) and trying to control the inevitable splatters. My easy version eliminates the mess by cooking the polenta in a very large bowl in the microwave oven. Plus, this technique frees you to do other things while the polenta cooks, so it is also a real time-saver. This is the way I always make my polenta, and it is virtually fail-proof and mess-free. I prefer to use broth because it heightens the flavor; if you use water, you may need a little more salt to compensate for the salt in broth.

1 cup gluten-free Bob's Red Mill yellow
   corn grits/polenta
3½ cups gluten-free chicken or vegetable
   broth or cold water
1 tablespoon butter or buttery spread
¼ cup grated Parmesan cheese or soy
   Parmesan
½ teaspoon salt, or to taste

1 Combine all of the ingredients in a large microwave-safe bowl. (I use an 8-cup glass Pyrex measuring cup, which is large enough to avoid boilovers.) Lay a sheet of waxed paper over the bowl and cook in the microwave on High in 10-minute increments, whisking between each increment, to reach the desired consistency. Cooking times may vary depending on your microwave; mine takes two 10-minute periods, for a total of 20 minutes. Serve immediately for hot, soft polenta. To make polenta rounds for Polenta-Parmesan Appetizers on page 75, proceed to Step 2.

2 To cool the polenta before making appetizers: Line a 7x11-inch rimmed baking pan with plastic wrap. Pour in all of the hot polenta, smooth the top evenly, cover, and refrigerate until firm and cold, 3 to 4 hours.

3 Place a large cutting board on top of the baking pan and, firmly holding opposite ends of the baking pan, flip the pan onto the cutting board. Remove the plastic wrap and cut the chilled polenta into 12 rounds with a 2-inch biscuit cutter. Or, for triangles, cut the slab of polenta in half lengthwise, then crosswise into 6 squares. Lift each square out with a spatula, place it on a cutting board, and cut diagonally into 2 triangles.

Q, V
Makes about 3 cups (4 servings as a side dish)
Makes 12 polenta rounds (4 servings as an appetizer)
Preparation time: 2 minutes
Cooking time: 20 minutes

Per serving:
74 calories;
3g protein;
2g total fat;
2g fiber;
11g carbohydrates;
4mg cholesterol;
343 mg sodium

Polenta-Parmesan Appetizers

Starting with a tube of store-bought polenta means you can make these crispy appetizers very quickly. But you can also make your own polenta, using the simple recipe on page 73. This recipe starts with a simple topping of Parmesan cheese and fresh herbs, but you can use anything you like, such as sliced olives, diced fresh tomatoes or sun-dried tomatoes, chopped fresh herbs, pâté, hummus, or tiny bits of prosciutto.

1 (18-ounce) tube gluten-free prepared polenta
¼ cup cornstarch
2 tablespoons olive oil (or more as needed)
Salt and freshly ground black pepper, to taste
¾ cup shredded Parmesan cheese or soy Parmesan
¼ cup chopped fresh parsley or your favorite fresh herb, for garnish

Q, V
Makes 12 rounds
Preparation time: 10 to 15 minutes
Baking time: 7 to 10 minutes

1 Place a rack in the middle of the oven. Preheat the oven to 300°F. Line a 9x13-inch baking sheet with aluminum foil or parchment paper.

2 Place the polenta on a large cutting board. With a sharp knife, cut the polenta into twelve ¼-inch-thick rounds and lay the rounds flat on the cutting board.

3 Lightly dust both sides of the rounds with cornstarch. In a heavy nonstick skillet (gray, not black), heat the oil over medium heat. Fry a few polenta rounds at a time, turning occasionally, until browned and crispy, 2 to 3 minutes per side. Transfer the rounds to the baking sheet. Repeat with the remaining polenta, adding more oil to the skillet as needed. Sprinkle each round with salt, pepper, and a tablespoon of Parmesan.

4 Bake in the oven until the Parmesan begins to melt, 7 to 10 minutes. Remove from the oven and immediately add any additional toppings, if desired (see headnote). Serve hot, garnished with the parsley.

Per round:
190 calories;
5g protein;
4g total fat;
4g fiber;
33g carbohydrates;
4mg cholesterol;
86mg sodium

Antipasto Plate

The beauty of this plate is that it can be assembled in seconds on a pretty tray and served to your guests. In fact, it will take you longer to go to the store and buy these items than it will take you to arrange them on the tray. I rely on my local natural foods stores for these items, after reading labels to make sure that each is gluten-free. If cheese is off-limits, replace it with stuffed grape leaves or vegetables (pickled or fresh) such as baby carrots, celery sticks, or broccoli florets.

Q

Makes 4 servings

Preparation time: 10 minutes

1 (4½-ounce) jar marinated artichokes, drained

4 ounces fresh mozzarella cheese balls or cheese alternative wedges

4 ounces cured Italian deli meats of your choice, thinly sliced

4 ounces pitted kalamata olives or a blend of pitted olives (or Warm Olives, page 69)

4 ounces roasted red peppers

4 ounces red or yellow grape tomatoes, washed and patted dry

1 (5-ounce) package gluten-free crackers or Italian breadsticks

❭ Nutrient value will vary based on items selected.

Assemble the items decoratively on a large tray, preferably one with indentations to collect any stray juices. Or, place each item in its own little bowl on a larger tray, surrounded by the crackers.

Panini

Panini are toasted, pressed sandwiches, usually made in a panini press or toasted-sandwich maker (available at kitchen stores)—or in a heavy skillet, much like making a grilled cheese sandwich but using another heavy skillet to press down on top. This ham-and-cheese sandwich is just one of many possible flavor combinations, so feel free to experiment with your own favorites.

8 slices gluten-free sandwich bread
5 tablespoons Dijon mustard
¼ cup mayonnaise or salad dressing
   spread
2 tablespoons sweet pickle relish
8 thin slices Black Forest ham or deli
   ham
4 slices provolone cheese or cheese
   alternative

Q
Makes 4
sandwiches
Preparation
time: 5 minutes
Grilling time:
about 8 minutes
per sandwich

Per sandwich:
355 calories;
22g protein;
16g total fat;
2g fiber;
30g
carbohydrates;
55mg
cholesterol;
1294mg sodium

1 Lay the bread slices on a flat surface, such as a large cutting board. In a small bowl, whisk together the mustard, mayonnaise, and pickle relish until well blended, and then spread a scant tablespoon of the mixture on each slice of bread. Layer four of the bread slices with a slice of ham, a slice of cheese, and another slice of ham. Top with the remaining slice of bread, spread side down.

2 Preheat a panini press on medium-high heat and cook the sandwiches according to the manufacturer's directions. Or place the sandwich on a heated grill pan or heavy skillet, place a heavy skillet on top, and press down while cooking until browned on the bottom, about 3 minutes. With a metal spatula, flip the sandwich, press down with the skillet, and cook until browned on the bottom, about 3 minutes more. With a sharp knife, halve the sandwiches diagonally, and serve immediately.

Gluten-Free Bread for Pressed Sandwiches

Pressed sandwiches are perfect for our somewhat delicate gluten-free bread because the process of toasting and pressing strengthens the bread, making a sandwich that holds together and is less likely to crumble. It is also a perfect way to use up stale bread. If your bread is hard or frozen, gently warm it on very Low power in the microwave oven before assembling the sandwich so it won't break apart when pressed in the sandwich maker.

Crostini

Crostini are small, thinly sliced little pieces of toasted bread. They can be topped with many different things, such as chopped tomatoes, pureed beans, diced vegetables, cream cheese, smoked salmon with dill, liver pâté, and so on. You could also simply use Parmesan cheese. If you don't want to make your own French baguette (see page 156), use halved slices of store-bought, gluten-free sandwich bread.

Q, V

Makes 24 crostini

Preparation time: 5 minutes

Baking time: 7 to 8 minutes

1 gluten-free French Baguette (page 156)
1 tablespoon olive oil
1 large garlic clove, halved
¾ cup low-fat cream cheese or cream cheese alternative
¾ cup diced red grape tomatoes
¼ cup chopped fresh basil
  Salt and freshly ground black pepper, to taste

Per crostini:
75 calories;
2g protein;
2g total fat;
1g fiber;
11g carbohydrates;
4mg cholesterol;
166mg sodium

1 Place a rack in the middle of the oven. Preheat the oven to 350°F. Line a 9x13-inch baking sheet with parchment paper or aluminum foil.

2 With a serrated knife or electric knife, cut the baguette on the diagonal into thin slices, about ⅓ inch thick (use discarded loaf ends to make bread crumbs; see Gluten-Free Bread Crumbs, page 104). With a pastry brush, brush both sides of the bread slices lightly with the oil and rub with the cut garlic. Arrange the bread slices on the baking sheet.

3 Bake until lightly crisped around the edges, 5 to 6 minutes. Depending on the bread's ingredients and moisture content, it may lightly brown as well. Flip the slices and bake for another 2 minutes. Cool the toasts on the pan on a wire rack until they are cool enough to handle.

4 Spread each toast with 1½ teaspoons of cream cheese, a few diced tomatoes, and a sprinkle of basil. Season generously with salt and pepper, and serve immediately.

Creative Crostini

Crostini are the perfect solution for leftover gluten-free bread, and they are delicious whether lightly toasted or deeply browned. Ingredients in the bread (such as cow's milk) can increase browning. Use any topping you like, but for best results use a cream or paste as the first layer (such as cream cheese, hummus, or pâté) to anchor the other toppings so they are less likely to fall off when you take a bite. Try to blend complementary flavors, such as the basil with tomato in this recipe, or smoked salmon with dill. Or try sweet ingredients, such as chutney or hot pepper jelly on cream cheese, or a sprinkle of raisins, currants, or dried cranberries for a pleasing counterbalance to savory toppings.

Prosciutto-Wrapped Breadsticks

I have certainly eaten my share of prosciutto-wrapped melon, especially when traveling in Italy. But why not shake up this tradition and wrap the prosciutto around the gluten-free Italian breadsticks known as grissini? Found in natural foods stores, grissini are a satisfyingly crisp contrast to the salty prosciutto.

Q

Makes 12 breadsticks

Preparation time: 5 minutes

Per breadstick:
125 calories;
16g protein;
5g total fat;
1g fiber;
2g carbohydrates;
40mg cholesterol;
1567mg sodium

3   thin slices prosciutto
12   gluten-free Italian breadsticks (grissini)

Divide each prosciutto slice lengthwise into 1-inch-wide strips. Wrap each strip around a breadstick at an angle, slightly overlapping the prosciutto to make it fit tightly. Leave one end of the breadstick unwrapped so it can be used as a handle. To serve, stand the breadsticks, wrapped end up, in a large glass or vase, or lay decoratively on a serving platter.

Basic Breading Batter

This batter makes a nice, crispy coating on fried foods. Peanut oil is the best option because it is least likely to burn; however, canola or vegetable oil works well, too. The granular nature of cornmeal and white rice flour lend a pleasing crunchiness. This batter works equally well with chicken, fish, or vegetables. The carbonization from the sparkling water adds lightness.

¼ cup Gluten-Free Flour Blend (page 27)
¼ cup cornmeal or white rice flour
2   teaspoons sugar

½ teaspoon baking powder
¼ teaspoon salt
¼ teaspoon freshly ground white pepper
1   cup sparkling water or club soda

In a bowl, whisk the flour blend, cornmeal, sugar, baking powder, salt, pepper, and sparkling water together until well blended and about the consistency of heavy cream. Chill for 1 hour, and then use as directed. Discard unused batter.

V

Makes 1 cup batter (4 servings)

Per serving:
35 calories;
0g protein;
0g total fat;
1g fiber;
9g carbohydrates;
2mg cholesterol;
195mg sodium

French-Fried Onions

French-fried onions are hardly a meal and perhaps not really an appetizer, but most gluten-free people crave them. And it's something we can't order in a restaurant because, like French fries, they are contaminated with gluten from the non-dedicated fryer. So, why not make them at home as an appetizer? Imagine your guests gathered around your stovetop, drinking gluten-free beer, and absolutely delighted when you serve these morsels piping hot and crisp from the fryer. Plus, you can use them on top of the traditional green bean casserole at holiday time or to adorn a grilled steak. Any way you use them, you will love this recipe and use the versatile breading batter often.

2   large onions, peeled and cut into
     ¼-inch slices
¼   teaspoon salt
¼   teaspoon garlic powder
1   cup Basic Breading Batter (see sidebar
     page 80)
     Peanut oil, for frying

V
Makes 4 servings
Preparation time: 10 minutes
Frying time: variable

Per serving:
115 calories;
4g protein;
15g total fat;
2g fiber;
25g carbohydrates;
2mg cholesterol;
360mg sodium

1 Place the onions on a cutting board or large plate. In a small bowl, whisk the salt and garlic powder into the Basic Breading Batter. Dip the sliced onions into the mixture, coating them thoroughly.

2 Heat 2 inches of oil to 375°F in a narrow heavy saucepan. Or, following the manufacturer's directions, add the recommended amount of oil to a temperature-controlled deep fryer. Add a small portion of the onions to the hot oil (be careful not to crowd the pieces) and fry until golden brown on both sides, turning once. (Frying time will vary with the size of the onions, the temperature of the batter, and whether you use a temperature-controlled deep fryer or a saucepan on the stovetop.) Drain the onions on paper towels. Fry the remaining onions in the same manner, adding more oil, if necessary, to keep the onions completely immersed. Serve immediately.

Soups & Salads 〉

Frequently including soups and salads in your weekly meals can be an excellent way to eat healthfully, and most are quite simple and inexpensive to make. They are also easy to modify to suit the taste and dietary needs of your family or friends. For example, soups can be made with or without meat or dairy and can be made on the stovetop or in a slow cooker. Salads can be made from mixed greens, whole grains, or lentils, with different dressings to lend variety.

However, when dining out in restaurants or as a guest in someone's home, soups and salads—two seemingly innocent foods—can be minefields. Soups can be thickened with wheat flour—the most common thickener—and store-bought broths may contain gluten. And salad dressing can be made with wheat-based soy sauce.

Here is a collection of soups and salads that provides a foundation of healthy choices that you can safely eat and modify to meet your needs. And the techniques you learn here (such as how to thicken a soup or use a slow cooker or make salad dressings and vinaigrettes) can be applied to your own recipes.

Many of these recipes can be made into light meals or appetizers (see Small Bites chapter) for guests simply by serving smaller portions. Plus, there are simple salads based on beans and whole grains so that you can see how easy it is to incorporate these wholesome foods into your diet.

Soups

Lentil Soup

Black Bean Soup

Cream of Mushroom Soup

   Cream of Chicken Soup

Chicken Soup with Dumplings

Beef Stew in a Slow Cooker

Chicken Broth

   Beef Broth

   Vegetable Broth

Onion Soup Mix

Salads

Simple Vinaigrette

White Bean Salad with Peppers and Olives

Pasta Salad with Italian Dressing

Whole-Grain Sorghum Salad

Q	**V**
Quick	**Vegetarian**

Lentil Soup

Lentils belong to the legume family—which includes beans—but they tend to cook faster than beans, so they're great for quick meals. Because lentils cook extra fast, you can have a meal on the table in about 30 minutes; plus, lentils are very economical. You can replace the cumin with your favorite herb: perhaps a tablespoon of fresh chopped herbs or a teaspoon of dried herbs such as thyme, marjoram, savory, or basil. If you use vegetable broth, this soup is vegan as well.

1 (14-ounce) can gluten-free low-sodium chicken or vegetable broth
1½ cups tomato juice
½ cup brown lentils
¼ teaspoon celery salt
¼ teaspoon ground cumin
⅛ teaspoon sugar (optional)
Salt and freshly ground black pepper to taste

Q, V
Makes 4 servings (about ¾ cup each)
Preparation time: 2 minutes
Cooking time: 30 minutes

In a medium saucepan, add all of the ingredients and stir until well blended. Bring to a boil over high heat, then reduce the heat to low and simmer, covered, until done, about 30 minutes. Taste and add additional salt and pepper, if desired. Serve hot.

Slow cooker option: Place all of the ingredients in a slow cooker and let cook on Low for 6 to 8 hours or all day.

Per serving:
110 calories; 12g protein; 1g total fat; 18g fiber; 8g carbohydrates; 0mg cholesterol; 425mg sodium

Black Bean Soup

Black beans are nutritional powerhouses, and this really simple soup makes it so easy to get them into your diet because you probably have all the ingredients in your pantry. Depending on the salt levels in the beans, broth, and salsa, you may need to add very little additional salt, or perhaps none at all. Let your palate be the judge. Likewise, if your store-bought salsa is too mild, boost the heat with a pinch of cayenne pepper.

Q, V

Makes 4 servings (about 1 cup each) **Preparation time:** 2 minutes **Cooking time:** 10 minutes

2 (14-ounce) cans black beans, thoroughly rinsed and drained (3 cups cooked beans)
2 cups gluten-free low-sodium broth (chicken, beef, or vegetable: see page 90 for recipes)
1 cup mild or medium Mexican salsa
Salt and freshly ground black pepper to taste
Garnishes: shredded cheese of choice, chopped green onions, fresh cilantro, sour cream (optional)

Per serving:
205 calories;
17g protein;
2g total fat;
11g fiber;
36g carbohydrates;
0mg cholesterol;
211mg sodium

1 Place the beans, broth, and salsa in a medium heavy saucepan. Bring to a boil over medium heat and simmer, covered, for 10 minutes.

2 To thicken the soup, remove the pan from the heat. Place an immersion/stick blender below the surface of the soup and buzz it a few times to puree the soup, leaving some whole beans for texture. Or use a potato masher to mash enough of the beans to produce the texture you like. Stir the soup, return the pot to the heat, and bring to serving temperature. Season with salt and pepper. Serve hot, topped with your choice of garnishes.

Beans

Dried beans, dried peas, and lentils (called legumes in the United States and pulses in Canada and Europe) are powerhouses of nutrition because they are rich in protein, fiber, and complex carbohydrates. They are also low in fat and contain a wide variety of vitamins and minerals—especially the B vitamins that gluten-free people need for good health when they can no longer eat vitamin B-fortified foods such as wheat cereal and pasta. Canned beans save time and are very inexpensive, but they contain sodium, so rinse them very, very thoroughly to remove up to nearly 40 percent of that sodium. Or cook your own beans from scratch for a fraction of the cost and add salt to suit your palate. Just be sure to carefully pick over the beans to remove any stones or twigs. Then rinse thoroughly to remove any dirt that naturally occurs in foods that come directly from the earth.

Cream of Mushroom Soup

Many casseroles require cream of mushroom soup as a base. This versatile recipe helps you make your own. It will yield the equivalent of one can of soup, reconstituted. You can use it in casseroles or eat it as is. To bump up the mushroom flavor, steep ¼ cup dried mushrooms in ½ cup boiling water for 10 minutes, then drain through a coffee filter—but save the strained liquid. Add the mushrooms and the strained liquid to the soup. Canned mushrooms make lighter-colored soup; fresh mushrooms make it darker.

2 tablespoons butter or buttery spread
1 cup chopped mushrooms (canned or fresh; a 10-ounce jar yields 1 cup drained)
1 small garlic clove, minced, or ¼ teaspoon garlic powder
1¼ cups milk of choice
½ cup fat-free half-and-half, canned coconut milk, or plain coffee creamer
1 tablespoon dried minced onions

½ teaspoon celery salt
½ teaspoon salt
½ teaspoon dry mustard
⅛ teaspoon freshly ground white pepper
1 tablespoon sweet rice flour
1 tablespoon dry sherry (optional)
2 tablespoons slivered or sliced almonds, toasted
2 tablespoons chopped fresh chives or parsley

Q, V
Makes 4 servings (about ½ cup each)
Preparation time: 10 minutes

1 In a medium saucepan, heat 1 tablespoon of the butter over medium heat. Cook the mushrooms and garlic until the mushroom juices are no longer visible. Remove the pan from the heat and add 1 cup of the milk, the half-and-half, and the remaining 1 tablespoon butter, plus the onions, celery salt, salt, mustard, and white pepper. Simmer on low heat for 5 minutes, but do not boil.

2 In a small bowl, whisk the sweet rice flour into the remaining ¼ cup milk until it is smooth to make a slurry. Whisk the slurry into the pan, return the pan to medium heat, and cook, whisking constantly, until the mixture thickens, about 30 seconds. Remove from the heat and stir in the sherry (if using). Serve hot, garnished with the toasted almonds and chopped chives.

Cream of Chicken Soup

Add 2 tablespoons gluten-free chicken bouillon granules to the dry ingredients and ¼ cup finely chopped chicken. Omit the celery salt, mushrooms, and salt. Prepare as directed, but taste and add more salt and pepper, if desired.

Per serving:
170 calories;
5g protein;
9g total fat;
1g fiber;
16g carbohydrates;
17mg cholesterol;
538mg sodium

Per serving:
160 calories;
6g protein;
8g total fat;
1g fiber;
13g carbohydrates;
26mg cholesterol;
126mg sodium

Thickeners for Soups

There are many ways to thicken soups without using wheat flour; this chapter illustrates several options. For example, bean soup can be thickened by mashing some of the beans; beef stew can be thickened by mashing some of the potatoes. Dumplings simmering in chicken soup give off starches that thicken the broth. Sweet rice flour gives this soup a hearty, opaque thickness without the unwanted shiny translucency that cornstarch (the most common gluten-free thickener) gives to soups.

Chicken Soup with Dumplings

Chicken soup is America's comfort food, and when you add dumplings (one of my most requested recipes), it is hearty, filling, and perfect on a cold winter night. Using leftover cooked chicken is the easiest and shortest route to this soothing soup—whether it is chopped chicken or whole cooked pieces, such as thighs or legs. Use whatever you have and it will be delicious.

Makes 6 servings (about 1½ cups each)
Preparation time: 10 minutes
Cooking time: 40 minutes

Soup

- 1 teaspoon canola oil
- ½ cup thinly sliced celery stalks
- ½ cup chopped onion
- 6 cups gluten-free low-sodium chicken broth
- 1 small carrot, thinly sliced
- 1 teaspoon poultry seasoning
- 1 bay leaf
- 1½ cups diced cooked chicken or 4 cooked chicken legs or thighs
- ¼ teaspoon salt, or to taste
- ¼ teaspoon freshly ground white pepper
- ⅛ teaspoon ground nutmeg (optional)

Dumplings

- 1 cup Gluten-Free Flour Blend (page 27)
- 1 teaspoon baking powder
- ½ teaspoon salt
- ¼ teaspoon xanthan gum
- 1½ teaspoons cold butter or buttery spread
- ½ cup milk of choice
- 2 tablespoons snipped fresh chives (optional)
- ¼ cup chopped fresh parsley
- 1 tablespoon lemon juice

Per serving:
285 calories;
24g protein;
11g total fat;
2g fiber;
25g carbohydrates;
46mg cholesterol;
931mg sodium

1 Make the soup: In a large soup pot or Dutch oven, heat the oil over medium heat. Cook the celery and onion in the oil, stirring occasionally, until translucent, about 5 minutes. Add the broth, carrot, poultry seasoning, bay leaf, and chicken. Bring to a boil, reduce the heat to low, and simmer for 20 minutes. Season with salt and pepper and add the nutmeg (if using). (Depending on the saltiness of the broth you use, you may need more or less than the recommended ¼ teaspoon salt. Tasting is important at this stage.) Continue to simmer while making the dumplings.

2 Make the dumplings: In a medium bowl, whisk together the flour blend, baking powder, salt, and xanthan gum until well blended. With a fork or pastry cutter, mash the butter into the mixture until it resembles pea-size crumbles. Add the milk and stir with a spatula until a stiff dough forms. Stir in the chives (if using). With your hands, shape the dough into 1½-inch balls. Or use a small spring-action, metal ice cream scoop to shape balls of dough.

3 With the broth at a simmer, gently add the dumplings with a spoon or ladle. Cook, covered with a tight-fitting lid, for 15 minutes. Do not remove the lid during this time or the steam that cooks the dumplings will escape and the dumplings may not cook all the way through. Just before serving, add the parsley and lemon juice. Serve hot.

Cooking Dumplings

Dumplings cook by steaming in a covered pot of simmering water. If the water boils, the action of the water may cause the dumplings to disintegrate. But how do you know if the water is simmering or boiling? To avoid the temptation to peek, use a glass lid so you can see what's going on in there. You can also vary the size of the dumplings, but keep in mind that making them smaller (as in this recipe) means greater control over cooking time and texture.

Making the Most of Your Slow Cooker

Slow cookers are a wonderful invention, but they are more of a time-shifter than a time-saver. The slow cooker doesn't measure, cut, or brown the food—you still have to do that. But you can perform these tasks when you choose (either the night before or in the morning). Also, the food cooks without your attention, rather than your having to stir a pot on the stovetop or check a dish in the oven over the span of several hours. Experienced users of slow cookers know that planning ahead is critical, so always leave time the night before or in the morning to prepare the food for slow cooking.

- **Choose the right size.** Based on the number of servings you need to feed your family, use the size that allows you to fill the slow cooker about half full, but no more than two-thirds full. An overfilled slow cooker won't cook food quickly enough, raising food-safety issues, while an underfilled slow cooker can burn food. Generally, a 5- to 6-quart cooker works for most purposes, but if you cook for a larger crowd, a 7-quart version may be better.

- **Decide what features are important.** Slow cookers range from very basic to having lots of bells and whistles. Some slow cookers switch to Warm when the cooking is done (so the food doesn't overcook); others have multiple heat settings (to suit the food being cooked) and programmable timers (to control cooking time length). Most have glass lids (to see the food without lifting the lid and losing precious heat). Some are round or oval, while others are square (which may fit better on the shelf). Older and smaller models don't have removable crocks (like the kind I started out with years ago), but today's crocks (also called inserts) are removable and dishwasher-safe. On some models, these inserts can be used to both brown meats on the stovetop and cook the food in the slow cooker, eliminating the need for a separate skillet to do the browning.

- **Maximize flavor.** You can just add all the raw ingredients to the pot and let them cook. But, browning ingredients such as beef, poultry, and onions will lend deeper flavor to the food, especially if you deglaze the pan with some of the liquid from the recipe and add it to the slow cooker. This technique captures those flavorful bits, called fond, from the bottom of the skillet so you can add them to your dish.

Avoid the "danger zone." Bacteria thrive most readily between the temperatures of 40°F and 140°F, so here are steps to avoid this "danger zone":
* Make sure the food heats to 140°F quickly. Always bring sauces, broth, and other liquids to a simmer before adding them to the slow cooker. Always thaw any food (especially meat or poultry) before adding to the slow cooker. Don't use extremely large pieces of meat such as whole chickens or roasts; cut them into smaller pieces instead so they cook more quickly and evenly.
* Make sure the food stays hot while cooking. This means no peeking, so resist the temptation to lift the lid. Do so only near the end of cooking to stir and adjust seasonings. Some experts say it takes 15 to 30 minutes to resume the temperature after the lid is lifted from a slow cooker because so much heat escapes—so leave the lid on.

Beef Stew in a Slow Cooker

Hearty and filling, this one-pot meal cooks all day and greets you with a delicious aroma at dinnertime. I relied on my slow cooker to make this weekly standby when I had an hour-long commute to and from work, and it was a great way to use up leftover roast beef and potatoes. Don't let the long list of ingredients deter you—this dish is a complete meal of meat, potatoes, and vegetables. If you don't have thyme, it works equally well with other herbs such as oregano, marjoram, or savory.

Makes 6 servings (about 2 cups each)
Preparation time: 20 minutes
Cooking time: 8 to 9 hours

- 1 tablespoon canola oil
- 1 pound lean beef stew meat, cut in ½-inch cubes
- ½ teaspoon salt, or to taste
- ¼ teaspoon freshly ground black pepper, or to taste
- 1 (14-ounce) can gluten-free low-sodium beef broth
- 1 (28-ounce) can whole tomatoes, undrained
- 4 small red potatoes, scrubbed and quartered

- 1 small white onion, chopped
- 2 cups peeled baby carrots
- 1 tablespoon gluten-free Worcestershire sauce
- 1½ tablespoons chopped fresh thyme or 1 teaspoon dried, or to taste
- ½ teaspoon sugar
- 1 bay leaf (optional)
- 1 small garlic clove, minced
- ¼ cup chopped fresh parsley

Per serving:
300 calories;
21g protein;
14g total fat;
4g fiber;
24g carbohydrates;
46mg cholesterol;
477mg sodium

1 In a medium heavy skillet, heat the oil over medium heat. Season the stew meat with salt and pepper, add to the skillet, and cook until all sides are deeply browned, 3 to 5 minutes. Transfer the beef to the slow cooker. Add the broth to the skillet and cook, stirring constantly with a heatproof spatula, to scrape all the browned bits from the bottom of the skillet. Add the broth to the slow cooker.

2 Add the tomatoes to the skillet (chop them if they're too big for your taste) and heat to boiling, then add to the slow cooker. Add all of the remaining ingredients except for the parsley to the slow cooker and stir to combine.

3 Cover and cook on Low until the vegetables and beef are tender, 8 to 9 hours. For a thicker stew, transfer about ½ cup of the cooked potatoes to a small bowl just before serving and mash them thoroughly with a fork; stir back into the stew. Remove the bay leaf (if using) and serve hot, garnished with the parsley.

Choosing Tomatoes for Soups

A tomato is a tomato, right? Not necessarily. Canned whole tomatoes are used in this stew because they break down, give off juices, and become smoother during cooking, creating a more soup-like consistency. If the tomato pieces are too big, chop them into smaller sizes with kitchen scissors. In contrast to whole tomatoes, diced tomatoes (another option for this recipe) are treated with calcium chloride, which causes them to stay firm during cooking. While this firmness might be nice in a salsa or Mexican dish where juice is less desirable, it makes for a chunkier, thicker stew, so you might need to add more liquid (such as broth or water) to this stew to reach the right consistency. For that reason—and because the canned whole tomatoes taste better—I prefer whole tomatoes for this dish.

Chicken Broth

It is so easy to use store-bought broth. But for the freshest, purest broth, make your own. That way, you know there is no gluten in it, as there can be in store-bought versions. It is not hard, but it does require tending the pot for a couple of hours while it simmers on the stove. Or, cook it in a slow cooker all day, with no need to tend. I almost always make chicken broth after I serve roast chicken so that I can make use of the bones, which usually have a bit of meat clinging to them.

V

Makes 8 cups
Preparation time: 5 minutes
Cooking time: 2 hours

Bones of ½ chicken (leave a little meat on the bones for flavor)
2 stalks of celery, trimmed and halved crosswise
2 whole carrots, halved crosswise
1 small onion, halved
½ bunch fresh parsley
2 tablespoons chopped fresh thyme or 1 teaspoon dried
8 cups water
2 teaspoons salt
6 black peppercorns
1 large bay leaf

Per serving (1 cup):
35 calories;
3g protein;
2g total fat;
1g fiber;
4g carbohydrates;
10mg cholesterol;
558mg sodium

1 Place all of the ingredients in a Dutch oven and slowly bring to a simmer over medium heat. Cover and simmer for 2 hours. The broth will become cloudy if it boils, so always keep it at just a simmer for clearer broth. Simmering rather than boiling also reduces foam, but if any foam forms, simply skim it off the top with a spoon. The foam won't harm the broth; it just looks unsightly.

2 Remove the Dutch oven from the heat and cool for 20 minutes. Taste the broth and add more salt, if desired. Strain the broth through a wire sieve to remove solids and transfer to storage containers. Refrigerate until cold, and then skim off any fat, if desired. Freeze, clearly labeled, for up to 3 months.

Beef Broth

Replace the chicken bones with 8 ounces beef bones (leave a little meat on bones) and prepare as directed.

Vegetable Broth

Replace the chicken bones with 1 cup sliced mushrooms and prepare as directed.

Handling Homemade Broth Safely

It's tempting to put the whole pot of broth in the refrigerator to let it cool and then divvy it up into containers later. Don't do it. The hot Dutch oven and its huge mass of broth take a long time to cool down in the refrigerator, making it linger too long in that danger zone of 40°F to 140°F. And, it warms up the other foods in the refrigerator. So as soon as the broth is cool enough to handle safely, ladle it into your chosen containers—freezer bags, glass canning jars (leave 1 inch at the top for expansion), plastic pop-top containers, or ice cube trays (freeze, then store cubes in plastic bags for when you need just a little). Always thaw broth in the refrigerator rather than at room temperature to avoid having it in that temperature danger zone.

Onion Soup Mix

Onion soup mix has so many versatile uses. Keep this easy version on your pantry shelf if you can't find gluten-free commercial brands or you prefer to make your own. Whenever your recipe calls for onion soup mix, use the same amount of this handy mix. You can easily double or even triple this recipe, if you like.

½ cup dried minced onions
1 tablespoon sweet rice flour
1 teaspoon onion salt
½ teaspoon gluten-free chicken or
   vegetable bouillon powder

¼ teaspoon garlic powder
¼ teaspoon sugar
¼ teaspoon celery seeds
⅛ teaspoon xanthan gum

Combine all of the ingredients in a screw-top jar and shake to thoroughly combine. Or, for a finer texture, whirl in a blender for a few seconds to pulverize the minced onions. Store in a dark, dry place.

V, Q
Makes a scant 6 tablespoons
Preparation time: 5 minutes

Per 1 tablespoon:
30 calories;
1g protein;
0g total fat;
1g fiber;
8g carbohydrates;
0mg cholesterol;
271mg sodium

Simple Vinaigrette

The freshness and purity of homemade salad dressing can't be beat. If you use a simple 1-3-5 ratio, you can make perfect salad dressing every time. You decide what "part" means. It could mean "teaspoon" as in the Mustard Vinaigrette for One Salad. Or it could be "tablespoons" as in the Mustard Vinaigrette for Several Salads. Modify the proportions to suit your taste.

Q, V

Vinaigrette 1-3-5 Ratio
1 part Dijon mustard
3 parts of choice (not malt vinegar)
5 parts extra-virgin olive oil

Q, V
Makes 4 teaspoons

Mustard Vinaigrette for One Salad
1 teaspoon Dijon mustard
3 teaspoons vinegar of choice (not malt vinegar)
5 teaspoons extra-virgin olive oil

Q, V
Makes 9 tablespoons (a generous ½ cup)

Per 1 teaspoon:
50 calories;
0g protein;
6g total fat;
0g fiber;
0g carbohydrates;
0mg cholesterol;
16mg sodium

Mustard Vinaigrette for Several Salads
1 tablespoon Dijon mustard
3 tablespoons vinegar of choice (not malt vinegar
5 tablespoons extra-virgin olive oil

In a glass jar, whisk together the mustard and vinegar until well blended. Drizzle in the olive oil, whisking continuously, until the mixture thickens. Or, blend all of the ingredients in a blender until thickened. Refrigerate for up to 1 month.

White Bean Salad with Peppers and Olives

Cannellini beans are actually white kidney beans, and their pleasing size and shape make them perfect for bean salads. This recipe will also work with other types of canned beans, but white beans contrast nicely with the bright green of the fresh herbs and the red bell pepper. It's important to let the salad sit for 20 minutes before serving, because the flavors will intensify as the dish warms up. You can use other fresh herbs in place of the thyme, such as basil, sage, or tarragon. For meat eaters, add pieces of chopped prosciutto, salami, or ham. Although you could serve this salad right after it's prepared, it's better to let it sit a bit so the flavors meld.

¼ cup extra-virgin olive oil
3 garlic cloves, minced
½ cup finely diced white onion
¼ cup sherry vinegar or red wine vinegar
½ diced cup red bell pepper
½ cup chopped fresh thyme, plus fresh
   sprigs for garnish
½ cup chopped kalamata olives
3 (15-ounce) cans cannellini beans,
   rinsed and drained
   Salt and freshly ground black pepper to
   taste

Q, V
Makes 6 servings (about ¾ cup each)
Preparation time: 10 minutes
Chilling time: 4 hours

1 Heat the oil, garlic, and onion in a small saucepan over medium heat until the garlic and onion are fragrant, about 1 minute. Remove the pan from the heat and stir in the vinegar. While the dressing is still warm, stir in the bell pepper, thyme, olives, and beans and toss until thoroughly combined. Season with salt and black pepper to taste.

2 Refrigerate, covered, for up to 4 hours, then let stand at room temperature for 20 minutes. Serve, garnished with the sprigs of fresh thyme.

Per serving:
405 calories;
21g protein;
11g total fat;
15g fiber;
58g carbohydrates;
0mg cholesterol;
130mg sodium

Pasta Salad with Italian Dressing

Pasta salad is a great dish for hot days. The versatile dressing can be used on other salads, too. Briefly boiling the green vegetables (such as broccoli) for a few seconds and then plunging into ice water (blanching) preserves the bright color. To add vegetarian protein, toss in cubed hard cheese, crumbled feta, chickpeas, or nuts. For meat eaters, add shrimp or chopped cooked chicken.

V

Makes 8 servings (about 1¼ cups each)
Preparation time: 15 minutes
Cooking time: depends on brand of pasta
Chilling time: 2 hours

Per serving:
375 calories;
9g protein;
17g total fat;
2g fiber;
46g carbohydrates;
4mg cholesterol;
265mg sodium

Italian Dressing
- ½ cup red or white wine vinegar
- 1 tablespoon balsamic vinegar
- 1 tablespoon Dijon mustard
- 1½ teaspoons dried Italian seasoning
- ¼ teaspoon sugar
- ¼ teaspoon salt
- 1 small garlic clove, minced (optional)
- ½ cup olive oil

Pasta and Vegetables
- 1 pound gluten-free penne or spiral pasta
- 1 cup small broccoli florets or snow peas
- ½ cup chopped red bell pepper
- ½ cup black olives
- ¼ cup chopped fresh parsley or basil
- ¼ cup chopped red onion
- ¼ teaspoon freshly ground black pepper, plus more to taste
- ½ cup Parmesan cheese or soy Parmesan
  Salt to taste

1 Make the dressing: In a jar with a tight-fitting lid, place the red or white wine vinegar, balsamic vinegar, mustard, Italian seasoning, sugar, salt, and garlic (if using). Seal tightly with the lid and shake until well blended. Add the oil, and shake until the dressing thickens (or whirl all ingredients in a blender until thickened). Refrigerate.

2 In a large pot of salted boiling water, cook the pasta according to package directions until almost done (it will continue to cook after draining.) Add the broccoli during the last minute of cooking to slightly cook the florets. Drain the pasta and broccoli thoroughly and put the broccoli in cold water to stop cooking, then drain it thoroughly.

3 Place the cooked pasta and broccoli in a large serving bowl and add the red bell pepper, olives, parsley, onion, black pepper, and Parmesan. Toss gently with enough of the dressing to thoroughly coat. Taste and add salt and more black pepper, if desired. Chill for at least 2 hours or up to all day. Let stand at room temperature for 20 minutes before serving.

Gluten-Free Pasta
Commercial gluten-free pasta can be made from several different grains—such as beans, corn, quinoa, or rice, or combinations of these grains—so different brands have different cooking times. Cooking pasta to the al dente stage ("to the tooth" in Italian) means it is almost done, but not quite. This is important in pasta salads because pasta continues to cook—even after it is drained—due to residual heat, so overcooking can lead to mushiness. Follow the manufacturer's directions for your particular brand of pasta, but check the pasta a minute or two before it is scheduled to be done so that you can remove it from the heat while it is still al dente. Cooking to the al dente stage helps keep the pasta strong enough to stand up to the salad dressing without breaking apart.

Whole-Grain Sorghum Salad

One serving of this salad puts you closer to your quota of three to five servings of whole grains per day, as recommended by the Whole Grains Council. Soak the sorghum in water overnight or it will take a full hour to cook. For meat eaters, add cooked shrimp or chopped chicken.

Dressing

- 2 tablespoons red wine vinegar
- 2 tablespoons lemon juice or orange juice
- 2 tablespoons agave nectar
- 1 tablespoon Dijon mustard
- 1 small garlic clove, minced
- ¼ teaspoon salt
- ⅛ teaspoon freshly ground black pepper
- ¼ cup extra-virgin olive oil

Salad

- 1 cup whole-grain sorghum (soaked in water overnight and drained)
- 2 medium navel oranges or 1 (11-ounce) can mandarin oranges, drained
- 2 cups strawberries, halved (reserve 6 whole strawberries for garnish)
- 3 tablespoons minced shallot or onion
- 2 cups packed baby spinach
- ½ cup pecan halves
  Salt and freshly ground black pepper
- ½ cup feta cheese (optional)

V

Makes 6 servings (about 1⅓ cups each)
Preparation time: 15 minutes
Cooking time: 45 minutes
Chilling time: 4 hours

Per serving: 350 calories; 7g protein; 19g total fat; 8g fiber; 43g carbohydrates; 11mg cholesterol; 272mg sodium

1 Make the dressing: Whisk the vinegar, lemon juice, agave nectar, mustard, garlic, salt, pepper, and oil until slightly thickened.

2 Make the salad: In a large pot, bring 6 cups salted water to a boil. Add the sorghum and bring to a boil, then reduce the heat to low, cover, and simmer, stirring occasionally, until the sorghum is tender, about 45 minutes. Drain and set aside to cool. (The sorghum can be cooked up to 3 days ahead and refrigerated.)

3 Meanwhile, finely grate the zest of 1 orange into a large serving bowl. Using a sharp knife, remove the peel and white pith from the outside of both oranges. On a cutting board, chop the oranges into bite-size pieces and set aside to stir in just before serving.

4 Add the cooked sorghum to the large bowl and toss with enough of the dressing to thoroughly coat. (Refrigerate leftover dressing for another salad.) Refrigerate for up to 4 hours to let the flavors meld. Then, just before serving, gently stir in the oranges, strawberries, shallots, spinach, and pecans. Taste and add salt and pepper, if desired. Serve, topped with the feta (if using) and the whole strawberries.

Cooking Whole Grains

The traditional method of cooking whole grains is to cook them in a covered pan, with an exact ratio of 2 parts water to 1 part grain. However, my method yields a firmer, less mushy cooked grain: For every 1 cup of sorghum or brown rice (or any other grain), measure four times as much water or broth (in this recipe, that equals 6 cups for every 1 cup sorghum) into a large pot. Bring to a boil, add the grain and return to a boil, and cook uncovered until tender (the time will vary depending on the grain). Drain the grains, but leave them in the pot and set aside to steam, covered, for 10 minutes. Then proceed with your recipe.

Main Dishes 〉

Casseroles and other comfort food dishes often define our childhoods, so it's only natural that we want to continue eating them and serving them to our families, despite having to avoid gluten. Meat Loaf, Macaroni & Cheese, Spaghetti & Meatballs, Chicken-Fried Steak with Gravy, and Tuna-Noodle Casserole are just a few of the dishes in this chapter that take you down memory lane. Ease and efficiency are important to beginning cooks, so I added one-pot meals, slow cooker dishes, simple roasts, and cooking techniques that save time but yield maximum flavor with the least amount of effort. Gather the family around the dinner table and enjoy these classic favorites.

Q	**V**
Quick	Vegetarian

Beef, Pork, and Ham

Chicken-Fried Steak with Gravy
Chili Corn Bread Casserole
Ham & Scalloped Potatoes
Marinated Flank Steak with Herbs
One-Skillet Tortilla Casserole
Meat Loaf
One-Pot Penne with Ground Beef
Pan-Roasted Pork Tenderloin with Honey-
   Mustard Pan Sauce
Six-Layer Casserole
Slow Cooker Pork Shoulder Roast
Spaghetti & Meatballs
Stuffed Bell Peppers
Stuffed Pork Chops with White Sauce
Swiss Steak

Chicken & Fish

Mexican Casserole
Roasted Chicken with Gravy
Chicken Potpie with Herbed Biscuit Topping
Chicken Potpie with Herbed Piecrust Topping
Oven-Fried Chicken
Chicken Fingers
   Spicy Chicken Fingers
Fish Sticks
One-Pot Roasted Salmon with Mediterranean
   Vegetables and Rice
Baked Sea Bass Packets
Tuna-Noodle Casserole

Vegetarian

Veggie Pizza
Hash Brown Casserole
Macaroni & Cheese

Chicken-Fried Steak with Gravy

This is the comfort food many of us associate with diners and home cooking—especially Southern cooking—although it was a dinner staple while I was growing up in eastern Nebraska.

Steak
4 cube steaks (4 to 6 ounces each)
⅓ cup Gluten-Free Flour Blend (page 27)
½ teaspoon salt
½ teaspoon freshly ground black pepper
½ teaspoon paprika
¼ teaspoon onion powder
2 tablespoons canola oil

Gravy
2 teaspoons cornstarch or potato starch
1 cup milk of choice
¼ teaspoon salt
¼ teaspoon freshly ground black pepper

Makes 4 servings (1 cube steak each)
Preparation time: 15 minutes
Cooking time: about 10 minutes

Per steak: 340 calories; 23g protein; 21g total fat; 1g fiber; 14g carbohydrates; 66mg cholesterol; 486mg sodium

1 Make the steak: Pat the steaks dry with paper towels and place on a cutting board.

2 On a plate, combine the flour blend, salt, pepper, paprika, and onion powder. Dip the steaks in the flour mixture and place on the cutting board. Pound each with a meat mallet or a spatula to make the flour mixture stick to the meat.

3 Heat the oil in a nonstick 10-inch skillet (gray, not black). Brown the steaks on both sides; then cook to desired doneness. Cooking time will depend on the thickness of the steaks. Transfer the steaks to a serving platter and cover with aluminum foil to keep warm.

4 Make the gravy: Whisk the cornstarch into ¼ cup of the milk; then stir it into the skillet over medium-low heat, scraping up the browned bits in the skillet with a heatproof spatula. Add the remaining ¾ cup milk and cook, stirring constantly, until the mixture thickens. Add the salt and pepper. Pour the gravy into a warmed bowl or gravy server and cover to keep warm.

5 If needed, return the steaks to the skillet and gently rewarm over low heat. Serve the steaks immediately with the gravy on the side.

Chili Corn Bread Casserole

You can make the chili ahead of time and freeze it. Then, when you're pressed for time and need a quick meal, defrost the chili in the microwave while you mix up the corn bread crust. I usually serve this casserole with slices of avocado for a Southwestern touch. The leftovers are great when simply reheated in the microwave.

Makes 8 servings
Preparation time: 15 minutes
Chili cooking time: 2 hours
Baking time: 20 to 25 minutes

Chili
- 1 pound lean ground beef
- 1 cup finely chopped onions
- 1 (15-ounce) can pinto or kidney beans
- 1 (15-ounce) can canned tomatoes
- 2 teaspoons chili powder
- ½ teaspoon ground cumin
- ½ teaspoon ground coriander
- 1 teaspoon salt
- Water, if needed

Corn Bread Crust
- ⅔ cup Gluten-Free Flour Blend (page 27)
- ½ cup yellow cornmeal
- 2 tablespoons sugar
- 1 teaspoon baking powder
- ½ teaspoon baking soda
- ½ teaspoon salt
- ½ teaspoon xanthan gum
- 1 large egg
- ⅔ cup buttermilk or buttermilk substitute (see Buttermilk Substitutes, page 148)
- 2 tablespoons canola oil
- ¼ cup cheddar cheese (optional)

Per serving:
480 calories;
27g protein;
17g total fat;
16g fiber;
57g carbohydrates;
67mg cholesterol;
727mg sodium

1 Make the chili: In a Dutch oven or large heavy skillet, combine the ground beef and onions. Cook over medium heat until both are gently browned and all juices are absorbed. Add the remaining chili ingredients, cover, and simmer on low heat for 2 hours. Or, cook in a slow cooker on Low for 4 to 6 hours. At this point, you can refrigerate or freeze the chili or proceed to Step 2.

2 Place a rack in the middle of the oven. Preheat the oven to 375°F. Grease a 9x13-inch pan or 10-inch cast-iron skillet. Pour in the chili and set aside while you make the crust. (If the chili is not hot, put it in the oven to heat while making the crust.)

3 Make the crust: In a medium bowl, whisk together the flour blend, cornmeal, sugar, baking powder, baking soda, salt, and xanthan gum until well blended. Add the egg, buttermilk, and oil and beat with an electric mixer on low speed until the batter is smooth, 30 to 40 seconds. Pour the cornbread batter evenly over the chili filling, spreading it to the edges of the pan.

4 Bake until the corn bread crust is firm and lightly browned, 20 to 25 minutes. Sprinkle with the cheese (if using) and return to the oven until the cheese melts, about 5 minutes. Serve immediately.

Ham & Scalloped Potatoes

This has long been one of our family's favorite dishes. It's actually quite easy to make and is terrific as leftovers. It is also an excellent way to use up leftover bits of ham from those holiday dinners. Vegetarians can omit the ham or replace it with a soy-based meat alternative or mushrooms.

4 medium russet potatoes, peeled and sliced
1 cup cubed ham
1 tablespoon dried minced onion
½ teaspoon onion salt
¼ teaspoon freshly ground white pepper
2 tablespoons potato starch or sweet rice flour
½ teaspoon dry mustard

⅛ teaspoon ground nutmeg
2 cups milk of choice
1 tablespoon canola oil
2 tablespoons Parmesan cheese or soy Parmesan
1 tablespoon butter or buttery spread, cubed
Pinch of paprika

1 Preheat the oven to 350°F. Coat a 2-quart casserole with cooking spray.

2 In the baking dish, toss the potatoes and ham with the onion, onion salt, and pepper. In a jar with a screw-top lid, shake together the potato starch, dry mustard, and nutmeg until blended and then add the milk, oil, and 1 tablespoon of the Parmesan, and shake thoroughly until ingredients are blended. Or, blend in a blender until smooth.

3 Pour the milk mixture over the potatoes and ham, then scatter the butter cubes on top. Lightly sprinkle with the paprika. Cover with a lid or aluminum foil and bake for 50 minutes. Uncover, sprinkle with the remaining 1 tablespoon Parmesan, and bake until bubbly and the potatoes are lightly browned on top, about 10 minutes more. Serve hot.

V
(without ham)

Makes 4 servings
Preparation time: 15 minutes
Cooking time: about 1 hour

Per serving:
260 calories;
13g protein;
12g total fat;
1g fiber;
25g carbohydrates;
34mg cholesterol;
786mg sodium

Marinated Flank Steak with Herbs

Planning ahead is important for all cooks, but especially for new cooks. So, always keep this dish in your freezer for those occasions when you need a last-minute dinner and won't have much time beforehand to prepare it. The steak marinates while it thaws in the refrigerator overnight. I like rosemary, thyme, or savory in this dish, but use the herbs you like. You can grill the steak on the barbecue or on a grill pan on your stovetop, or you can broil it in the oven. Serve the meat plain or in fajitas, tacos, or sandwiches.

Q

Makes 4 servings
Preparation time: 5 minutes
Marinating time: thawing in refrigerator overnight
Cooking time: 10 to 14 minutes, plus resting time of 5 minutes

Per serving: 305 calories; 28g protein; 18g total fat; 1g fiber; 6g carbohydrates; 72mg cholesterol; 486mg sodium

¼ cup red wine vinegar
2 tablespoons gluten-free Worcestershire sauce
1 tablespoon olive oil
1 tablespoon Dijon mustard
1 tablespoon sugar
2 garlic cloves, minced
2 tablespoons dried herbs of choice
½ teaspoon salt, plus more to taste
¼ teaspoon freshly ground black pepper, plus more to taste
1¼ pounds flank steak or skirt steak

1 In a heavy-duty, gallon-size resealable freezer storage bag, place the vinegar, Worcestershire sauce, oil, mustard, sugar, garlic, herbs, salt, and pepper.

2 Add the flank steak, label, and seal the bag (with the steak flattened, so it thaws more quickly and marinates evenly) and place flat in the freezer. The day before you want to cook it, transfer to the refrigerator to thaw overnight.

3 Preheat a barbecue grill to medium heat or heat a grill pan on the stovetop until very hot. Grill the steak to the desired degree of doneness, 5 to 7 minutes per side. Transfer to a cutting board and let rest, covered with aluminum foil, for 5 minutes. Thinly slice the meat into thin strips on the diagonal (see Cutting Meat on the Diagonal below). Arrange on a serving platter and serve immediately.

Cutting Meat on the Diagonal

Flank steak and skirt steak are less tender cuts of meat. The first secret to tenderness is to slice off any membrane before cooking. Second, slice the meat in very thin slices on the diagonal or bias, which means against the grain. Look for the lines on the cooked meat; they indicate the grain's direction. Then, holding a very sharp knife at a 45-degree angle to the meat, slice it as thinly as possible in the opposite direction of the grain. This severs the meat's fibers and increases tenderness.

One-Skillet Tortilla Casserole

This dish will become one of your go-to choices for those nights when you need dinner on the table pronto. You control the heat with the spiciness of the salsa (mild, medium, or hot), so choose accordingly. It is very colorful to serve it with avocado slices and sour cream.

8 ounces lean pork sausage

2 cups tomato juice

2 (15-ounce) cans pinto beans, rinsed and drained

½ cup Mexican salsa, plus more for garnish

2 cups corn tortilla chips

½ cup shredded Monterey Jack cheese or cheddar cheese or both, or cheese alternative

½ cup chopped fresh cilantro

1 small head iceberg lettuce, chopped

Q
Makes 6 servings
Cooking time: 15 minutes

1 In a large, heavy, deep skillet, cook the sausage over medium heat, breaking it up with a spatula, until deeply browned, about 5 minutes. Pour off the fat and drain the meat on paper towels to remove excess fat. Return the meat to the skillet.

2 Add the tomato juice, beans, and salsa and stir to combine. Bring to a boil over high heat, reduce the heat to low, and simmer, covered, for 5 minutes. Remove the lid and stir in the tortilla chips. Sprinkle with the cheese and cilantro, cover, and heat over low heat just until the cheese melts, 3 to 5 minutes. Serve immediately over a bed of the lettuce, garnished with a drizzle of salsa.

Per serving:
480 calories;
20g protein;
23g total fat;
14g fiber;
49g carbohydrates;
34mg cholesterol;
778mg sodium

Meat Loaf

Meat loaf is the perfect main dish for beginners because it is so easy to make, you can shape it in a variety of forms, and any extra makes great meat loaf sandwiches. It is also quite versatile, so feel free to use ground turkey or ground pork in place of ground beef (or a mixture of all three) and to vary the spices to suit your palate.

Makes 4 servings
Preparation time: 10 minutes
Baking time: 45 minutes for large loaf; 30 to 35 minutes for small loaves

Per serving: 485 calories; 26g protein; 26g total fat; 2g fiber; 34g carbohydrates; 132mg cholesterol; 954mg sodium

1 (8-ounce) can tomato sauce
¼ cup packed brown sugar
½ teaspoon dry mustard
½ teaspoon chili powder
¼ teaspoon ground cloves
1 garlic clove, minced
1 teaspoon gluten-free Worcestershire sauce

1 pound lean ground beef
1 large egg, beaten
1 cup gluten-free bread crumbs (see below)
½ teaspoon salt
¼ teaspoon freshly ground black pepper
1 tablespoon dried minced onion

1 Preheat the oven to 350°F. Grease a 5x9-inch loaf pan or a 9x13-inch rimmed baking sheet.

2 In a large bowl, whisk together the tomato sauce, sugar, mustard, chili powder, cloves, garlic, and Worcestershire sauce until thoroughly blended. Transfer half (about ½ cup) of the tomato mixture to a small bowl to drizzle over the meat loaf.

3 In the same large bowl with the remaining tomato mixture, add the ground beef, egg, bread crumbs, salt, pepper, and onion. Mix well with your hands until well blended. (Or, put everything in a gallon-size plastic bag and massage until all of the ingredients are well blended.)

4 Place the meat loaf mixture in the loaf pan or shape into a free-form loaf or four smaller, free-form loaves on the rimmed baking sheet. (The advantage of smaller loaves is that there is more crust and they bake faster.) Make an indentation down the center of each loaf (or loaves) and pour the reserved tomato mixture into this indentation.

5 Bake until the top is nicely browned and an instant-read thermometer registers 160°F when inserted into the center, about 45 minutes for a large loaf or 30 to 35 minutes for four smaller loaves. Serve hot.

Gluten-Free Bread Crumbs

Although you can buy gluten-free bread crumbs, it is much cheaper and better-tasting to make your own. For bread crumbs that are lighter in color and that brown uniformly, cut the crusts from the bread. This makes 2 cups.

For regular or Italian bread crumbs: In a food processor, place 4 cups of bread torn into small pieces. For Italian bread crumbs, add 1 teaspoon onion powder and 4 teaspoons dried Italian seasoning. Pulse on and off until the crumbs reach desired consistency. Store tightly covered in the refrigerator for up to 2 weeks, or freeze for up to 3 months.

For extra-crisp bread crumbs: Spread the crumbs on a rimmed baking sheet (not nonstick) and toast in a 250°F oven until lightly browned—the amount of time will vary depending on the moisture content of the bread. The more moisture, the longer to brown. Store tightly covered in the refrigerator for up to 2 weeks, or freeze for up to 3 months.

One-Pot Penne with Ground Beef

This was an old standby for busy nights when I was late getting home from work. I could have a meal on the table in about 20 minutes! This easy pasta dish cooks on the stove while you fix a salad to go with it.

Q

Makes 4 servings
Cooking time: 15 to 20 minutes

8   ounces lean ground beef
2   cups gluten-free penne or spiral pasta
1   (15-ounce) can diced tomatoes
1   tablespoon dried minced onion
1   teaspoon gluten-free Worcestershire sauce
1   teaspoon onion powder
1   teaspoon seasoning salt

Per serving:
380 calories;
18g protein;
12g total fat;
3g fiber;
47g carbohydrates;
43mg cholesterol;
403mg sodium

1 In a large skillet or saucepan with a lid, cook the ground beef until deeply browned. Stir in the pasta, along with all of the remaining ingredients, until well blended.

2 Bring to a boil, cover, and reduce the heat to medium-low. Cook, stirring occasionally to prevent sticking, until the pasta is done, 8 to 12 minutes, depending on the brand of pasta. The dish is done when all of the liquid has been absorbed by the pasta. If the mixture appears too dry, add a little water, as needed. Serve immediately.

Pan-Roasted Pork Tenderloin with Honey-Mustard Pan Sauce

Pork tenderloin is one of my favorite meat cuts because it is very versatile, it cooks quickly because it is thin, and there's no waste. The method used here is pan roasting, an extremely easy, no-fail technique that helps busy cooks get a meal on the table quickly. I use it often because it frees me up to attend to the other parts of the meal while the pork finishes in the oven. When you put these two together—pork tenderloin and pan roasting—you have a dish that you will make again and again.

2 teaspoons dry mustard	3 tablespoons cider vinegar
1½ teaspoons salt	2 tablespoons milk of choice
¼ teaspoon freshly ground black pepper	2 tablespoons Dijon mustard
1 pound pork tenderloin, trimmed of fat	1 tablespoon honey or agave nectar
2 teaspoons canola oil	1 tablespoon chopped fresh thyme or ¼
¼ teaspoon cornstarch	teaspoon dried

Makes 4 servings
Preparation time: 5 minutes
Cooking time: 30 to 35 minutes

Per serving: 190 calories; 25g protein; 7g total fat; 1g fiber; 6g carbohydrates; 74mg cholesterol; 736mg sodium

1 Place a rack in the middle of the oven. Preheat the oven to 425°F.

2 In a small bowl, combine the dry mustard, salt, and pepper, and rub evenly over the pork. Heat a large ovenproof skillet over medium-high heat until the skillet is very hot. Add the oil. When it is hot, add the pork and brown on all sides, 5 to 8 minutes.

3 Transfer the skillet to the oven and roast until the internal temperature registers 145°F on an instant-read thermometer, 15 to 20 minutes. Transfer the pork to a cutting board and let rest, covered with aluminum foil, for 5 minutes. The pork will continue to cook and the temperature will continue to rise.

4 While the meat rests, make the pan sauce: In a small bowl, whisk the cornstarch into the vinegar and add to the skillet along with the milk, Dijon mustard, honey, and thyme. Bring to a boil over medium-high heat, scraping up any browned bits with a wooden spoon or heatproof spatula, about 30 seconds. Reduce the heat to low and simmer until the sauce thickens, 2 to 3 minutes.

5 Remove the foil from the pork, slice, and place on a serving platter. Drizzle the pan sauce over the pork and serve immediately.

Six-Layer Casserole

My mother-in-law made this casserole for my husband when he was a child. When we married, he asked me to continue making it for him; it was one of my first experiences with casseroles. It is a super-easy, one-dish meal that can be assembled the night before and then baked the next day. Plan ahead, because it takes 2 hours to bake, but it's worth the wait! Leftovers are yummy!

Makes 6 servings (about 1½ cups each)
Preparation time: 15 minutes
Baking time: 2 hours

1 large russet potato, thinly sliced
⅓ cup white rice
8 ounces lean ground beef
1 small onion, finely diced
1 cup finely diced carrots
½ cup green peas
4 cups diced canned tomatoes
2 teaspoons salt
1 teaspoon sugar
½ teaspoon dried thyme
½ teaspoon freshly ground black pepper

Per serving: 200 calories; 10g protein; 8g total fat; 3g fiber; 22g carbohydrates; 28mg cholesterol; 758mg sodium

1 Preheat the oven to 350°F. Grease a deep, 2-quart baking dish.

2 Layer the potatoes evenly in the bottom of the dish. Top with the rice, then the ground beef, followed by the onions, carrots, and peas.

3 Mix the tomatoes with the salt, sugar, thyme, and pepper and pour evenly over the dish. Cover with a tight-fitting lid or aluminum foil. Place on a baking sheet to catch any boilovers or spills.

4 Bake until the vegetables are done, the beef is cooked through, and the rice is tender, about 2 hours. Remove the lid or foil during the last 15 minutes of baking for better browning.

Slow Cooker Pork Shoulder Roast

Slow cookers are great; they do the cooking for you while you're free to do other things. Moist, lean pork shoulder is great for slow cookers and is extremely versatile. It is delicious for dinner, sliced and drizzled with the flavorful sauce created by the juices as it cooks. Or, transfer the roast to a plate, shred the meat (see How to Shred Meat below), and serve with taco fixings for a Southwestern dinner. Use any leftover meat in a soup or stew.

1 cup orange juice
½ cup diced onion
2 tablespoons red wine vinegar
1 teaspoon dried oregano
½ teaspoon ground cumin
¼ teaspoon chipotle chile powder, or
   more to taste

2 large garlic cloves, peeled
1 (1¼-pound) boneless pork shoulder or
   Boston butt, trimmed of fat
2 tablespoons canola oil
¾ teaspoon salt
½ teaspoon freshly ground black pepper

Makes 4 servings
Preparation time: 40 minutes
Cooking time: about 6 to 8 hours or all day

Per serving: 325 calories; 28g protein; 18g total fat; 1g fiber; 10g carbohydrates; 96mg cholesterol; 504mg sodium

1 In a medium bowl, combine the orange juice, onion, vinegar, oregano, cumin, chile powder, and garlic to make the marinade.

2 Heat the oil in a medium heavy skillet over medium-high heat. Pat the pork dry with paper towels and season with the salt and pepper. Brown on all sides, about 8 minutes. Remove the browned pork from the pan and place in the slow cooker. Add the marinade to the skillet and bring to a boil, scraping the skillet with a spatula to loosen the browned bits. Add the hot marinade to the slow cooker.

3 Cook 6 to 8 hours or all day on Low. Remove the pork from the slow cooker, let rest for 10 minutes (covered), then slice and serve, drizzled with the juices. Or, shred the pork and return to the slow cooker juices to moisten, and then serve in tacos.

How to Shred Meat
First, let the cooked meat stand for 15 minutes, wrapped in aluminum foil, after cooking to let the meat reabsorb its juices. Unwrap the meat and place it on a flat surface, such as a cutting board. Then, holding a fork in each hand, place the first fork into the meat aligned with the grain and hold it steady. Then place the second fork into the meat and pull it away from the first fork. Repeat this process until all of the meat is shredded into small pieces.

Spaghetti & Meatballs

This is my family heirloom recipe; I promise that you'll love it. It is very bold and flavorful because of all the herbs and spices. It actually works better with dried herbs because the equivalent amount of fresh herbs turns the sauce an unappetizing green color. If you don't want to use all beef, use half ground beef and half ground pork or turkey. The sauce cooks best in a slow cooker so that the flavors can meld all day with no tending.

Makes 8 servings (2 meatballs each)
Preparation time: 15 minutes
Baking time for meatballs: 20 minutes
Cooking time for sauce: 6 to 8 hours or all day

Per serving: 315 calories; 18g protein; 15g total fat; 6g fiber; 29g carbohydrates; 96mg cholesterol; 1676mg sodium

Meatballs

- 1 pound lean ground beef
- ¼ teaspoon salt
- ½ teaspoon freshly ground black pepper
- ¼ cup gluten-free bread crumbs (see page 104)
- 1 large egg
- 2 tablespoons dried parsley
- 1½ teaspoons dried basil
- ½ teaspoon dried oregano
- 1 garlic clove, minced
- 2 tablespoons grated Romano cheese (optional)
- ¼ teaspoon crushed red pepper flakes

Spaghetti Sauce

- 1 (24-ounce) can tomato juice
- 2 (6-ounce) cans tomato paste
- 1½ tablespoons dried parsley
- 1½ tablespoons sugar
- 1 tablespoon dried basil
- 1½ teaspoons dried rosemary
- 1 bay leaf
- 1 teaspoon dried oregano
- 1 teaspoon salt, or to taste
- ½ teaspoon freshly ground black pepper
- 2 tablespoons grated Romano cheese (optional)
- 2 pounds gluten-free spaghetti, cooked

1 Place a rack in the middle of the oven. Line a 9x13-inch rimmed baking sheet with aluminum foil. Preheat the oven to 350°F.

2 Make the meatballs: In a large bowl, combine all of the meatball ingredients and mix well with your hands. Shape into 16 meatballs, about 2 tablespoons each or 1½ inches in diameter, and place on the baking sheet.

3 Bake until the meatballs are browned, about 20 minutes. Remove from the oven and cool for 15 minutes on the sheet on a wire rack. The meatballs can be made ahead and reheated at serving time.

4 Make the sauce: In a slow cooker, combine all of the sauce ingredients and stir well. Cook 6 to 8 hours or all day on Low, stirring occasionally. Add the Romano cheese (if using) just before serving.

5 To serve, add the meatballs to the sauce and serve, 2 meatballs per person, over the hot spaghetti.

Stuffed Bell Peppers

This dish is perfect for using up leftover cooked rice. Brown rice offers far more nutrients than white rice and counts toward your daily quota of whole grains, but use what you have. No Italian sausage? Use plain sausage, but increase the Italian seasoning to 1 teaspoon. Vegetarians can replace the sausage with soy protein or cooked beans for added protein.

4 medium red bell peppers	1 teaspoon minced garlic
2 cups cooked brown rice or instant brown rice	½ teaspoon dried Italian seasoning
4 ounces Italian sausage, browned and drained	½ teaspoon salt, or to taste
	¼ teaspoon freshly ground black pepper
1 (14½-ounce) can diced tomatoes, drained	½ cup shredded low-fat mozzarella cheese or cheese alternative
	¼ cup chopped fresh parsley

1 Place a rack in the middle of the oven. Preheat the oven to 350°F. Coat a 9x13-inch microwave-safe baking dish with cooking spray.

2 Halve each pepper lengthwise, from stem to base, leaving the stems on if you wish for a prettier presentation but removing the seeds. Place in the baking dish, cut side up, cover with waxed paper, and cook in the microwave on High for 5 minutes to soften. Remove the dish from the microwave and let the peppers cool while making the filling.

3 In a large bowl, stir together the rice, sausage, tomatoes, garlic, Italian seasoning, salt, and pepper. Stuff the pepper halves with the rice mixture and then cover the dish with aluminum foil.

4 Bake until the filling is heated through, about 20 minutes. Remove the foil, sprinkle the peppers with the cheese, and bake until the cheese is melted, 5 to 10 minutes. Remove from the oven and serve immediately, garnished with the parsley.

V
(without sausage)

Makes 4 servings

Preparation time: 30 minutes

Baking time: 25 to 30 minutes

Per serving: 310 calories; 11g protein; 14g total fat; 5g fiber; 37g carbohydrates; 34mg cholesterol; 548mg sodium

Stuffed Pork Chops with White Sauce

An all-American dish, stuffed pork chops are hearty, filling, and perfect for a chilly day when you want an oven meal. This dish consists of three distinct recipes that you can use separately for other dishes—pork chops, stuffing, and white sauce—but together, they spell comfort food. Vary the spices in the stuffing to suit your taste and feel free to double or triple it for stuffing a turkey. You can also use corn bread instead of regular bread. The white sauce, or béchamel, is very versatile and can be used on other meats and vegetables.

Makes 4 servings
Preparation time: 15 minutes
Baking time: 40 to 55 minutes

Stuffing
Per serving:
310 calories;
14g protein;
6g total fat;
3g fiber;
54g carbohydrates;
1mg cholesterol;
970mg sodium

Pork Chop
Per pork chop:
135 calories;
20g protein;
5g total fat;
0g fiber;
0g carbohydrates;
56mg cholesterol;
623mg sodium

Stuffing
- 1 (14-ounce) loaf gluten-free bread, lightly toasted and cut into 1-inch cubes (about 8 cups)
- 1 teaspoon canola oil
- 1 small onion, finely chopped
- 2 celery stalks, finely chopped
- 2 teaspoons dried sage
- 1 teaspoon poultry seasoning
- 1 teaspoon celery salt
- 1 teaspoon celery seeds
- 1 teaspoon dried parsley
- ¼ teaspoon freshly ground white pepper
- 2 cups gluten-free chicken broth or homemade Chicken Broth, page 90

Pork Chops
- 4 thick bone-in pork chops (1½ to 2 inches; about 1 pound total)

- 2 teaspoons dried sage
- ½ teaspoon salt
- ¼ teaspoon freshly ground black pepper

White Sauce
- 1 cup milk of choice (the richer the milk, the richer the sauce)
- 1 cup gluten-free chicken broth
- 1 small onion, quartered
- 2 tablespoons butter or buttery spread
- 1 small bay leaf
  Pinch of ground nutmeg (optional)
- 3 tablespoons cornstarch
  Salt and white pepper to taste (optional; depending on saltiness of the broth)

  Pinch of paprika

1 Make the stuffing: Place the bread cubes in a large bowl. In a medium skillet, heat the oil over medium heat and cook the onion and celery until just tender and slightly translucent, about 5 minutes. Add to the bread cubes, along with all of the remaining stuffing ingredients. Toss until all the cubes are moist.

2 Make the pork chops: Preheat the oven to 350°F. Grease a 7x11-inch baking dish. Place the pork chops on a cutting board and trim any excess fat. Holding a knife horizontal to the cutting board, cut a deep slash in the meaty side almost—but not quite—to the bone to create a pocket. Rub ¼ teaspoon sage onto each side of the pork chop and then sprinkle with salt and pepper. Press about ½ cup stuffing into the pocket of each pork chop. Lightly arrange the remaining stuffing evenly on the bottom of the baking dish and then lay the pork chops on top. Cover with aluminum foil.

3 Bake for 30 minutes. Remove the foil and bake until the pork registers 145°F when an instant-read thermometer is inserted in the thickest part, another 10 to 15 minutes.

4 Meanwhile, make the white sauce: In a small heavy saucepan, combine ¾ cup of the milk, the broth, onion, butter, bay leaf, and nutmeg (if using) and heat on medium heat just until bubbles form around the edge of the pan (don't boil); then remove from the heat and let stand for 10 minutes to let the flavors meld. Discard the onion and bay leaf.

5 Whisk the cornstarch into the remaining ¼ cup milk until smooth, and then whisk it into the saucepan and heat over medium heat, whisking constantly, until the mixture thickens, about 1 minute. Add salt and pepper to taste.

6 Serve the pork chops with the stuffing, drizzled with the sauce and a sprinkle of paprika.

White Sauce
Per serving:
125 calories;
5g protein;
6g total fat;
1g fiber;
11g carbohydrates;
18mg cholesterol;
220mg sodium

Swiss Steak

This was an old standby when my son was growing up and I needed a meal on the table quickly after I got home from work. I served it over cooked rice, but it also works with mashed potatoes. A mixed green salad completed the meal (along with our favorite dessert, chocolate pudding). We all loved it; in fact, we had it once a week ("if it's Tuesday, then it must be Swiss Steak").

> 1   tablespoon canola oil
> 1   pound lean round steak (1 inch thick)
> ¼   cup chopped onion
> 1   (16-ounce) can diced tomatoes
> 1   tablespoon diced green bell pepper
> 1   teaspoon beau monde seasoning
> ¼   teaspoon dried basil
> ¼   teaspoon salt

In a large skillet with a lid, heat the oil over medium heat. Add the steak and cook until well browned on both sides, about 5 minutes. Add all of the remaining ingredients, bring to a boil, and then reduce the heat to low. Cover and simmer for 30 minutes. Cut the steak into serving pieces and serve hot, topped with the juices.

Q
Makes 4 servings
Preparation time: 35 minutes
Cooking time: 30 minutes

Per serving:
275 calories;
23g protein;
17g total fat;
1 gram fiber;
6g carbohydrates;
68mg cholesterol;
541mg sodium

Mexican Casserole

Bold and flavorful, this layered, make-ahead casserole is perfect for busy weeknights, but it also makes a great dish for entertaining friends. Add a mixed green salad, a frosty mug of gluten-free beer, and Lemon Bars (page 190) or Mexican Wedding Cakes (page 183) for dessert and you have a winning meal. If you like it spicier, increase the amount of chili powder to ½ teaspoon.

1 cup gluten-free low-sodium chicken broth
1 cup Mexican-style diced tomatoes
1 medium onion, finely diced
1 (4-ounce) can diced green chiles
½ teaspoon dried oregano
¼ teaspoon ground cumin
¼ teaspoon dried sage
¼ teaspoon chili powder

¼ teaspoon garlic powder
½ teaspoon salt
2 cups cubed cooked chicken
1 cup grated cheddar cheese or cheese alternative
1 cup grated Monterey Jack cheese or cheese alternative
2 cups lightly crushed corn tortilla chips
2 tablespoons chopped fresh cilantro

Makes 6 servings
Preparation time: 10 minutes
Baking time: 35 to 40 minutes

1 Preheat the oven to 350°F. In a medium bowl, stir together the chicken broth, tomatoes, onions, green chiles, oregano, cumin, sage, chili powder, garlic powder, and salt to form the sauce. Set aside.

2 Grease a 10x14-inch casserole dish with 3-inch sides. Layer half of the chicken, then half of the sauce, half of the cheddar and Monterey Jack cheeses, and half of the tortilla chips in the dish. Repeat the layers, ending with a final sprinkling of the cheeses.

3 Bake until the casserole is hot and bubbly around the edges, 35 to 40 minutes. Let sit for a few minutes so any moisture in the dish absorbs back into the casserole, then serve hot, garnished with the cilantro.

Per serving: 330 calories; 27g protein; 19g total fat; 2g fiber; 13g carbohydrates; 76mg cholesterol; 631mg sodium

Roasted Chicken with Gravy

Makes 4 servings
Preparation time: 15 minutes
Roasting time: 1½ to 2 hours

A whole roasted chicken is the perfect Sunday dinner, leaving you with leftovers for casseroles and sandwiches later in the week. It is also fail-proof for beginning cooks and an easy way to entertain guests. Don't forget to save the chicken bones to make Chicken Broth (page 90). This is a very basic recipe, but you may add carrots, potatoes, and onions to the pot and stuff the cavity with fresh herbs or lemon slices for added flavor.

Chicken
Per serving:
635 calories;
50g protein;
36g total fat;
1g fiber;
1g carbohydrates;
262mg cholesterol;
516mg sodium

Chicken

- 1 (3½- to 4-pound) chicken
- 2 tablespoons butter or buttery spread, softened, or olive oil
- ½ teaspoon salt, or to taste
- ¼ teaspoon freshly ground black pepper, or to taste
- ½ cup hot water
  Cooking spray

Gravy

- 2 cups gluten-free low-sodium chicken broth or homemade Chicken Broth, page 90
- 2 tablespoons cornstarch or ¼ cup sweet rice flour
- ¼ teaspoon salt, plus more to taste
- ¼ teaspoon freshly ground black pepper, plus more to taste
- ¼ teaspoon dried sage
- ¼ teaspoon dried thyme
- ¼ teaspoon poultry seasoning

Gravy
Per ¼ cup gravy:
80 calories;
3g protein;
6g total fat;
1g fiber;
2g carbohydrates;
6mg cholesterol;
198mg sodium (nutrients can vary with the amount of fat and salt in the pan drippings)

1 Make the chicken: Place a rack in the lower third of the oven and remove the top racks to allow enough room in the top of the oven for the chicken. Preheat the oven to 425°F. Coat a roasting pan or Dutch oven with cooking spray and place an ovenproof wire rack inside; coat the rack with cooking spray. Pat the chicken dry with paper towels and rub with the softened butter. Sprinkle generously with the salt and pepper.

2 Place the chicken on the rack, breast side up, and pour the hot water on the bottom of the roasting pan. Roast for 15 minutes. Reduce the heat to 350°F and continue roasting until the chicken is browned and crisp and the internal temperature registers 180°F when tested with an instant-read thermometer, 60 to 75 minutes (the juices will run clear). Baste the chicken occasionally with the pan drippings while it roasts. Transfer the chicken to a serving platter. Let the chicken rest, covered with aluminum foil, for 15 minutes before carving.

3 Make the gravy: While the chicken rests, remove the wire rack from the roasting pan, strain the pan juices through a sieve to remove any solids, and reserve ½ cup of the juices (or add water to the juices to equal ½ cup). Return the juices to the roasting pan (or to a medium heavy saucepan) and add 1¾ cups of the broth, mixing well. Place the pan on the stovetop. Whisk the cornstarch into the remaining ¼ cup broth until smooth, and add to the pan, along with the salt, pepper, sage, thyme, and poultry seasoning. Bring to a boil over high heat, and cook, stirring constantly, until the mixture thickens into gravy. Taste and add additional salt and pepper, if desired.

4 Carve the chicken, and serve hot with the gravy.

Roasted Chicken from the Deli?

Why not buy a roasted chicken from the deli instead of roasting it at home? Well, even if the ingredients are gluten-free, you don't know whether the chicken came into contact with gluten during preparation or roasting at the deli. It should have a gluten-free label, and unless you know for sure, it is safer (and cheaper) to roast your own chicken.

Simple Ways to Vary Roast Chicken

Roast Chicken is a crowd-pleaser and easy to make regularly once you get the basic technique. You can also easily add different flavorings in Step 1 for a change of pace with only a little extra effort. (Read the labels to make sure that the added seasonings are gluten-free.) If you're using one of the seasoning blends suggested below, add salt and pepper only if it isn't already included in the blend. For best results, add these ingredients in the order in which they're listed. Note that seasoning variations here will flavor the drippings, which will in turn flavor the gravy. Certain flavors may taste wonderful on roast chicken, but not on mashed potatoes. Let the variation you choose determine how you use the gravy—or whether you make it at all.

1) For Greek chicken: Instead of butter, rub skin with olive oil, drizzle with fresh lemon juice, sprinkle with chopped fresh oregano or dried oregano
2) For Italian chicken: Instead of butter, rub skin with olive oil, sprinkle with Italian herb seasoning
3 For Provençal chicken: Instead of butter, rub skin with olive oil, sprinkle with herbs de Provence
4) For Southwestern chicken: Instead of butter, rub skin with canola oil, sprinkle with a Southwest seasoning blend
5) For Asian chicken: Instead of butter, rub skin with canola oil, sprinkle with an Asian seasoning blend

Chicken Potpie with Herbed Biscuit Topping

At my house, if we have roast chicken for dinner, it's a sure bet that we'll have chicken potpie later that week. I often roast potatoes, carrots, and onions along with the chicken so that I can use them later in this dish. Some of the cold chicken goes for sandwiches, and then I use the bones to make chicken broth. That way, one food preparation leads to several easier meals later in the week. Although this recipe appears to have lots of ingredients, if you start with cooked ingredients for the filling it goes together very quickly, and it is a complete meal in itself. This is a very rustic dish; if you prefer a more refined potpie, try the next recipe, which uses a piecrust topping.

Makes 6 servings
Preparation time: 20 minutes
Baking time: 50 to 55 minutes

Filling

- 2 cups cubed cooked chicken
- 1 cup mixed frozen vegetables (such as carrots, corn, and peas)
- 1 small cooked russet potato, peeled and cubed
- ½ cup finely chopped yellow onion
- 2 tablespoons chopped fresh thyme or 1 teaspoon dried
- 1 tablespoon Dijon mustard
- 1 teaspoon tomato paste
- 1 teaspoon gluten-free soy sauce
- 1 teaspoon salt
- ¼ teaspoon freshly ground black pepper
- 1 garlic clove, minced
- 1½ cups gluten-free low-sodium chicken broth
- 1 tablespoon cornstarch
- 2 tablespoons water

Herbed Biscuit Topping

- 1 cup Gluten-Free Flour Blend (page 27)
- ½ cup cornstarch or potato starch
- 1 tablespoon sugar
- 2 teaspoons baking powder
- 1 teaspoon xanthan gum
- ½ teaspoon salt
- ¼ teaspoon baking soda
- 2 tablespoons chopped fresh thyme or 1 teaspoon dried
- ¼ cup butter, buttery spread, or shortening
- ¾ cup milk of choice, or as needed to make a soft dough
- 1 large egg, separated, at room temperature
- 1 tablespoon water

Per serving:
350 calories;
20g protein;
11g total fat;
3g fiber;
43g carbohydrates;
93mg cholesterol;
1130mg sodium

1 Make the filling: Preheat the oven to 375°F. Grease a 2-quart baking dish. Place all of the filling ingredients except the cornstarch and water in the dish and mix together thoroughly. Whisk the cornstarch into the water until smooth and stir into the filling until well blended. Bake, covered, for 30 minutes to heat the filling.

2 Meanwhile, prepare the biscuit topping: In a food processor, pulse the dry ingredients (flour blend through thyme) until thoroughly blended. Add the butter, milk, and the egg white. Blend until the dough forms a ball, scraping down the sides of the bowl with a spatula, if necessary. The dough will be somewhat soft. If it is too stiff, add more milk, a tablespoon at a time, until the dough easily falls from a spatula.

3 Remove the baking dish from the oven and drop the biscuit dough by tablespoons onto the hot filling. The dough does not have to cover all of the filling; it will spread out as it bakes. Whisk the egg yolk with the water and brush it over the dough to encourage browning. Return the dish to the oven and continue baking until the topping is nicely browned, 20 to 25 minutes. Serve immediately.

Chicken Potpie with Herbed Piecrust Topping

This is the recipe I use when I want a crisp piecrust topping on my potpie, rather than a bready biscuit topping, like the previous version. It is filling, homey, and very comforting. The piecrust doesn't have to be rolled perfectly round because you tuck it in around the edges of the round baking dish.

1 batch Chicken Potpie Filling (opposite)	2 tablespoons chopped fresh thyme or
1 cup Gluten-Free Flour Blend	1 teaspoon dried
(page 27)	½ teaspoon salt
⅔ cup tapioca flour	½ cup shortening
½ cup sweet rice flour	2 tablespoons butter or buttery spread
1 tablespoon sugar	¼ cup milk of choice
¾ teaspoon xanthan gum	1 large egg, beaten, for egg wash

Makes 6 servings
Preparation time: 20 minutes
Baking time: 50 to 55 minutes

Per serving: 490 calories; 20g protein; 21g total fat; 3g fiber; 58g carbohydrates; 71mg cholesterol; 826mg sodium

1 Preheat the oven to 375°F. Grease a deep, 2-quart round baking dish. Place the filling in the dish and bake, covered, until the filling is heated, about 30 minutes.

2 Place the flour blend, tapioca flour, sweet rice flour, sugar, xanthan gum, thyme, salt, shortening, and butter in a food processor. Process until the mixture resembles green peas. Add the milk and process until the dough forms a soft ball. If it doesn't form a ball, add a tablespoon of water and process again. Knead the ball of dough with your hands until it is very soft and pliable. Divide the dough in half; freeze one half, tightly wrapped, for another use.

3 Roll the remaining half of the dough into a circle (the same size as the diameter of the baking dish) between two pieces of heavy-duty plastic wrap. Use a damp paper towel between the countertop and the plastic wrap to anchor the plastic wrap. Be sure to move the rolling pin from the center of the dough toward the outer edge, moving around in a clockwise fashion, to ensure uniform thickness.

4 Remove the baking dish from the oven. Remove the top plastic wrap and invert the crust onto the baking dish, centering it over the filling. Remove the remaining plastic wrap, being careful not to touch the hot filling or the hot baking dish with your hands. With a spatula, tuck the outer edges of the crust down around the edge of the baking dish, and brush the piecrust with the beaten egg. Return the baking dish to the oven and bake until the crust is nicely browned, 20 to 25 minutes. Serve immediately.

Oven-Fried Chicken

Fried chicken is one of America's favorites, but this version is far healthier because it is baked rather than fried. Don't worry, though; it is still crispy and crunchy and goes perfectly with your favorite coleslaw. If you need to serve more than 4 people—or you are especially hungry—you can double the recipe.

Makes 4 servings
Preparation time: 10 minutes
Baking time: 45 to 60 minutes

Per serving: 120 calories; 15g protein; 3g total fat; 1g fiber; 7g carbohydrates; 58mg cholesterol; 358mg sodium

½ cup buttermilk or buttermilk substitute (see Buttermilk Substitutes, page 148)
¼ teaspoon cayenne pepper
¼ teaspoon garlic powder
¼ cup brown rice flour

3 tablespoons cornmeal
½ teaspoon salt
¼ teaspoon freshly ground white pepper
¼ teaspoon paprika
4 large boneless, skinless chicken thighs (about 1 pound total)
Cooking spray

1 Preheat the oven to 400°F. Grease a 9x13-inch nonstick rimmed baking sheet (gray, not black).

2 In a small shallow bowl, whisk together the buttermilk, cayenne pepper, and garlic powder until thoroughly blended. In another shallow bowl, whisk together the flour, cornmeal, salt, white pepper, and paprika until well combined.

3 Dip each chicken thigh into the buttermilk mixture and then into the flour mixture, shaking gently to remove any excess. Place the chicken on the prepared baking sheet. Gently mist the chicken pieces with cooking spray to encourage browning.

4 Bake, turning once, until the chicken is browned and juices are no longer pink when the centers of the thickest pieces are cut, 45 to 60 minutes. Serve immediately.

Additional Breading Ideas

Fried chicken (or any fried meat or vegetable) can be breaded with any of the following items. Dip in milk, buttermilk, or beaten egg first. Each breading produces a different texture and taste, so experiment to see what you like best. Don't forget to read labels to make sure all are gluten-free.

Cornflakes
Cornmeal
Cream of rice cereal
Crushed corn tortilla chips
Crushed rice crackers
Gluten-free bread crumbs
Mashed potato flakes

Chicken Fingers

Chicken is easier to slice if it's cold, so pop the breasts into the freezer for 15 minutes before cutting. These chicken fingers are very similar to those on the menu at fast-food restaurants. Kids (young and old) will enjoy them as a meal or a hearty treat that is healthier since they are baked rather than fried. The herbs and spices lend a nice flavor, but for a spicier version, use the Spicy Chicken Fingers variation below.

Makes 4 servings
Preparation time: 15 minutes
Baking time: 30 minutes

Per serving:
295 calories;
31g protein;
3g total fat;
2g fiber;
32g carbohydrates;
116mg cholesterol;
375mg sodium

Spicy Chicken Fingers
Per serving:
185 calories;
24g protein;
6g total fat;
1g fiber; 8g carbohydrates;
101mg cholesterol;
684mg sodium

4 very cold boneless, skinless chicken breast halves
1 very cold large egg, beaten
½ cup very cold milk of choice
1 cup Basic Seasoned Breading Mix for Frying (recipe follows)

1 Preheat the oven to 350°F. Coat a 9x13-inch nonstick rimmed baking sheet (gray, not black) with cooking spray.

2 On a cutting board with a sharp knife, slice each chicken breast diagonally into ½-inch-wide strips. In a shallow bowl, whisk together the egg and milk until very smooth. In another shallow bowl, place the breading mix.

3 Using tongs, dip each chicken strip into the egg mixture, then into the breading mix, and lay it on the baking sheet.

4 Bake, turning once, until nicely browned and crispy, about 30 minutes.

Spicy Chicken Fingers
Use this spicy mixture instead of the Basic Seasoned Breading Mix for Frying before baking.

1 cup very finely crushed corn tortilla chips
1 teaspoon salt
½ teaspoon garlic powder
½ teaspoon ground cumin
½ teaspoon freshly ground black pepper
¼ teaspoon cayenne pepper

Basic Seasoned Breading Mix for Frying

Whip up a batch of this flavorful breading mix and keep it on hand so that you're ready to coat whatever needs frying, quickly and easily.

1 cup yellow or white cornmeal
1 cup cornstarch
1 teaspoon dried thyme
1 teaspoon dried oregano
1 teaspoon onion powder
1 teaspoon paprika
1 teaspoon salt
½ teaspoon cayenne pepper
¼ teaspoon garlic powder
¼ teaspoon sugar

Mix all of the ingredients together and store in an airtight container in a dark, dry place for up to 3 months. Use as a breading mix for meats, seafood, or vegetables in frying and baking. Do not reuse the mix after dipping.

Makes 2 cups

Per 1 tablespoon:
30 calories; 0g protein; 0g total fat; 1g fiber; 7g carbohydrates; 0mg cholesterol; 67mg sodium

Fish Sticks

Kids love fish sticks, but adults certainly can enjoy them too. Plus, they are a great way to use up leftover cooked fish. Have the ketchup ready for dipping!

1 pound cooked white fish, such as cod, perch, sole, or snapper

2 large eggs

1 cup gluten-free bread crumbs (see Gluten-Free Bread Crumbs, page 104)

1 tablespoon Dijon mustard

½ teaspoon dried thyme

¼ teaspoon salt

¼ teaspoon freshly ground black pepper

2 tablespoons chopped green onions (white parts only)

2 tablespoons canola or peanut oil

1 Place half of the fish, one of the eggs, ¼ cup of the bread crumbs, and all of the mustard, thyme, salt, and pepper in a food processor. Puree until smooth.

2 In a medium bowl, flake the remaining fish with a fork and stir in the pureed fish mixture plus the onions. Shape the mixture into 4 patties or 8 fish sticks.

3 In a separate bowl, whisk the remaining egg until foamy. Place the remaining bread crumbs on a plate. Dip the fish patties or sticks into the egg mixture, then into the bread crumbs.

4 In a medium, heavy, nonstick skillet (gray, not black), heat the oil over medium-high heat. Fry the fish in batches until golden brown on one side. Turn and fry until cooked through and browned on the other side (2 to 3 minutes per side). Serve hot.

Makes 4 servings (1 patty or 2 sticks each)

Preparation time: 10 minutes

Frying time: 4 to 6 minutes per batch

Per patty or 2 fish sticks: 335 calories; 34g protein; 12g total fat; 1g fiber; 21g carbohydrates; 171mg cholesterol; 560mg sodium

One-Pot Roasted Salmon on Mediterranean Vegetables and Rice

Cooking everything—meat, starch, and vegetable—in a single pan is an incredible time-saver. It is more efficient, and you have fewer pans to wash, plus some dishes—like this one—are so pretty that it is perfectly acceptable to serve them right in the cooking vessel.

2 cups gluten-free low-sodium chicken broth or homemade Chicken Broth, page 90, heated to boiling
1 cup long-grain white rice
5 ounces baby spinach
1 (6½-ounce) jar marinated artichokes, drained
2 garlic cloves, minced
1 cup red grape tomatoes, halved
½ cup pitted black olives, sliced
4 small salmon fillets (about 4 ounces each)

2 tablespoons olive oil
2 tablespoons dry white wine or lemon juice
¼ teaspoon salt, plus more to taste
¼ teaspoon freshly ground black pepper, plus more to taste
1 teaspoon lemon-pepper seasoning or lemon-herb seasoning

Makes 4 servings
Preparation time: 10 minutes
Roasting time: 35 to 37 minutes

1 Place a rack in the lower third of the oven. Preheat the oven to 400°F. Place the boiling broth and the rice in a deep, 2-quart baking dish.

2 In a large bowl, toss the spinach, artichokes, and garlic together and place on top of the rice. Arrange the tomatoes and black olives around the edges of the dish. Arrange the salmon fillets on top of the spinach, drizzle with the oil and wine, and sprinkle with the salt, pepper, and lemon-pepper seasoning. Cover tightly with a lid or aluminum foil.

3 Roast in the oven for 30 minutes. Remove the lid and continue roasting until the fish flakes easily with a fork, 5 to 7 minutes, depending on the thickness of the fish. Serve immediately.

Per serving:
470 calories; 35g protein; 15g total fat; 4g fiber; 46g carbohydrates; 59mg cholesterol; 894mg sodium

Baked Sea Bass Packets

This is the perfect dish for both weekday meals and entertaining—especially for beginners—because you prepare it the night before, refrigerate the cute little packets, and bake for only 15 to 20 minutes. Presto! You have a gorgeous, flavorful dish that's worthy of any occasion and that turns out perfect every time. You can use parchment paper instead of aluminum foil (see Cooking in Parchment below) for an even prettier presentation, like they do in restaurants. Talk to the fish seller and use fish fillets that are fresh.

Q
Makes 4 servings
Preparation time: 10 minutes
Baking time: 15 to 20 minutes

¼ cup olive oil
4 (6-ounce) sea bass fillets (or cod, halibut, red snapper, or tilapia)
½ teaspoon salt, or to taste
¼ teaspoon freshly ground black pepper, or to taste
2 medium plum tomatoes, chopped
¼ cup chopped pitted olives
¼ cup drained capers
4 teaspoons chopped fresh rosemary or thyme leaves
1 small shallot, chopped

Per serving:
325 calories;
36g protein;
18g total fat;
1g fiber;
3g carbohydrates;
54mg cholesterol;
513mg sodium

1 Place a rack in the middle of the oven. Preheat the oven to 450°F.

2 Cut four 12-inch squares of aluminum foil and lay them on the countertop. Drizzle a little of the oil on each square of foil to prevent the fish from sticking and then lay a fillet on each square. Drizzle each fillet with the remaining oil and season with the salt and pepper.

3 In a small bowl, toss together the tomatoes, olives, capers, rosemary, and shallot and divide evenly among each fillet. (If there is any brine from the jar of capers or olives, drizzle a tablespoon over each fillet.) Fold the foil up to make tightly sealed packets and place seam side up on a rimmed baking sheet. You can refrigerate overnight or proceed to Step 4.

4 Bake for 15 to 20 minutes. Serve immediately; place each packet on a dinner plate, open the foil (be careful of the steam), and roll the foil back to reveal the fish.

Cooking in Parchment

For a special occasion, replace the foil with parchment paper and fold it like you are wrapping a sandwich in waxed paper, but twist the ends together to prevent leaking. Or, if this is too cumbersome, buy PaperChef Culinary Parchment Cooking Bags (less than $5 for 10 bags) and simply slide the food into the bag and fold the open end shut. Bake as directed above.

Tuna-Noodle Casserole

You don't have to give up this favorite family casserole. This is a basic version, but you can jazz it up with water chestnuts, chopped pimiento, a topping of crushed potato chips, or a sprinkle of Parmesan cheese for added flavor. I like using penne or spiral pasta because it holds its shape so well after cooking, but you can use the traditional elbow macaroni, if you like.

1 (6-ounce) can low-sodium tuna in water, drained
1 (18-ounce) can Progresso creamy mushroom soup
½ cup green peas
1 tablespoon dried minced onion
¼ teaspoon celery salt

¼ teaspoon dried dill weed or 1 teaspoon chopped fresh (optional)
⅛ teaspoon freshly ground white pepper
4 cups cooked gluten-free penne pasta or elbow macaroni
Pinch of paprika

1 Preheat the oven to 350°F. Grease a 9-inch square glass baking dish.

2 In a large bowl, thoroughly combine the tuna, soup, peas, onion, celery salt, dill (if using), and pepper. Gently stir in the cooked pasta just until blended; the mixture may be soupy. Spread evenly in the prepared baking dish.

3 Bake until hot and bubbly around the edges, 15 to 20 minutes. Serve hot, garnished with the paprika.

Q
Makes 4 servings
Preparation time: 10 minutes
Baking time: 15 to 20 minutes

Per serving: 345 calories; 19g protein; 8g total fat; 3g fiber; 48g carbohydrates; 17mg cholesterol; 579mg sodium

Veggie Pizza

Pizza is one of the top foods people ask me about when they go gluten-free. I've been refining this pizza crust process for years, and now the result is so good that it has received national acclaim. You can hold it in your hand and it won't crumble! Gluten-free pizza dough is very soft and sticky—without the elasticity of wheat flour dough—so it is patted into the pan rather than rolled or stretched. The dough adheres to the pan better when it is greased with shortening rather than cooking spray. You can use store-bought pizza sauce, but try mine—it is thicker so it won't make the crust soggy and you can make it up to 1 week ahead. I used bell peppers, tomatoes, onion, and olives to top this veggie pizza, but you can use any toppings you like, such as other vegetables or cooked meats.

V

Makes 1 (12-inch) pizza (6 slices)
Pizza sauce preparation time: 15 minutes
Crust and topping preparation time: 15 minutes
Baking time: 30 to 35 minutes

Per slice:
260 calories;
10g protein;
10g total fat;
4g fiber;
35g carbohydrates;
27mg cholesterol;
730mg sodium

Pizza Sauce
1 (8-ounce) can tomato sauce
1½ teaspoons dried Italian seasoning
½ teaspoon fennel seeds (optional)
¼ teaspoon garlic powder or 1 garlic clove, minced
1 teaspoon sugar
¼ teaspoon salt

Crust
1 tablespoon active dry yeast
1 teaspoon sugar
¾ cup warm (110°F) milk of choice
⅔ cup brown rice flour, plus more for sprinkling
¼ cup potato starch
¼ cup tapioca flour
1 teaspoon xanthan gum
1 teaspoon dried Italian seasoning
½ teaspoon salt
2 teaspoons olive oil
2 teaspoons cider vinegar

Toppings
1 tablespoon olive oil (for cooking vegetables), plus more for brushing the crust (optional)
2 cups vegetables (see sidebar below)

Cheese
1½ cups (6 ounces) shredded mozzarella cheese or cheese alternative

---

Vegetables to Use Uncooked
Artichoke hearts (marinated), thinly sliced
Olives, sliced or halved
Fresh plum tomatoes, thinly sliced or diced
Fresh cherry or grape tomatoes, halved
Sun-dried tomatoes, chopped

Vegetables to Precook
Asparagus, chopped
Bell peppers (green, red, yellow), thinly sliced
Broccoli, thinly sliced
Mushrooms, thinly sliced
Red or white onion, thinly sliced
Zucchini, thinly sliced

(continued)

1 Make the pizza sauce: In a small heavy saucepan, combine all of the sauce ingredients and simmer, uncovered and stirring occasionally, for 15 minutes. Set aside.

2 Make the crust: Arrange oven racks in the bottom and middle positions of the oven. Preheat the oven to 400°F. Grease (use shortening or butter, not oil or cooking spray) a 12-inch nonstick pizza pan (gray, not black). Dissolve the yeast and sugar in the warm milk for 5 minutes.

3 In a food processor, blend all of the crust ingredients, including the yeast mixture, until the dough forms a ball. The dough will be very, very soft. (Or, blend in a medium bowl, using an electric mixer on low speed, until well blended.) Put the dough in the center of the pizza pan. Liberally sprinkle rice flour onto the dough; then press the dough into the pan with your hands, continuing to dust the dough with flour to prevent it from sticking to your hands. At first, it will seem as though there is not enough dough to cover the pan, but don't worry—it is just the right amount. Make the edges thicker to contain the toppings, taking care to make the dough as smooth as possible. The smoother you can shape the dough, especially around the edges, the prettier the crust will be. Bake the pizza crust for 10 minutes on the bottom rack.

4 While the crust bakes, make the toppings: Heat the oil in a large skillet over medium heat. Add the vegetables and cook, stirring frequently, until slightly softened, 3 to 5 minutes.

5 Remove the pizza crust from the oven and brush the top with the pizza sauce. Sprinkle with the cheese and arrange the vegetables on top. Return the pizza to the oven and bake on the middle rack until nicely browned, 15 to 20 minutes. Remove the pizza from the oven and cool on a wire rack for 5 minutes. You may brush the crust edges with a little olive oil, if you like. Cut it into 6 slices and serve warm.

How to Shape Pizza Crust Dough

See a step-by-step guide to making gluten-free pizza at www.glutenfree101.com. Click on Videos, then on Pizza 101.

Make-Ahead Pizza Dough

Wouldn't it be nice to have a pizzeria in your own kitchen? Well, that may be asking a bit much. But you can have pizza often and with little effort, with a little advance preparation. Make the pizza dough ahead of time and freeze it, tightly covered, for up to 1 month. Thaw the dough overnight, tightly covered, in the refrigerator before shaping the dough on the pizza pan following Step 3. Or, make the dough on weekends, refrigerate, tightly covered, and bake it up to 3 days later. The only change required for make-ahead dough is to use cold rather than warm milk so that the yeast won't activate until the pizza goes into the oven. While the chilled dough is easier to shape, it may take longer to rise because it is cold, so let the shaped crust sit on the countertop for 10 minutes to warm up a bit before baking.

Bake-Ahead Pizza Crust

Remember when we could buy a pizza crust at the grocery store—the ones that are already baked and just need toppings and a warm-up in the oven? Well, you can make your own. Prepare the pizza dough and shape it following Step 3. Then, bake on the bottom rack of a preheated oven for 10 minutes, but then—instead of adding the toppings—shift the pizza pan to the middle rack and bake just until the crust is a light golden brown and firm to the touch, 10 to 15 minutes. (The goal is to bake it just long enough to cook the dough but not brown it so much that it burns during the final baking.) Remove the pizza crust from the oven and cool it completely on a wire rack. Then wrap it tightly in aluminum foil and freeze for up to 1 month.

   When you're ready to bake the pizza, preheat the oven, remove the foil from the crust, and place it on a lightly greased 12-inch pizza pan. Let the crust thaw for about 10 minutes while you prepare the toppings. Add the toppings and bake the pizza on the middle rack just until the cheese is melted and lightly browned, 15 to 20 minutes (depending on toppings). Serve immediately.

❰ Gluten-free pizza dough is very soft and sticky—without the elasticity of wheat flour dough—so it is patted into the pan rather than rolled or stretched. Fill a flour shaker with brown rice flour and sprinkle it on the dough to prevent it from sticking to your hands.

Hash Brown Casserole

This is the home-style casserole that is famous at potlucks, family reunions, and Sunday dinners, but it is also perfect for vegetarians. If you want to enhance this homey dish while keeping it vegetarian, you can add green peas, edamame, or mushrooms. Non-vegetarians can add tuna or chopped cooked chicken or ham.

V

Makes 4 servings
Preparation time: 10 minutes
Baking time: 1 hour

Per serving:
345 calories;
18g protein;
8g total fat;
3g fiber;
48g carbohydrates;
23mg cholesterol;
768mg sodium

- 3 cups frozen hash browns (about one-quarter of a 32-ounce bag)
- 1 cup shredded low-fat cheddar cheese or cheese alternative
- 1 cup sour cream or sour cream alternative
- ½ cup milk of choice
- ¼ cup grated Parmesan cheese or soy Parmesan
- 1 teaspoon onion powder
- 1 garlic clove, minced
- ½ teaspoon salt
- ¼ teaspoon freshly ground black pepper
- 1 tablespoon canola oil
- ½ small onion, finely chopped
- ½ cup gluten-free bread crumbs (see Gluten-Free Bread Crumbs, page 104)

1 Generously grease an 8-inch square baking dish. Preheat the oven to 350°F. Place the hash browns in a large bowl.

2 In a small bowl, toss together the cheese, sour cream, milk, 3 tablespoons of the Parmesan, the onion powder, garlic, salt, and pepper until completely blended.

3 In a small skillet, heat the oil over medium heat. Cook the onion until tender, about 5 minutes. Stir into the cheese–sour cream mixture until well blended. Then stir into the hash browns until thoroughly blended. Spread evenly in the prepared baking dish. Sprinkle with the remaining 1 tablespoon Parmesan, and then with the bread crumbs. Lay a sheet of aluminum foil on top.

4 Bake for 30 minutes. Remove the foil and bake until the casserole is bubbly around the edges and the bread crumbs are browned, about 30 minutes longer. Serve hot.

Macaroni & Cheese

Mac and cheese is such a beloved, satisfying comfort food, for young and old alike. Many of us grew up making it from a box, and we take that little box for granted until we can't have it (because both the pasta and the flavor packet include gluten). But trust me—this homemade version is truly flavorful. And worthy. Use sharp cheddar for fuller flavor, although children may prefer a milder cheddar.

8 ounces gluten-free elbow macaroni	1¾ cups milk of choice
2 tablespoons cornstarch or 1 tablespoon sweet rice flour	1 teaspoon gluten-free Worcestershire sauce
½ teaspoon dry mustard	2 cups grated low-fat sharp cheddar cheese or cheese alternative
¼ teaspoon freshly ground white pepper	Pinch of paprika
⅛ teaspoon cayenne pepper	
½ teaspoon beau monde seasoning	

1 Cook the pasta according to the package directions. Drain and keep warm.

2 In a large pan, whisk together the cornstarch, dry mustard, pepper, cayenne, and beau monde seasoning. Stir this mixture into ½ cup of the milk. Add this mixture, the remaining 1¼ cups milk, and the Worcestershire sauce to the pan. Place the pan over medium heat and cook, whisking, until the mixture thickens. Add the cheese and cook, stirring, until melted, then toss with the cooked pasta. Serve immediately with a sprinkle of paprika.

V

Makes 4 servings
Preparation time: 15 minutes

Per serving: 370 calories; 25g protein; 6g total fat; 1g fiber; 53g carbohydrates; 16mg cholesterol; 587mg sodium

Breads 〉

"Do I have to give up bread? What about toast for breakfast and sandwiches for lunch and rolls with dinner?" This is what I hear from newly diagnosed people who have just learned that they must avoid gluten. The good news is that you can enjoy bread with the easy recipes in this chapter. We yearn for yeast bread, so there are many varieties here, from Basic Sandwich Bread to Hearty Whole-Grain Bread. French Bread is even simpler and faster and—with my innovative cold-oven start—you can have bread in about 40 minutes. You will find recipes for yeast buns, rolls, and flatbreads that are simple to make and sure to delight your family and friends. If you use a bread machine, there are instructions for that too. Quick breads such as corn bread, muffins, scones, and popovers round out the selection. Everything you need to satisfy that yen for bread is here. But first, be sure to read about baking bread in the Gluten-Free Kitchen chapter (page 30), and then get busy in the kitchen and start baking.

Q	**V**
Quick	Vegetarian

Basic Muffins

Muffins are one of the simplest, most fail-proof of gluten-free breads, so I suggest that beginning bakers make them first to gain confidence. Plus, muffins are small, so they bake more quickly than a large loaf of bread and you have gratification in much less time. Use this recipe when you want a plain and simple muffin and follow the variations on next page to modify it to your tastes. With a good basic muffin recipe to build upon, many variations are possible.

2⅓ cups Gluten-Free Flour Blend (page 27)
¾ cup sugar, plus more for sprinkling
2 teaspoons baking powder
1½ teaspoons xanthan gum
¾ teaspoon salt

¼ teaspoon baking soda
1 cup milk of choice
⅓ cup canola oil
2 large eggs, at room temperature
1 teaspoon pure vanilla extract

V
Makes 12 muffins
Preparation time: 10 minutes
Baking time: 20 to 25 minutes

Per muffin:
210 calories;
3g protein;
7g total fat;
1g fiber;
36g carbohydrates;
32mg cholesterol;
260mg sodium

1 Place a rack in the lower third of the oven. Preheat the oven to 375°F. Generously grease a standard 12-cup nonstick muffin pan (gray, not black) or use paper liners.

2 In a large bowl, whisk together the flour blend, sugar, baking powder, xanthan gum, salt, and baking soda until well blended. With an electric mixer on low speed, beat in the milk, oil, eggs, and vanilla until thoroughly blended. Increase the speed to medium-low and beat until the batter is slightly thickened, about 30 seconds. Divide the batter evenly among the muffin cups and sprinkle the tops with a little sugar. (A 1½-inch spring-action metal ice cream scoop helps ensure uniformly sized muffins.)

3 Bake until the muffin tops are lightly browned, 20 to 25 minutes. Cool the muffins in the pan on a wire rack for 10 minutes, then remove the muffins from the pan and cool on the wire rack for another 10 minutes. Serve slightly warm.

Blueberry-Lemon Muffins

Prepare the batter as directed. Gently stir 1 cup fresh blueberries and 1 tablespoon grated lemon peel into the batter before pouring into the cups. Bake as directed.

Per muffin: 220 calories; 3g protein; 7g total fat; 2g fiber; 38g carbohydrates; 32mg cholesterol; 260mg sodium

Cranberry-Orange Muffins

Gently stir 1 cup sweetened dried cranberries and 1 tablespoon grated orange zest into the batter before pouring into the cups. Bake as directed.

Per muffin: 215 calories; 3g protein; 7g total fat; 2g fiber; 36g carbohydrates; 32mg cholesterol; 260mg sodium

Lemon–Poppy Seed Muffins

Add 1 tablespoon poppy seeds and 1 tablespoon grated lemon zest to the batter in Step 2. Bake as directed.

Per muffin: 215 calories; 3g protein; 8g total fat; 1g fiber; 36g carbohydrates; 32mg cholesterol; 261mg sodium

Raspberry Muffins

Add ½ teaspoon ground cinnamon to the dry ingredients, and gently stir 1 cup fresh raspberries into the batter before pouring into the cups. Bake as directed.

Per muffin: 220 calories; 3g protein; 7g total fat; 2g fiber; 37g carbohydrates; 32mg cholesterol; 260mg sodium

❱ Portioning soft, sticky, gluten-free muffin batter into liners is easy with a spring-action metal ice cream scoop. Equal amounts of batter in each liner ensure equal-size muffins that bake uniformly and evenly.

Cranberry-Orange Muffins

Bran-Spice Muffins

These flavorful muffins make a hearty breakfast choice and also travel very well. Freeze single muffins in resealable food storage bags and take one to work or when traveling on a plane or in the car. By the time you're ready to eat it, it will be thawed.

V

Makes 12 muffins

Preparation time: 15 minutes

Baking time: 20 to 25 minutes

- 2 cups Gluten-Free Flour Blend (page 27)
- ¾ cup packed brown sugar
- ½ cup oat bran* or rice bran
- 2 teaspoons baking powder
- 1½ teaspoons ground cinnamon
- 1½ teaspoons xanthan gum
- ¾ teaspoon salt
- ½ teaspoon ground nutmeg
- ¼ teaspoon ground cloves
- ¼ teaspoon ground allspice
- ¼ teaspoon baking soda
- 1 cup milk of choice
- ⅓ cup canola oil
- 2 large eggs, at room temperature
- 1 tablespoon molasses
- 1 teaspoon pure vanilla extract
- ½ cup raisins

Per muffin:
240 calories;
4g protein;
8g total fat;
2g fiber;
43g carbohydrates;
37mg cholesterol;
675mg sodium

1 Place a rack in the lower third of the oven. Preheat the oven to 375°F. Generously grease a standard 12-cup nonstick muffin pan (gray, not black) or use paper liners.

2 In a large bowl, whisk together the flour blend, sugar, bran, baking powder, cinnamon, xanthan gum, salt, nutmeg, cloves, allspice, and baking soda until well blended. With an electric mixer on low speed, beat in the milk, oil, eggs, molasses, and vanilla until thoroughly blended. Increase the speed to medium-low and beat until the batter is slightly thickened, about 30 seconds. Stir in the raisins. Divide the batter evenly among the muffin cups. (A 1½-inch spring-action metal ice cream scoop helps ensure uniformly sized muffins.)

3 Bake until the muffin tops are lightly browned, 20 to 25 minutes. Cool the muffins in the pan on a wire rack for 10 minutes, then remove the muffins from the pan and cool on the wire rack for another 10 minutes. Serve slightly warm.

❮ *Check with your physician before eating gluten-free oats.

Biscuits

Biscuits are perfect for breakfast or with a hearty soup or stew for lunch or dinner. Serve them warm with butter and honey, or with your favorite jam or jelly. I prefer using parchment paper rather than greasing the baking sheet (see Rolling Biscuits on Parchment Paper below) because this biscuit dough is quite soft and the parchment paper allows me to easily transfer the biscuits to the baking sheet.

½ cup cornstarch or potato starch, plus more for dusting
1 cup Gluten-Free Flour Blend (page 27)
1 tablespoon sugar
2 teaspoons baking powder
¼ teaspoon baking soda
1 teaspoon xanthan gum
1 teaspoon guar gum
½ teaspoon salt
¼ cup vegetable shortening
½ cup milk of choice
1 large egg white

V
Makes 10 biscuits
Preparation time: 10 minutes
Baking time: 12 to 15 minutes

1 Place a rack in the lower third of the oven. Preheat the oven to 350°F. Grease a 9x13-inch rimmed baking sheet (not nonstick) or line with parchment paper. Dust the surface lightly with cornstarch.

2 In a food processor, pulse the flour blend, cornstarch, sugar, baking powder, baking soda, xanthan gum, guar gum, and salt to mix thoroughly. Add the shortening, milk, and egg white. Process until the dough forms a ball, scraping down the bowl with a spatula as needed. The dough will be very soft and sticky, but dusting with cornstarch will make it easier to handle.

3 Place the dough on the prepared baking sheet and lightly dust the dough with cornstarch to prevent your hands from sticking. Gently pat the dough to a ¾-inch-thick circle. Cut the dough into ten 2-inch circles with a floured metal biscuit cutter (metal cuts better than plastic). Push the biscuit cutter straight down into the dough rather than twisting it as you cut. Shape the remaining dough into a ¾-inch-thick round and cut again. If the dough is sticky, lightly dust with more cornstarch. Arrange the biscuits on the baking sheet.

4 Bake until the biscuits are lightly browned, 12 to 15 minutes. Serve immediately.

Shortcakes

Increase the amount of sugar to ¼ cup and prepare as directed. Bake as directed, and serve with strawberries and whipped cream.

Per biscuit:
130 calories;
1g protein;
5g total fat;
1g fiber;
20g carbohydrates;
1mg cholesterol;
248mg sodium

Shortcakes
Per shortcake:
145 calories;
1g protein;
5g total fat;
1g fiber;
25g carbohydrates;
1mg cholesterol;
248mg sodium

Rolling Biscuits on Parchment Paper

Gluten-free biscuit dough is soft and sticky, so it requires special handling. Parchment paper is ideal for biscuit dough because it is coated with silicone to prevent sticking. Try rolling the biscuits directly on the parchment paper on the countertop and cut them out with a biscuit cutter, then transfer the parchment (with the biscuits on it) directly to the baking sheet. Re-roll scraps on another sheet of parchment paper and transfer to the baking sheet with a thin spatula. Be sure to use metal rather than plastic biscuit cutters for a cleaner cut, which enables better rising.

Scones

Although they sound like a delicate pastry served by the English at afternoon tea, scones are actually quite rustic-looking and surprisingly easy to make. Once the dough is mixed, work quickly to shape it and get it into the oven so that the leaveners can do their job well.

V

Makes 8 scones
Preparation time: 10 minutes
Baking time: 20 to 25 minutes

Per scone:
215 calories;
3g protein;
5g total fat;
2g fiber;
42g carbohydrates;
34mg cholesterol;
306mg sodium

⅓ cup butter or buttery spread, at room temperature
½ cup milk of choice, at room temperature, plus more for brushing the dough
1 large egg, at room temperature
2 tablespoons sugar, plus more for sprinkling

1¾ cups Gluten-Free Flour Blend (page 27)
½ cup tapioca flour
2 teaspoons xanthan gum
1½ teaspoons cream of tartar
¾ teaspoon baking soda
½ teaspoon salt
½ cup dried currants

1 Place a rack in the lower third of the oven. Preheat the oven to 375°F. Grease a 9x13-inch rimmed baking sheet (not nonstick) or line with parchment paper.

2 In a food processor, blend the butter, milk, and egg together until well mixed. Add the sugar, flour blend, tapioca flour, xanthan gum, cream of tartar, baking soda, and salt. Process just until mixed. Toss in the currants and pulse twice to incorporate. The dough will be soft. Transfer the dough to the baking sheet and pat with a wet spatula into a smooth 8-inch circle, ¾ inch thick. Make the dough thickness uniform across the circle, rather than tapering the outer edges, so the scones brown evenly. Brush the top with milk and sprinkle with sugar.

3 Bake until the top is browned and crisp, 15 to 20 minutes. Remove the pan from the oven, but leave the oven on. With a serrated knife, cut the dough into 8 wedges, and pull the wedges slightly away from the center so the innermost edges are exposed to the heat and can crisp up a little. Return the pan to the oven and bake for another 5 minutes. Cool the scones on the pan for 10 minutes, then serve slightly warm.

❨ For gluten-free scones that are crisp on all sides, pull the partially baked wedges slightly away from the center so the innermost edges are exposed to the heat and can crisp up a little during the final 5 minutes of baking.

Basic Quick Bread

Quick breads are so-named because their leavening causes them to rise right after the batter is exposed to moisture and heat—without the prolonged waiting for leavening such as yeast to do its job. This simple bread can serve as the basis for many flavor variations (see below for some ideas).

V

Makes 12 slices

Preparation time: 10 minutes

Baking time: 35 to 40 minutes for small loaves; 50 to 55 minutes for large loaf

2 large eggs, at room temperature
⅓ cup canola oil
1 teaspoon pure vanilla extract
1 cup milk of choice, at room temperature
1 teaspoon grated lemon zest

2⅓ cups Gluten-Free Flour Blend (page 27)
¾ cup sugar
2 teaspoons baking powder
1½ teaspoons xanthan gum
1 teaspoon salt
¼ teaspoon baking soda

1 Place a rack in the lower third of the oven. Preheat the oven to 375°F. Generously grease three 4x6-inch or one 5x9-inch nonstick loaf pan(s) (gray, not black).

2 In a large bowl, beat the eggs, oil, vanilla, milk, and lemon zest with an electric mixer on low speed until thoroughly blended. In a medium bowl, whisk together the flour blend, sugar, baking powder, xanthan gum, salt, and baking soda until well blended. Gradually beat the flour mixture into the egg mixture just until blended. Increase the speed to medium-low and beat until the batter slightly thickens, about 30 seconds. Spread the batter evenly in the prepared pan(s).

3 Bake the bread until nicely browned and a toothpick inserted into the center comes out clean, 35 to 40 minutes for the small loaves; 50 to 55 minutes for the large loaf. Cool the bread in the pan on a wire rack for 10 minutes, then remove the bread and cool on the wire rack for another 10 minutes. With a serrated knife or an electric knife, cut into slices, and serve slightly warm.

Per slice:
210 calories;
3g protein;
7g total fat;
1g fiber;
36g carbohydrates;
32mg cholesterol;
260mg sodium

Blueberry-Lemon Quick Bread
Gently stir 1 cup fresh blueberries and 1 tablespoon grated lemon zest into the batter, just before spreading it into the pan. Bake as directed.

Per slice:
220 calories; 3g protein; 7g total fat; 2g fiber; 38g carbohydrates; 32mg cholesterol; 260mg sodium

Cranberry-Orange Quick Bread
Omit the lemon zest. Gently stir 1 cup sweetened dried cranberries and 1 tablespoon grated orange zest into the batter, just before spreading it into the pan. Bake as directed.

Per slice:
215 calories; 3g protein; 7g total fat; 1g fiber; 36g carbohydrates; 32mg cholesterol; 260mg sodium

Banana Quick Bread

Banana bread evokes fond memories of childhood, home, and family. So, save those extra-ripe bananas for this quintessential comfort food favorite. It freezes and travels very well. Vary it by adding chocolate chips and different kinds of nuts. Replace the raisins with dried cherries, cranberries, or currants.

2 large eggs, at room temperature
⅓ cup canola oil
1 cup milk of choice, at room temperature
1 teaspoon pure vanilla extract
2 mashed ripe medium bananas (about 1 cup)
2⅓ cups Gluten-Free Flour Blend (page 27)

¾ cup packed brown sugar
1½ teaspoons xanthan gum
2 teaspoons baking powder
1 teaspoon ground cinnamon
1 teaspoon salt
¼ teaspoon baking soda
½ cup chopped walnuts
½ cup raisins

V

Makes 12 slices
Preparation time: 10 minutes
Baking time: 35 to 40 minutes for small loaves; 50 to 60 minutes for large loaf

Per serving: 300 calories; 5g protein; 10g total fat; 3g fiber; 51g carbohydrates; 32mg cholesterol; 311mg sodium

1 Place a rack in the lower third of the oven. Preheat the oven to 375°F. Generously grease three 4x6-inch or one 5x9-inch nonstick loaf pan(s) (gray, not black).

2 In a large bowl, beat the eggs, oil, milk, vanilla, and bananas with an electric mixer on low speed until thoroughly blended. In a medium bowl, whisk together the flour blend, sugar, xanthan gum, baking powder, cinnamon, salt, and baking soda until well blended. With the mixer on low speed, gradually beat the flour mixture into the egg mixture just until blended. Increase the speed to medium-low and beat until the batter slightly thickens, about 30 seconds. Stir in the nuts and raisins. Spread the batter evenly in the prepared pan(s).

3 Bake until the top is nicely browned and a toothpick inserted into the center comes out clean, 35 to 40 minutes for the small loaves; 50 to 60 minutes for the large loaf. Cool the bread in the pan on a wire rack for 10 minutes, then remove the bread and cool on the wire rack for another 10 minutes. With a serrated knife or an electric knife, cut into slices, and serve slightly warm.

Corn Bread

Corn bread is an all-American quick bread that is so easy to prepare. It bakes quickly and so it is a great choice to accompany dinner. Put it in the oven first and prepare the rest of the meal while it bakes. For a lighter texture, sift the dry ingredients together after measuring. I was raised in the Midwest, so my corn bread is more cake-like and sweeter than the Southern version. We eat it with the meal as a savory side, then drizzle another piece with butter and honey for dessert.

V

Makes 12 slices

Preparation time: 10 minutes

Baking time: 25 to 30 minutes

Per serving: 175 calories; 3g protein; 7g total fat; 2g fiber; 26g carbohydrates; 31mg cholesterol; 282mg sodium

1¼ cups cornmeal
1 cup Gluten-Free Flour Blend
    (page 27)
⅓ cup sugar
2 teaspoons baking powder

1 teaspoon xanthan gum
1 teaspoon salt
⅛ teaspoon baking soda
2 large eggs, at room temperature
1 cup water, at room temperature
⅓ cup canola oil

1 Place a rack in the lower third of the oven. Preheat the oven to 350°F. Generously grease a 4x8-inch or 8-inch round or square nonstick baking pan (gray, not black).

2 In a large bowl, whisk together the cornmeal, flour blend, sugar, baking powder, xanthan gum, salt, and baking soda until well blended. With an electric mixer on low speed, beat in the eggs, water, and oil until just blended. Increase the speed to medium-low and beat until the batter is slightly thickened, about 30 seconds. The batter will be the consistency of thick cake batter. Spread the batter evenly in the pan.

3 Bake until the top is firm and a toothpick inserted into the center comes out clean, 25 to 30 minutes. Cool the corn bread in the pan on a wire rack for 10 minutes. Serve warm.

Pumpkin Quick Bread

The plentiful spices in this quick bread make your kitchen smell absolutely heavenly and also make for a very flavorful bread. It is especially delightful on a crisp autumn day, when these spices feel just perfect for the season. Brew a cup of tea and enjoy a slice.

2 large eggs, at room temperature	¾ cup sugar
1 cup milk of choice, at room temperature	2 teaspoons baking powder
½ cup canned pumpkin puree (not pumpkin pie filling)	1½ teaspoons pumpkin pie spice
⅓ cup canola oil	1½ teaspoons xanthan gum
1 teaspoon pure vanilla extract	1 teaspoon salt
2⅓ cups Gluten-Free Flour Blend (page 27)	¼ teaspoon baking soda
	¼ teaspoon ground allspice
	¼ teaspoon ground ginger
	½ cup golden raisins

1 Place a rack in the lower third of the oven. Preheat the oven to 375°F. Generously grease three 4x6-inch or one 5x9-inch nonstick loaf pan(s) (gray, not black).

2 In a large bowl, beat the eggs, milk, pumpkin, oil, and vanilla with an electric mixer on low speed until thoroughly blended. In a medium bowl, whisk together the flour blend, sugar, baking powder, pumpkin pie spice, xanthan gum, salt, baking soda, allspice, and ginger until well blended. With the mixer on low speed, gradually beat the flour mixture into the egg mixture just until blended. Increase the speed to medium-low and beat until the batter slightly thickens, about 30 seconds. Stir in the raisins. Spread the batter evenly in the pan(s).

3 Bake until the top is nicely browned and a toothpick inserted into the center comes out clean, 35 to 40 minutes for the small loaves; 50 to 60 minutes for the large loaf. Cool the bread in the pan on a wire rack for 10 minutes, then remove the bread and cool on the wire rack for another 10 minutes. With a serrated knife or an electric knife, cut into slices, and serve slightly warm.

V

Makes 12 slices
Preparation time: 10 minutes
Baking time: 35 to 40 minutes for small loaves; 50 to 60 minutes for large loaf

Per serving:
235 calories;
3g protein;
7g total fat;
2g fiber;
42g carbohydrates;
32mg cholesterol;
261mg sodium

Zucchini Quick Bread

Though zucchini is a vegetable that divides people into "love it" or "hate it" camps, most of us like it in zucchini bread, so bake a batch and enjoy this classic.

V

Makes 12 slices

Preparation time: 15 minutes

Baking time: 45 to 55 minutes for small loaves; 60 to 70 minutes for large loaf

Per slice: 270 calories; 3g protein; 13g total fat; 2g fiber; 38g carbohydrates; 31mg cholesterol; 207mg sodium

2 cups Gluten-Free Flour Blend (page 27)
¾ cup sugar
2 teaspoons baking powder
1 teaspoon ground cinnamon
1½ teaspoons xanthan gum
¾ teaspoon salt
¼ teaspoon baking soda

2 large eggs, at room temperature
½ cup canola oil
1 teaspoon pure vanilla extract
2 cups grated zucchini (about 1 medium or 2 small)
½ cup raisins
½ cup chopped pecans

1 Place a rack in the lower third of the oven. Preheat the oven to 350°F. Generously grease three 4x6-inch or one 5x9-inch nonstick loaf pan(s) (gray, not black).

2 In a medium bowl, whisk together the flour blend, sugar, baking powder, cinnamon, xanthan gum, salt, and baking soda until well blended. In a large bowl, beat the eggs with an electric mixer on medium speed until light yellow and frothy, about 30 seconds. Add the oil and vanilla and beat on low speed until well blended. With the mixer on low speed, beat the flour mixture gradually into the egg mixture until the batter is smooth and slightly thickened. The batter will be very stiff, but then beat in the grated zucchini and it will become softer. With a spatula, stir in the raisins and nuts. Spread the batter evenly in the pan(s).

3 Bake until the top is nicely browned and a toothpick inserted into the center comes out clean, 45 to 55 minutes for the small loaves; 60 to 70 minutes for the large loaf. Cool the bread in the pan for 10 minutes on a wire rack. Remove the bread from the pan(s) and cool completely on the wire rack. Slice with a serrated knife or an electric knife, and serve slightly warm.

Cheese Bread Rounds

These tapioca-based breads are from Brazil, where they are called *pão de quiejo.* They're quick, easy to make, and very, very tasty. My dear sister-in-law makes them for me when she hosts holiday dinners so that I will have bread to eat along with everyone else. Use them as snacks or dinner rolls—or slice them in half, toast them, and use them for sandwiches (see below). They'll be crisp on the outside and pleasingly sticky on the inside, and are a nice choice for people who avoid yeast.

> 1   cup milk of choice
> ¼   cup light olive oil, plus more for oiling
>   your hands (optional)
> 1½ cups tapioca flour
> 1   large egg
> ½   cup grated Parmesan cheese or soy
>   Parmesan
> ¼   teaspoon salt

1 Preheat the oven to 375°F. Line a 9x13-inch rimmed baking sheet (not nonstick) with parchment paper.

2 In a medium heavy saucepan, bring the milk and oil to a rolling boil. Remove the pan from the heat and immediately stir in the tapioca flour with a wooden spoon until thoroughly blended. Let the tapioca mixture cool in the saucepan for 5 minutes.

3 Place the tapioca mixture in a food processor and add the egg, Parmesan, and salt. Process until the dough is smooth and forms a ball.

4 With a 1½- or 2-inch spring-action metal ice cream scoop, drop 12 balls of dough about 2 inches apart onto the baking sheet. For smoother rounds, roll between oiled hands before placing on the baking sheet.

5 Bake until the rounds are lightly browned and crisp, 30 to 35 minutes. They are best served warm or at room temperature, but not cold.

Cheese Bread Sandwich Buns

Prepare the dough as directed. Shape the dough into 8 balls, place on the baking sheet, and flatten slightly with a wet spatula. Bake as directed. Turn the buns over midway through baking. When slightly cool, slice in half (crosswise). These are best when served slightly warm.

V
Makes 12 rounds
Preparation time: 15 minutes
Baking time: 30 to 35 minutes

Per round:
120 calories;
3g protein;
6g total fat;
0g fiber; 14g carbohydrates;
19mg cholesterol;
121mg sodium

Cheese Bread Sandwich Buns
Per bun:
180 calories;
4g protein;
9g total fat;
0g fiber;
21g carbohydrates;
29mg cholesterol;
182mg sodium

Irish Soda Bread

I get many requests for this bread, particularly from those who want yeast-free bread. My version departs from traditional Irish soda bread because it is a bit sweeter and contains caraway, currants, and orange zest—but these additions make it very flavorful. The rectangular loaf will work better for sandwiches.

V

Makes 1 (8-inch) round loaf or 1 (4x8-inch) rectangular loaf (10 slices)
Preparation time: 10 minutes
Baking time: 40 to 45 minutes

Per slice:
220 calories;
3g protein;
9g total fat;
2g fiber;
36g carbohydrates;
38mg cholesterol;
267mg sodium

2 cups Gluten-Free Flour Blend (page 27)	⅓ cup canola oil
⅓ cup sugar	2 teaspoons grated orange zest (optional)
1 teaspoon xanthan gum	½ cup buttermilk or plain kefir (see Buttermilk Substitutes below), at room temperature
1½ teaspoons baking powder	
½ teaspoon baking soda	
½ teaspoon salt	½ cup dried currants
2 large eggs, at room temperature (reserve 1 tablespoon egg for brushing the crust)	1 teaspoon caraway seeds

1 Place a rack in the lower third of the oven. Preheat the oven to 350°F. Generously grease an 8-inch round or 4x8-inch loaf or 8-inch nonstick springform pan with removable sides (gray, not black).

2 In a large bowl, whisk together the flour blend, sugar, xanthan gum, baking powder, baking soda, and salt until well blended. With an electric mixer on low speed, beat in the eggs, oil, orange zest (if using), and buttermilk until just blended, then beat on medium speed until the batter is very smooth, about 30 seconds. Stir in the currants and caraway seeds. Spread the dough in the pan with a wet spatula until the top is very smooth. Whisk the reserved 1 tablespoon of egg with 1 teaspoon of water and then brush on top of the dough for a shinier, crispier crust. Let the batter stand in the pan on the countertop for 10 minutes. With a sharp knife, make an "X" about ⅛ inch deep in the dough.

3 Bake until the bread is firm and browned and a toothpick inserted into the center comes out clean, 40 to 45 minutes. Cool the bread in the pan on a wire rack for 10 minutes, then remove the bread from the pan and cool completely on the wire rack. To serve, slice with a serrated knife or an electric knife.

Buttermilk Substitutes

Buttermilk does wonderful things for gluten-free baking but, unfortunately, it is made from cow's milk—which makes it inappropriate for dairy-sensitive people. There are two ways around this dilemma: You can make your own buttermilk by adding 1 tablespoon of vinegar or lemon juice to 1 cup of your milk of choice. Let stand for a few minutes to thicken slightly; do not stir. Or, use plain kefir (a fermented milk drink that is made from cow's milk but can also be made from coconut milk), which is similar in texture and acidity to buttermilk. Make sure to buy plain (rather than flavored) coconut kefir. It is usually quite thick, so use ¾ cup kefir and ¼ cup water to thin it down in a recipe that calls for 1 cup buttermilk. My favorite dairy-free kefir is cultured coconut milk sold under the brand name So Delicious; look for it in the refrigerated dairy section of natural foods stores. Don't worry—it won't make your baked goods taste like coconut.

Sweet Potato–Cranberry Quick Bread

This makes excellent holiday bread and is a great way to use leftover sweet potatoes. It is perfect for brunches, breakfast, or snacking. It also makes terrific bread pudding.

2 large eggs, at room temperature

1 cup milk of choice, at room temperature

½ cup cooked mashed sweet potatoes

⅓ cup canola oil

1 teaspoon pure vanilla extract

2⅓ cups Gluten-Free Flour Blend (page 27)

¾ cup sugar

2 teaspoons baking powder

1½ teaspoons xanthan gum

1½ teaspoons pumpkin pie spice

1 teaspoon salt

¼ teaspoon baking soda

½ cup sweetened dried cranberries

1 Place a rack in the lower third of the oven. Preheat the oven to 375°F. Generously grease three 4x6-inch or one 5x9-inch nonstick loaf pan(s) (gray, not black).

2 In a large bowl, beat the eggs, milk, sweet potatoes, oil, and vanilla with an electric mixer on low speed until thoroughly blended. In a medium bowl, whisk together the flour blend, sugar, baking powder, xanthan gum, pumpkin pie spice, salt, and baking soda until well blended. With the mixer on low speed, gradually beat the flour mixture into the egg mixture just until blended. Increase the speed to medium-low and beat until the batter slightly thickens, about 30 seconds. Stir in the cranberries. Spread the batter evenly in the prepared pan(s).

3 Bake until the top is nicely browned and a toothpick inserted into the center comes out clean, 35 to 40 minutes for the small loaves; 50 to 60 minutes for the large loaf. Cool the bread in the pan on a wire rack for 10 minutes, then remove the bread and cool on the wire rack for another 10 minutes. With a serrated knife or an electric knife, cut into slices, and serve slightly warm.

V

Makes 12 slices

Preparation time: 10 minutes

Baking time: 35 to 40 minutes for small loaves; 50 to 60 minutes for large loaf

Per serving: 225 calories; 3g protein; 7g total fat; 1g fiber; 38g carbohydrates; 32mg cholesterol; 313mg sodium

Basic Sandwich Bread

One easy recipe—in three different sizes—so you can choose the one that's right for you. The dough is light colored, which makes it versatile . . . use it for croutons, bread crumbs, toast, or sandwich bread. This recipe uses two gums—xanthan and guar—because their synergies produce a better bread.

Preparation time: 15 minutes
Rising time: 45 to 60 minutes
Baking time: 55 to 65 minutes

Per slice:
170 calories;
3g protein;
2g total fat;
2g fiber;
38g carbohydrates;
22mg cholesterol;
297mg sodium

Ingredients	1-Pound Loaf (4x8-inch pan) Makes 10 slices	1½-Pound Loaf (5x9-inch pan) Makes 15 slices	2-Pound Loaf (Two 4x8-inch pans) Makes 20 slices
Active dry yeast	2¼ teaspoons (1 packet)	2¼ teaspoons (1 packet)	2¼ teaspoons (1 packet)
Sugar	1 tablespoon	4½ teaspoons	2 tablespoons
Water (110°F)	1 cup	1½ cups	2 cups
Gluten-Free Flour Blend (page 27)	1½ cups	2¼ cups	3 cups
Potato starch	½ cup	½ cup	¾ cup
Nonfat dry milk powder or Better Than Milk soy powder	¼ cup	⅓ cup	½ cup
Xanthan gum	1½ teaspoons	2 teaspoons	3 teaspoons
Guar gum	1 teaspoon	1 teaspoon	1 teaspoon
Salt	¾ teaspoon	1 teaspoon	1¼ teaspoons
Large eggs, at room temperature	1	2	2
Butter/buttery spread	1 tablespoon	1½ tablespoons	2 tablespoons
Cider vinegar	½ teaspoon	½ teaspoon	1 teaspoon

Hand Method

1 Combine the yeast, 2 teaspoons of the sugar, and the warm water. Set aside to let the yeast foam for about 5 minutes. Generously grease your chosen nonstick pan(s) (gray, not black).

2 In the bowl of a heavy-duty stand mixer on low speed (using a regular beater, not the dough hook), beat the yeast mixture with all of the remaining ingredients (including the remaining sugar).

3 Blend on medium speed for 1 minute, scraping down the sides of the bowl with a spatula if necessary. Place the dough in the pan(s). Tent with oiled aluminum foil and let rise at room temperature (75°F to 85°F) until the dough is level with the top of the pan. Rising time will vary from 45 to 60 minutes, depending on altitude. (Bread rises more quickly at higher altitudes.)

4 Place a rack in the lower third of the oven. Preheat the oven to 375°F. With a sharp knife, make three diagonal slashes ⅛ inch deep on the top of the loaf so steam can escape during baking.

5 Bake until nicely browned and an instant-read thermometer registers 200°F to 205°F when inserted into the center, 55 to 65 minutes, depending on loaf size. Do not underbake. Cover loosely with aluminum foil after 20 minutes of baking to reduce overbrowning. Cool the bread in the pan on a wire rack for 10 minutes, then remove the bread from the pan and cool completely on the wire rack before slicing with a serrated knife or an electric knife.

Bread Machine Method

Follow your bread machine instructions, making sure your machine is the appropriate size for the recipe. If the recipe yield is too large, the dough will overflow the bucket or pan and cause a mess in your machine. With my machine, I whisk the dry ingredients together (including the yeast) and add to the pan. Then, I whisk the liquid ingredients together (with the water at room temperature) and pour carefully over the dry ingredients. Set controls and bake. I use the Normal setting.

Fennel Bread

To the Basic Sandwich Bread dough, add the following ingredients (being sure to use unsulfured regular—rather than blackstrap—molasses):

- 1-pound loaf: 1 tablespoon molasses and 1 tablespoon fennel seeds
- 1½-pound loaf: 1½ tablespoons molasses and 1½ tablespoons fennel seeds
- 2-pound loaf: 2 tablespoons molasses and 2 tablespoons fennel seeds

Bake as directed above.

Fennel Bread

Per slice:
180 calories;
3g protein;
2g total fat;
2g fiber;
40g carbohydrates;
22mg cholesterol;
298mg sodium

"Cracked Wheat" Bread

I learned to love this bread when my grandmother baked it for us. As an adult, I baked every weekend, and as soon as it came out of the oven, I sliced off the heel and slathered it with butter. With a cup of freshly brewed coffee, I was in heaven. Of course, real cracked wheat is off-limits on a gluten-free diet, so I devised this version using roasted cracked brown rice to get the same satisfying crunch.

V

Preparation time: 15 minutes
Rising time: 45 to 60 minutes
Baking time: 55 to 65 minutes

Per slice:
195 calories;
3g protein;
2g total fat;
2g fiber;
43g carbohydrates;
22mg cholesterol;
299mg sodium

Ingredients	1-Pound Loaf (4x8-inch pan) Makes 10 slices	1½-Pound Loaf (5x9-inch pan) Makes 15 slices	2-Pound Loaf (Two 4x8-inch pans) Makes 20 slices
Active dry yeast	2¼ teaspoons	2¼ teaspoons	2¼ teaspoons
Sugar	1 tablespoon	4½ teaspoons	2 tablespoons
Water (110°F)	1 cup	1½ cups	2 cups
Whole wehani rice or brown rice	¼ cup	⅓ cup	½ cup
Gluten-Free Flour Blend (page 27)	1½ cups	2¼ cups	3 cups
Potato starch	½ cup	½ cup	¾ cup
Nonfat dry milk powder or Better Than Milk soy powder	¼ cup	⅓ cup	½ cup
Xanthan gum	1½ teaspoons	2 teaspoons	3 teaspoons
Guar gum	1 teaspoon	1 teaspoon	1 teaspoon
Salt	¾ teaspoon	1 teaspoon	1¼ teaspoons
Large eggs	1	2	2
Butter/buttery spread	1 tablespoon	1½ tablespoons	2 tablespoons
Cider vinegar	½ teaspoon	½ teaspoon	1 teaspoon

Hand Method

1 Combine the yeast, 2 teaspoons of the sugar, and the warm water. Set aside to let the yeast foam for about 5 minutes. Generously grease your chosen nonstick pan(s) (gray, not black).

2 Pulverize the rice in a small coffee grinder until the kernels are slightly "cracked," then place in the bowl of a heavy-duty stand mixer along with the yeast mixture and all of the remaining ingredients (including the remaining sugar). With the mixer on low speed (using a regular beater, not the dough hook), beat for 1 minute, scraping down the sides with a spatula if necessary.

3 With a wet spatula, spread the dough evenly in the pan(s). Tent with oiled aluminum foil and let rise at room temperature (75°F to 85°F) until the dough is level with the top of the pan. Rising time will vary from 45 to 60 minutes, depending on altitude. (Bread rises more quickly at higher altitudes.)

4 Place a rack in the lower third of the oven. Preheat the oven to 375°F. With a sharp knife, make three diagonal slashes ⅛ inch deep on the top of the loaf so steam can escape during baking.

5 Bake until nicely browned and an instant-read thermometer registers 200°F to 205°F when inserted into the center, 55 to 65 minutes. Do not underbake. Cover loosely with aluminum foil after 20 minutes of baking to reduce overbrowning. Cool the bread in the pan on a wire rack for 10 minutes, then remove the bread from the pan, and cool completely on the wire rack before slicing with a serrated knife or an electric knife.

Bread Machine Method

Follow your bread machine instructions, making sure your machine is the appropriate size for the recipe. If the recipe is too big, the dough will overflow the bucket or pan and cause a mess in your machine. With my machine, I whisk the dry ingredients together (including the yeast) and add to the pan. Then, I whisk the liquid ingredients together (with the water at room temperature) and pour carefully over the dry ingredients. Set controls and bake. I use the Normal setting.

Popovers

The secret to successful popovers is having the ingredients at room temperature and heating the pans before baking. Popovers are a great alternative to yeast breads for sandwiches—just scoop out a little of the "bready" interior to create room for the filling. You can also make popover batter ahead of time for dinner guests; refrigerate the prepared batter, let it come to room temperature, and then bake just before dinner is served. You will have piping-hot popovers that will amaze everyone—and they are yeast-free, too!

V

Makes 6 popovers
Preparation time: 5 minutes
Baking time: 40 minutes

Per popover:
150 calories;
5g protein;
6g total fat;
1g fiber;
21g carbohydrates;
126mg cholesterol;
230mg sodium

Yorkshire Puddings
Per pudding:
190 calories;
5g protein;
10g total fat;
1g fiber; 21g carbohydrates;
126mg cholesterol;
230mg sodium

4 large eggs, at room temperature
¾ cup milk of choice, at
     room temperature
1 tablespoon canola oil
⅔ cup potato starch
¼ cup Gluten-Free Flour Blend
     (page 27)
½ teaspoon salt
¼ teaspoon xanthan gum
     Cooking spray

1 Place a rack in the lower third of the oven. Preheat the oven to 450°F.

2 In a blender, thoroughly blend all of the ingredients until very smooth.

3 Place a standard 6-cup nonstick muffin pan or 6-cup nonstick popover pan or a rimmed baking sheet with 6 custard cups arranged on it in the oven for 3 minutes. With oven mitts, remove the hot pan from the oven, place on a wire rack, and coat with cooking spray. Fill the indentations about three-quarters full of batter.

4 Bake for 20 minutes, then reduce the heat to 350°F and continue baking until the sides of the popovers are rigid, about 15 minutes longer. Do not open the oven during this time. Remove the popovers from the oven, pierce the side of each popover with a toothpick to let the steam escape, and return to the oven to bake for another 5 minutes. Serve immediately.

Yorkshire Puddings
Pour 1 teaspoon of hot beef drippings into each cup.

Fill three-quarters full with the popover batter and bake as directed.

French Bread

This is the bread I make most often for dinner guests. I love taking it out of the oven just before they arrive; the aroma of baking bread and the sight of a freshly baked loaf are an excellent prelude to a wonderful evening. Use a pan specially designed for French bread—one with two indentations that hold the bread in a French loaf shape. These pans are available at kitchen stores. The dough is too soft to hold its shape free-form on a regular baking sheet.

2 tablespoons active dry yeast
1 tablespoon sugar
1¼ cups warm (110°F) water
2 cups Gluten-Free Flour Blend
   (page 27)
1 cup potato starch
1 teaspoon xanthan gum
1 teaspoon guar gum
¼ cup nonfat dry milk powder or Better
   Than Milk soy powder

1¼ teaspoons salt
1 tablespoon butter or buttery spread, at
   room temperature
3 large egg whites, at room temperature
1 teaspoon cider vinegar
1 egg white, beaten to a foam for
   egg wash
1 tablespoon sesame seeds (optional)

V

Makes 2 loaves.
Serves 10
(2 slices)
Preparation time: 15 minutes
Rising time: 30 to 45 minutes
Baking time: 30 to 35 minutes

Per 2 slices:
125 calories;
4g protein;
2g total fat;
2g fiber;
26g carbohydrates;
3mg cholesterol;
306mg sodium

1 Dissolve the yeast and sugar in the warm water. Set aside to let the yeast foam for about 5 minutes.

2 Grease a French bread pan or line with parchment paper. If the pans are perforated, they must be lined with parchment paper or the dough will fall through the perforations.

3 In the bowl of a heavy-duty stand mixer, combine the yeast mixture and the flour blend, potato starch, xanthan gum, guar gum, dry milk powder, salt, butter, egg whites, and vinegar. Beat on low speed (using a regular beater, not the dough hook) just until blended. Increase the speed to medium-low and beat for 1 minute, scraping down the sides of the bowl with a spatula. The dough will be soft.

4 Divide the dough evenly between the two indentations in the pan. Smooth each half into a 12-inch log with a wet spatula, making the ends blunt rather than tapered for more even baking. Brush with the egg wash and let rise at room temperature (75°F to 85°F) until doubled in height.

5 Place a rack in the middle of the oven. Preheat the oven to 425°F. Just before baking, make 3 diagonal slashes (⅛ inch deep) in each loaf so steam can escape during baking. Sprinkle with the sesame seeds, if desired.

6 Bake until nicely browned and an instant-read thermometer registers 200°F to 205°F when inserted in the center of the loaf, 30 to 35 minutes. Tent with aluminum foil after 20 minutes of baking to prevent overbrowning. Remove the bread from the pan; cool completely on a wire rack before slicing with a serrated knife or an electric knife.

(continued)

French Baguettes
Per 3 slices:
85 calories;
3g protein;
1g total fat;
1g fiber;
17g
carbohydrates;
2mg
cholesterol;
204mg sodium

French Baguettes

Prepare the dough as directed for French Bread, but use a French baguette pan. It has three indentations rather than two, but because you are using the same amount of dough as French Bread, the loaves are narrower. Follow the baking directions, but bake for 25 to 30 minutes.

❰ Gluten-free bread dough is very soft and sticky. Portioning the dough into uniformly sized balls with a spring-action metal ice cream scoop makes it easier to handle. A spatula dipped in water makes it easier to shape the dough into equal-size logs on the parchment-lined baguette pan. The loaf ends are blunt rather than tapered for more even baking.

Starting Bread to Bake in a Cold Oven

It may seem unusual, especially when most of us have been taught the standard method of preheating the oven before baking anything. In reality though, the cold-oven method works quite nicely with narrow or thin loaves like French Bread (or Bagels or Breadsticks). (It does not work well with standard loaf sizes because they are too thick for the oven heat to penetrate quickly enough to bake properly.) Gluten-free bread dough is heavy and wet; as the oven preheats, it warms the wet dough and activates the yeast, causing the bread to rise quickly, but that's OK because the loaf is narrow, it doesn't have to rise as much as a 5x9-inch loaf, and the heat from the oven dries out the crust to make it crisp. It also means that a loaf of French bread takes 30 to 35 minutes compared to nearly an hour with the standard method that requires rising time outside of the oven and then baking time in the oven. The bottom line? You will have French Bread or French Baguettes much faster with the cold-oven method than the standard method.

How to Bake This French Bread in a Cold Oven

Starting bread to bake in a cold oven produces a more golden, crisper crust and a more uneven but attractive artisan-like crumb. The crust is crisper because it dries out a bit as the oven preheats. Gluten-free breads, which have moister doughs than traditional breads, often have a paler color and softer, cake-like texture if baked in preheated ovens because the bread doesn't have enough time or exposure to heat to get brown or get crisp.

Here is how to do it: Place a rack in the middle of the oven, but do not preheat the oven. Place the bread on the middle rack, then turn on the oven to 425°F and bake until the crust is nicely browned and an instant-read thermometer registers 200°F to 205°F when inserted into the center of a loaf, 30 to 35 minutes. Lay a sheet of aluminum foil over the bread after 15 minutes of baking if it starts to brown too much. This method works perfectly in my KitchenAid electric oven, but it doesn't work in all ovens—especially those with quick preheat cycles. Try it once in your oven; if it doesn't work, then use the traditional method of rising the bread outlined above.

Hearty Whole-Grain Bread

Many gluten-free cooks want to re-create the whole-grain bread they remember—but they need to do it without wheat. This recipe is for a hearty version using gluten-free whole grains to produce that nutty, wholesome flavor.

V

Preparation time: 15 minutes
Rising time: 45 to 60 minutes
Baking time: 55 to 65 minutes

Per slice:
190 calories; 4g protein; 3g total fat; 3g fiber; 43g carbohydrates; 22mg cholesterol; 188mg sodium

❱ *Kañiwa (also called baby quinoa) is related to quinoa, but has smaller kernels and a less intense flavor. Look for it at specialty stores.

Ingredients	1-Pound Loaf (4x8-inch pan) Makes 10 slices	1½-Pound Loaf (5x9-inch pan) Makes 15 slices	2-Pound Loaf (Two 4x8-inch pans) Makes 20 slices
Active dry yeast	2¼ teaspoons	2¼ teaspoons	2¼ teaspoons
Sugar	1 tablespoon	4½ teaspoons	2 tablespoons
Water (110°F)	1 cup	1½ cups	2 cups
Gluten-Free Flour Blend (page 27)	1½ cups	2¼ cups	3 cups
Potato starch	½ cup	½ cup	¾ cup
Nonfat dry milk powder or Better Than Milk soy powder	¼ cup	⅓ cup	½ cup
Xanthan gum	1½ teaspoons	2 teaspoons	3 teaspoons
Guar gum	1 teaspoon	1 teaspoon	1 teaspoon
Salt	¾ teaspoon	1 teaspoon	1¼ teaspoons
Large eggs	1	2	2
Butter/buttery spread	1 tablespoon	1½ tablespoons	2 tablespoons
Cider vinegar	½ teaspoon	½ teaspoon	1 teaspoon
Oat bran*, rice bran, or rice polish	½ cup	¾ cup	1 cup
Flax meal	2 teaspoons	1 tablespoon	4 teaspoons
Whole-grain teff or kañiwa*	2 teaspoons	1 tablespoon	4 teaspoons

*Check with your physician before eating gluten-free oats.

Hand Method

1 Combine the yeast, 2 teaspoons of the sugar, and the warm water. Set aside to let the yeast foam for about 5 minutes. Generously grease your chosen nonstick pan(s) (gray, not black).

2 In the bowl of a heavy-duty stand mixer (using a regular beater, not the dough hook), combine the yeast mixture with all of the remaining ingredients (including the remaining sugar).

3 Blend on medium speed for 1 minute, scraping down the sides of the bowl with a spatula if necessary.

4 With a wet spatula, spread the dough evenly in the pan(s). Tent with oiled aluminum foil and let rise at room temperature (75°F to 85°F) until the dough is level with the top of the pan. Rising time will vary from 45 to 60 minutes, depending on altitude. (Bread rises more quickly at higher altitudes.)

5 Place a rack in the lower third of the oven. Preheat the oven to 375°F. With a sharp knife, make three diagonal slashes $\frac{1}{8}$ inch deep in the loaf so steam can escape during baking.

6 Bake until nicely browned and an instant-read thermometer registers 200°F to 205°F when inserted into the center, 55 to 65 minutes, depending on loaf size. Do not underbake. Cover loosely with aluminum foil after 20 minutes of baking to reduce overbrowning. Cool the bread in the pan on a wire rack for 10 minutes, then remove the bread from the pan, and cool completely on the wire rack. Slice with a serrated knife or an electric knife.

Bread Machine Method
Follow your bread machine instructions, making sure your machine is the appropriate size for the recipe. If the recipe is too big, the dough will overflow the bucket or pan and cause a mess in your machine. With my machine, I whisk the dry ingredients together (including the yeast) and add to the pan. Then, I whisk the liquid ingredients together (with the water at room temperature) and pour carefully over the dry ingredients. Set controls and bake. I use the Normal setting.

Pumpernickel Bread

This bread makes a superb Reuben or terrific hearty sandwiches of pastrami, corned beef, or good old tuna salad. That unique "pumpernickel" flavor is produced with a creative blend of surprise ingredients such as cocoa powder, caraway seeds, molasses, onion powder, and grated orange zest.

V

Preparation time: 15 minutes
Rising time: 45 to 60 minutes
Baking time: 55 to 65 minutes

Per slice:
130 calories;
3g protein;
2g total fat;
2g fiber;
28g carbohydrates;
22mg cholesterol;
188mg sodium

Ingredients	1-Pound Loaf (4x8-inch pan) Makes 10 slices	1$\frac{1}{2}$-Pound Loaf (5x9-inch pan) Makes 15 slices	2-Pound Loaf (Two 4x8-inch pans) Makes 20 slices
Active dry yeast	2$\frac{1}{4}$ teaspoons	2$\frac{1}{4}$ teaspoons	2$\frac{1}{4}$ teaspoons
Sugar	1 tablespoon	4$\frac{1}{2}$ teaspoons	2 tablespoons
Water (110°F)	1 cup	1$\frac{1}{2}$ cups	2 cups
Gluten-Free Flour Blend (page 27)	1$\frac{1}{2}$ cups	2$\frac{1}{4}$ cups	3 cups
Potato starch	$\frac{1}{2}$ cup	$\frac{1}{2}$ cup	$\frac{3}{4}$ cup
Nonfat dry milk powder or Better Than Milk soy powder	$\frac{1}{4}$ cup	$\frac{1}{3}$ cup	$\frac{1}{2}$ cup
Xanthan gum	1$\frac{1}{2}$ teaspoons	2 teaspoons	3 teaspoons
Guar gum	1 teaspoon	1 teaspoon	1 teaspoon
Salt	$\frac{3}{4}$ teaspoon	1 teaspoon	1$\frac{1}{4}$ teaspoons
Large eggs	1	2	2
Butter/buttery spread	1 tablespoon	1$\frac{1}{2}$ tablespoons	2 tablespoons
Cider vinegar	$\frac{1}{2}$ teaspoon	$\frac{1}{2}$ teaspoon	1 teaspoon
Brown sugar (packed)	$\frac{1}{3}$ cup	$\frac{1}{2}$ cup	$\frac{2}{3}$ cup
Unsweetened cocoa powder	1 tablespoon	1$\frac{1}{2}$ tablespoons	2 tablespoons
Caraway seeds	1 tablespoon	1$\frac{1}{2}$ tablespoons	2 tablespoons
Molasses	2 teaspoons	3 teaspoons	4 teaspoons
Onion powder	$\frac{1}{2}$ teaspoon	$\frac{3}{4}$ teaspoon	1 teaspoon
Grated orange zest	1 teaspoon	1$\frac{1}{2}$ teaspoons	2 teaspoons

Hand Method

1 Combine the yeast, 2 teaspoons of the sugar, and the warm water. Set aside to let the yeast foam for about 5 minutes. Generously grease your chosen nonstick pan(s) (gray, not black).

2 In the bowl of a heavy-duty stand mixer, combine the yeast mixture with all of the remaining ingredients (including the remaining sugar).

3 Blend on medium speed for 1 minute (using a regular beater, not the dough hook), scraping down the sides of the bowl with a spatula if necessary.

4 With a wet spatula, spread the dough evenly in the greased pan(s). Tent with oiled aluminum foil and let rise at room temperature (75°F to 85°F) until the dough is level with the top of the pan. Rising time will vary from 45 to 60 minutes, depending on altitude. (Bread rises more quickly at higher altitudes.)

5 Place a rack in the lower third of the oven. Preheat the oven to 375°F. With a sharp knife, make three diagonal slashes $\frac{1}{8}$ inch deep in the loaf so steam can escape during baking.

6 Bake until nicely browned and an instant-read thermometer registers 200°F to 205°F when inserted into the center, 55 to 65 minutes, depending on loaf size. Do not underbake. Cover loosely with foil after 20 minutes of baking to reduce overbrowning. Cool the bread in the pan on a wire rack for 10 minutes, then remove the bread from the pan, and cool completely on the wire rack. Slice with a serrated knife or an electric knife.

Bread Machine Method

Follow your bread machine instructions, making sure your machine is the appropriate size for the recipe. If the recipe is too big, the dough will overflow the bucket or pan and cause a mess in your machine. With my machine, I whisk the dry ingredients together (including the yeast) and add to the pan. Then, I whisk the liquid ingredients together (with the water at room temperature) and pour carefully over the dry ingredients. Set controls and bake. I use the Normal setting.

Raisin Bread

Filling your kitchen with an enticing cinnamon aroma as it bakes, this tasty bread is ideal for breakfast, toasted and topped with cream cheese, peanut butter, or apple butter. It also makes phenomenal bread pudding or French toast. If you prefer, you can use the same amount of currants, which are smaller than raisins.

Ingredients	1-Pound Loaf (4x8-inch pan) Makes 10 slices	1½-Pound Loaf (5x9-inch pan) Makes 15 slices	2-Pound Loaf (Two 4x8-inch pans) Makes 20 slices
Active dry yeast	2¼ teaspoons	2¼ teaspoons	2¼ teaspoons
Sugar	1 tablespoon	4½ teaspoons	2 tablespoons
Water (110°F)	1 cup	1½ cups	2 cups
Gluten-Free Flour Blend (page 27)	1½ cups	2¼ cups	3 cups
Potato starch	½ cup	½ cup	¾ cup
Nonfat dry milk powder or Better Than Milk soy powder	¼ cup	⅓ cup	½ cup
Xanthan gum	1½ teaspoons	2 teaspoons	3 teaspoons
Guar gum	1 teaspoon	1 teaspoon	1 teaspoon
Salt	¾ teaspoon	1 teaspoon	1¼ teaspoons
Large eggs	1	2	2
Butter/buttery spread	1 tablespoon	1½ tablespoons	2 tablespoons
Cider vinegar	½ teaspoon	½ teaspoon	1 teaspoon
Ground cinnamon	1 teaspoon	1½ teaspoons	2 teaspoons
Raisins	½ cup	¾ cup	1 cup

V

Preparation time: 15 minutes
Rising time: 45 to 60 minutes
Baking time: 55 to 65 minutes

Per slice:
145 calories;
3g protein;
2g total fat;
2g fiber;
32g carbohydrates;
22mg cholesterol;
188mg sodium

(continued)

Hand Method

1 Combine the yeast, 2 teaspoons of the sugar, and the warm water. Set aside to let the yeast foam for about 5 minutes. Generously grease your chosen nonstick pan(s) (gray, not black).

2 In the bowl of a heavy-duty stand mixer (using a regular beater, not the dough hook), combine the yeast mixture with all of the remaining ingredients except for the raisins (including the remaining sugar).

3 Blend on medium speed for 1 minute, scraping down the sides of the bowl with a spatula if necessary. Stir in the raisins.

4 Place the dough in the pan(s). Tent with oiled aluminum foil and let rise at room temperature (75°F to 85°F) until the dough is level with the top of the pan. Rising time will vary from 45 to 60 minutes, depending on altitude. (Bread rises more quickly at higher altitudes.)

5 Place a rack in the lower third of the oven. Preheat the oven to 375°F. With a sharp knife, make three diagonal slashes ⅛ inch deep in the loaf so steam can escape during baking.

6 Bake until nicely browned and an instant-read thermometer registers 200°F to 205°F when inserted into the center, 55 to 65 minutes, depending on loaf size. Do not underbake. Cover loosely with aluminum foil after 20 minutes of baking to reduce overbrowning. Cool the bread in the pan on a wire rack for 10 minutes, then remove the bread from the pan, and cool completely on the wire rack. Slice with a serrated knife or an electric knife.

Bread Machine Method
Follow your bread machine instructions, making sure your machine is the appropriate size for the recipe. If the recipe is too big, the dough will overflow the bucket or pan and cause a mess in your machine. In my machine, I whisk the dry ingredients together (including the yeast) and add to the pan. Then, I whisk the liquid ingredients together (with the water at room temperature) and pour carefully over the dry ingredients. Set controls and bake. I use the Normal setting. Add the raisins as directed by your machine directions.

Potato Bread

Potato bread evokes nostalgia and happy memories for many people. It is a staple in those spiral-ringed, old-time cookbooks that were fund-raisers in many communities (like mine in Nebraska). It's also a great way to use up leftover mashed potatoes, which make the bread very moist and supple.

2 teaspoons active dry yeast

2 tablespoons sugar

¾ cup warm (110°F) water or potato water (water in which potatoes are boiled)

1 cup potato starch

½ cup Gluten-Free Flour Blend (page 27)

½ cup tapioca flour

2 teaspoons xanthan gum

¾ teaspoon salt

⅓ cup nonfat dry milk powder or Better Than Milk soy powder

2 large eggs, at room temperature

½ cup mashed potatoes

¼ cup butter or buttery spread, melted

1 teaspoon cider vinegar

1 Combine the yeast, 2 teaspoons of the sugar, and the warm water. Set aside to let the yeast foam for about 5 minutes. Generously grease three 4x6-inch or one 4x8-inch nonstick pan(s) (gray, not black).

2 In the bowl of a heavy-duty stand mixer, combine all of the ingredients (including the remaining sugar). Beat on low speed (using a regular beater, not the dough hook) until well blended. Increase the speed to medium-low and beat for 1 minute, scraping down the sides of the bowl if necessary.

3 Divide the dough evenly in the pan(s), cover loosely with oiled aluminum foil, and let rise at room temperature (75°F to 85°F) until the dough is level with the top of the pan. Rising time will vary from 45 to 60 minutes, depending on altitude. (Bread rises more quickly at higher altitudes.)

4 Place a rack in the lower third of the oven. Preheat the oven to 375°F. Bake until the bread is nicely browned and an instant-read thermometer registers 200°F to 205°F when inserted into the center, 25 to 30 minutes for small loaves; 45 to 50 minutes for the large loaf. Cool the bread in the pan on a wire rack for 10 minutes, then remove the bread from the pan, and cool completely on the wire rack. Slice with a serrated knife or an electric knife.

V

Makes 1 (1-pound) loaf or 3 (6-ounce) loaves. Serves 12 (1 large loaf slice; 4 small loaf slices)

Preparation time: 15 minutes

Rising time: 45 to 60 minutes

Baking time: 25 to 30 minutes for small loaves; 45 to 50 minutes for large loaf

Per slice of large loaf or 4 slices of small loaf:
175 calories; 3g protein; 6g total fat; 1g fiber; 30g carbohydrates; 50mg cholesterol; 256mg sodium

Bagels

We can now buy gluten-free bagels, but homemade ones are fantastic and actually quite easy. With a little practice, you'll be a pro! These bagels are best when slightly warm, slathered with cream cheese. Or add a little lox for a heartier bite. I once schlepped a Champagne breakfast to the top of a mountain with fellow hikers and our reward was bagels, lox, and cream cheese, with a flute of Champagne to toast our good fortune at being on top of a mountain in Colorado.

V

Makes 8 bagels
Preparation time: 20 minutes
Baking time: 35 to 40 minutes

4 teaspoons active dry yeast
3 tablespoons sugar
⅔ cup warm (110°F) water
1 cup Gluten-Free Flour Blend (page 27)
1 cup potato starch
½ cup nonfat dry milk powder or Better Than Milk soy powder
2 teaspoons salt

2 teaspoons xanthan gum
1 teaspoon guar gum
2 tablespoons canola oil
1 large egg
1 teaspoon cider vinegar
   Brown rice flour, for dusting
1 tablespoon baking soda
   Poppy seeds, for garnish (optional)

Per bagel:
175 calories;
4g protein;
3g total fat;
2g fiber;
37g carbohydrates;
24mg cholesterol;
565mg sodium

Onion Bagels
Per bagel:
175 calories;
4g protein;
3g total fat;
2g fiber;
37g carbohydrates;
24mg cholesterol;
565mg sodium

1 Dissolve the yeast and 1 teaspoon of the sugar in the warm water and set aside to let the yeast foam for about 5 minutes. Grease a 9x13-inch rimmed baking sheet or line with parchment paper.

2 In the bowl of a heavy-duty stand mixer, combine the yeast mixture, 1 tablespoon plus 2 teaspoons of the remaining sugar, and the flour blend, potato starch, dry milk powder, salt, xanthan gum, guar gum, 1 tablespoon of the oil, the egg, and vinegar. Beat on low speed (using a regular beater, not the dough hook) just until blended. Increase the speed to medium-low and beat for 2 minutes, scraping down the sides of the bowl with a spatula if necessary. The dough will be stiff.

3 Divide the dough into 8 equal portions. Generously dust each portion with rice flour; then shape it into a ball. Flatten to a 3-inch circle, dust again with rice flour, and punch a hole in the center. Pull the dough gently away from the hole to form a 3-inch-diameter bagel with a 1-inch hole in the center. Place the shaped bagel on the baking sheet.

4 Place a rack in the lower third of the oven. Place the bagels in the cold oven; set the temperature to 325°F. Bake for 10 minutes. Remove the bagels from the oven, but leave them on the baking sheet and increase the oven temperature to 350°F.

5 Meanwhile, bring 3 inches of water, the remaining 1 tablespoon sugar, the baking soda, and the remaining 1 tablespoon oil to boil in a Dutch oven. Boil the bagels in batches for 30 seconds, drain them on paper towels, and return them to the baking sheet. Sprinkle with the poppy seeds, if using.

6 Return the baking sheet of bagels to the oven. Bake until the bagels are nicely browned, 25 to 30 minutes. Cool the bagels on the baking sheet on a wire rack for 15 minutes. Transfer the bagels to the wire rack to cool for another 10 minutes. Serve slightly warm.

Onion Bagels
Add 1 tablespoon dried minced onions to the dough in Step 2 and proceed as directed.

Cinnamon-Currant Bagels

If your tastes lean toward a sweeter bagel, this one's for you! It's like a round raisin bread, with a hole in the center. It is fabulous with cream cheese, but I also slather it with chocolate-hazelnut spread for a treat that resembles dessert.

4 teaspoons active dry yeast
¼ cup sugar
⅔ cup warm (110°F) water
1 cup Gluten-Free Flour Blend
   (page 27)
1 cup potato starch
½ cup nonfat dry milk powder or Better
   Than Milk soy powder
1 teaspoon ground cinnamon

2 teaspoons salt
2 teaspoons xanthan gum
1 teaspoon guar gum
2 tablespoons canola oil
1 large egg
1 teaspoon cider vinegar
½ cup dried currants (or raisins)
   Brown rice flour, for dusting
1 tablespoon baking soda

V
Makes 8 bagels
Preparation time: 20 minutes
Baking time: 35 to 40 minutes

1 Dissolve the yeast and 1 teaspoon of the sugar in the warm water and set aside to let the yeast foam, about 5 minutes. Grease a 9x13-inch rimmed baking sheet or line with parchment paper.

2 In the bowl of a heavy-duty stand mixer, combine the yeast mixture, 2 tablespoons plus 2 teaspoons of the remaining sugar, and the flour blend, potato starch, dry milk powder, cinnamon, salt, xanthan gum, guar gum, 1 tablespoon of the oil, the egg, and vinegar. Beat on low speed (using a regular beater, not the dough hook) just until blended. Add the currants, increase the speed to medium-low, and beat for 1 minute, scraping down the sides of the bowl with a spatula. The dough will be stiff.

3 Divide the dough into 8 equal portions. Generously dust each portion with rice flour; then shape it into a ball. Flatten to a 3-inch circle, dust again with rice flour, and punch a hole in the center. Pull the dough gently away from the hole to form a 3-inch-diameter bagel with a 1-inch hole in the center. Place the shaped bagel on the baking sheet.

4 Place a rack in the lower third of the oven. Place the bagels in the cold oven; set the temperature to 325°F. Bake for 10 minutes. Remove the bagels from the oven, but leave them on the baking sheet and increase the oven temperature to 350°F.

5 Meanwhile, while the bagels are baking, bring 3 inches of water, the remaining 1 tablespoon sugar, the baking soda, and the remaining 1 tablespoon oil to boil in a Dutch oven. Boil the bagels in batches for 30 seconds, drain them on paper towels, and return them to the baking sheet.

6 Return the baking sheet of bagels to the oven. Bake until the bagels are nicely browned, 25 to 30 minutes. Cool the bagels on the baking sheet on a wire rack for 15 minutes. Transfer the bagels to the wire rack to cool another 10 minutes. Serve slightly warm.

Per bagel:
205 calories;
4g protein;
3g total fat;
3g fiber;
44g carbohydrates;
24mg cholesterol;
566mg sodium

Breadsticks

These cute little breadsticks are so easy that you'll make them again and again. For bigger breadsticks, extend the rising time or cut a bigger hole in the resealable freezer bag (which must be heavy duty or it might break) so that it releases a thicker strip of dough. Adjust the baking time accordingly. These are best when cooled for 15 minutes, although you will have a hard time resisting the temptation to bite into one right after they come out of the oven!

V

Makes 10 breadsticks

Preparation time: 15 minutes

Rising time: 20 to 30 minutes

Baking time: 15 to 20 minutes

Per breadstick: 90 calories; 3g protein; 3g total fat; 1g fiber; 14g carbohydrates; 4mg cholesterol; 190mg sodium

1 tablespoon active dry yeast

1 teaspoon sugar

⅔ cup warm (110°F) milk of choice

½ cup Gluten-Free Flour Blend (page 27)

½ cup potato starch

½ cup grated Parmesan cheese or soy Parmesan

1 tablespoon olive oil

2 teaspoons xanthan gum

1 teaspoon onion powder

½ teaspoon salt

1 teaspoon cider vinegar

1 teaspoon dried Italian seasoning

1 teaspoon sesame seeds (optional)

1 Place a rack in the lower third of the oven. Preheat the oven to 400°F for 10 minutes; then turn it off and leave the oven door closed. Dissolve the yeast and sugar in the warm milk and set aside to let the yeast foam for 5 minutes. Grease a 9x13-inch rimmed baking sheet (not nonstick) or line with parchment paper.

2 In a medium bowl, beat the yeast mixture and all of the remaining ingredients (except the Italian seasoning and sesame seeds) with a heavy-duty stand mixer on low speed for 30 seconds, and then on medium speed for 1 minute. The dough will be soft and sticky.

3 Transfer the dough to a gallon-size, heavy-duty resealable storage bag. With scissors, cut a ½-inch diagonal hole in one of the bottom corners of the bag. (This makes a 1-inch circle.) Squeeze the dough out of the bag onto the baking sheet in 10 strips, each 1 inch wide by 6 inches long. For best results, hold the bag of dough upright as you squeeze, rather than at an angle. Also, hold the bag with the seam on top, rather than at the side. Spray the breadsticks with cooking spray; then sprinkle with the Italian seasoning and sesame seeds, if using.

4 Place the breadsticks in the oven to rise for 20 to 30 minutes. Then, leaving the breadsticks in the oven, turn the temperature to 400°F and bake the breadsticks until golden brown, 15 to 20 minutes. Rotate the position of the baking sheet halfway through baking to ensure even browning. Cool the breadsticks on the baking sheet on a wire rack for 10 minutes, then transfer the breadsticks to the wire rack to cool until just slightly warm. Serve warm.

Cinnamon Rolls

The aroma of cinnamon rolls baking in the oven is pure heaven. The extra softness of gluten-free dough makes shaping them a bit more involved, so they are baked in a muffin tin to retain their round shape. It's a little more work, but totally worth the effort. Serve these plain or drizzled with Vanilla Powdered Sugar Frosting (page 207).

Filling
1 cup packed brown sugar
¼ cup very finely chopped pecans
   or walnuts
1 teaspoon ground cinnamon

Dough
2¼ teaspoons active dry yeast (1 packet)
3 tablespoons sugar
1 cup warm (110°F) water
1½ cups Gluten-Free Flour Blend
   (page 27)

1 cup potato starch
¼ cup dry milk powder or Better Than
   Milk soy powder
1½ teaspoons xanthan gum
1 teaspoon guar gum
¾ teaspoon salt
1 large egg plus 1 egg yolk, at
   room temperature
¼ cup butter or buttery spread
½ teaspoon cider vinegar
   Brown rice flour, for rolling the dough

V
Makes 12 rolls
Preparation time: 20 minutes
Rising time: 20 to 30 minutes
Baking time: 25 to 30 minutes

Per roll:
245 calories;
2g protein;
7g total fat;
2g fiber;
48g carbohydrates;
44mg cholesterol;
194mg sodium

1 Make the filling: Generously grease a 12-cup nonstick standard muffin pan (gray, not black). In a small bowl, whisk together the brown sugar, nuts, and cinnamon until well blended. Set aside.

2 Make the dough: In a small bowl, combine the yeast, 2 teaspoons of the sugar, and the warm water. Set aside to let the yeast foam for about 5 minutes.

3 In the bowl of a heavy-duty stand mixer (using a regular beater, not the dough hook), combine the yeast mixture with the remaining sugar and the flour blend, potato starch, dry milk powder, xanthan gum, guar gum, salt, eggs, butter, and vinegar. Blend on medium speed for 1 minute, scraping down the sides of the bowl with a spatula if necessary.

4 Place one-quarter of the dough on a large cutting board or sheet of parchment paper that is liberally dusted with brown rice flour. (Keep the remaining dough covered until you're ready to roll it.) Dust the dough with rice flour to prevent sticking. With a rolling pin, roll the dough to a ½-inch thickness. Sprinkle evenly with one-quarter of the filling. With a sharp knife, cut the dough into three strips. Roll up each strip and place in a muffin cup, cut side down. Repeat with the remaining dough. Let rise at room temperature (75°F to 85°F) until the dough is not quite level with the top of the pan. Rising time will vary from 20 to 30 minutes, depending on altitude. (Bread rises more quickly at higher altitudes.)

5 Place a rack in the lower third of the oven. Preheat the oven to 375°F. Bake until the rolls are nicely browned and an instant-read thermometer registers 200°F to 205°F when inserted into the center of the pan, 25 to 30 minutes. If they start to brown too much, lay a sheet of aluminum foil on top. Cool the rolls in the pan on a wire rack for 15 minutes, then transfer the rolls to a plate. Serve slightly warm.

Dinner Rolls

I am often asked about making gluten-free dinner rolls. Naturally, we all want our dinner rolls with the big holiday meal, and this recipe makes it quite easy. The dough is very soft, but with my special handling tips it bakes up into a delectable roll that everyone will enjoy.

V

Makes 18 rolls
Preparation time: 15 minutes
Rising time: 25 to 30 minutes
Baking time: 20 to 25 minutes

Per roll:
115 calories;
2g protein;
1g total fat;
1g fiber;
16g carbohydrates;
12mg cholesterol;
195mg sodium

2¼ teaspoons active dry yeast (1 packet)
1 tablespoon sugar
1 cup warm (110°F) water
1½ cups Gluten-Free Flour Blend (page 27)
1¼ cups potato starch
¼ cup nonfat dry milk powder or Better Than Milk soy powder
1½ teaspoons xanthan gum

1 teaspoon guar gum
1 teaspoon salt
1 large egg
1 tablespoon butter or buttery spread, at room temperature, plus more for brushing (optional)
½ teaspoon cider vinegar
Brown rice flour, for rolling the dough (optional)

1 Generously grease a 7x11-inch or 9-inch square nonstick baking pan (gray, not black).

2 In a small bowl, combine the yeast, 2 teaspoons of the sugar, and the warm water. Set aside to let the yeast foam for about 5 minutes.

3 In the bowl of a heavy-duty stand mixer (using a regular beater, not the dough hook), combine the yeast mixture with the remaining sugar and the flour blend, potato starch, dry milk powder, xanthan gum, guar gum, salt, egg, butter, and vinegar. Blend on medium speed for 2 minutes, scraping down the sides of the bowl with a spatula if necessary. The dough will seem impossibly soft to handle.

4 With a 1½-inch spring-action metal ice cream scoop, place 18 balls of dough in the pan, very close together so they will rise up rather than spread out. For smoother rolls, roll a ball of dough in a bowl of brown rice flour so you can shape it in your hands until smooth before placing it in the pan. Lay a sheet of oiled aluminum foil on top and let rise at room temperature (75°F to 85°F) until the dough is level with the top of the pan, 25 to 30 minutes.

5 Place a rack in the lower third of the oven. Preheat the oven to 375°F. Bake until the tops are lightly browned and an instant-read thermometer registers 200°F to 205°F when inserted into the center, 20 to 25 minutes. Lay a sheet of aluminum foil on top if the rolls start to brown too much. Remove from the oven and brush the tops with melted butter, if desired. Cool the rolls in the pan on a wire rack for 20 minutes. Remove the rolls from the pan and cool on the wire rack for another 10 minutes. Serve slightly warm.

Focaccia Bread

Focaccia is a cross between pizza and flatbread. I serve it to everyone (gluten-free or not) because it is so flavorful, especially if you serve it with dipping oil as they do in restaurants. Sliced in half horizontally, it makes great sandwich bread, and I have used it to make little tea sandwiches for an afternoon tea.

Bread Dough
- 2¼ teaspoons active dry yeast (1 packet)
- 2 teaspoons sugar
- ¾ cup warm (110°F) milk of choice
- 1½ cups Gluten-Free Flour Blend (page 27)
- 1½ teaspoons xanthan gum
- 1 tablespoon chopped fresh rosemary or 1 teaspoon dried
- ½ teaspoon onion powder
- ½ teaspoon salt
- 2 large eggs, at room temperature
- 2 tablespoons olive oil
- 2 teaspoons cider vinegar

Topping
- 1 tablespoon olive oil
- 1¼ teaspoons dried Italian seasoning
- ¼ teaspoon kosher or coarse sea salt
- 2 tablespoons grated Parmesan cheese or soy Parmesan

Dipping Oil
- ¼ cup extra-virgin olive oil (the good stuff)
- ¼ teaspoon salt, or to taste
- ¼ teaspoon freshly ground black pepper, or to taste
- 2 tablespoons balsamic vinegar
- ½ teaspoon dried oregano
- ½ teaspoon dried thyme

1 Make the bread dough: Dissolve the yeast and sugar in the warm milk. Set aside to let the yeast foam for about 5 minutes. Grease a 7x11-inch nonstick pan (gray, not black).

2 In a medium bowl, beat the yeast-milk mixture and all of the remaining bread ingredients with a heavy-duty stand mixer on low speed until just blended. Then beat on medium-low speed until the dough is slightly thickened, about 30 seconds. The dough will be soft and sticky.

3 With a wet spatula, spread the dough evenly in the pan. Cover with an oiled aluminum foil tent and let rise at room temperature (75°F to 85°F) until the dough is level with the top of the pan, 30 to 40 minutes. Sprinkle the dough with the topping ingredients: the oil, Italian seasoning, salt, and Parmesan.

4 Place a rack in the lower third of the oven. Preheat the oven to 400°F. Bake until the top is golden brown and an instant-read thermometer registers 200°F to 205°F when inserted into the center, 25 to 30 minutes. Cool the focaccia in the pan on a wire rack. When slightly warm, transfer to a cutting board and cut into 10 slices with a serrated knife or an electric knife.

5 Make the dipping oil: In a small bowl, whisk together all of the dipping oil ingredients. For better flavor, refrigerate for an hour to let the flavors meld, but bring to room temperature before serving. Place a little dipping oil on each serving plate and serve it with the slightly warm sliced bread.

Focaccia Flatbread
Grease a 9x13-inch nonstick immed baking sheet (gray, not black). Prepare the dough as directed and place in the pan. Use a wet spatula to make sure the dough is as evenly spread in the pan as possible so that bakes uniformly. Sprinkle with the topping ingredients, place in a cold oven, and turn the oven to 400°F. Bake 20 to 25 minutes. Cool 5 minutes, then tear into 10 pieces and serve.

V

Makes 10 slices
Preparation time: 10 minutes
Rising time: 30 to 40 minutes
Baking time: 25 to 30 minutes

Per slice with dipping oil:
310 calories;
10g protein;
13g total fat;
13g fiber;
36g carbohydrates;
39mg cholesterol;
268mg sodium

Focaccia Flatbread
Per slice with dipping oil:
310 calories;
10g protein;
13g total fat;
13g fiber;
36g carbohydrates;
39mg cholesterol;
268mg sodium

Hamburger Buns

Fire up the grill for hamburgers! These easy buns won't crumble, and they freeze well. The soy lecithin makes a finer crumb, but it is optional. For softer tops, brush with melted butter after baking.

V

Makes 8 buns
Preparation time: 15 minutes
Rising time: 20 to 30 minutes
Baking time: 15 to 20 minutes

Per bun:
265 calories; 18g protein; 7g total fat; 12g fiber; 39g carbohydrates; 56mg cholesterol; 316mg sodium

Hot Dog & Herbed Buns

Per bun:
265 calories; 18g protein; 7g total fat; 12g fiber; 39g carbohydrates; 56mg cholesterol; 316mg sodium

1½ teaspoons active dry yeast
2 teaspoons sugar
1 cup warm (110°F) milk of choice
1½ cups Gluten-Free Flour Blend (page 27)
1 tablespoon dried minced onion
2 teaspoons xanthan gum
1 teaspoon baking powder
¾ teaspoon salt
¼ teaspoon soy lecithin (optional)
2 tablespoons butter or buttery spread, melted and cooled, plus more for brushing on top (optional)
2 large eggs, at room temperature
½ teaspoon cider vinegar
4 teaspoons sesame seeds or poppy seeds (optional)
Cooking spray (optional)

1 Dissolve the yeast and sugar in the warm milk. Set aside to let the yeast foam for about 5 minutes. Grease 8 English muffin rings (or see How to Make Foil Rings, opposite) and place on a 9x13-inch rimmed baking sheet (not nonstick) lined with parchment paper.

2 In a large mixing bowl, whisk together the flour blend, minced onion, xanthan gum, baking powder, salt, and soy lecithin (if using), until well blended. Add the melted butter, eggs, and vinegar and beat on low speed with a heavy-duty stand mixer (using a regular beater, not the dough hook) until just blended. Increase the speed to medium-low and beat until the dough thickens slightly, about 30 seconds. The dough will be very soft and sticky.

3 Divide the dough evenly among the muffin rings and use a wet spatula to spread the dough to the edges of the rings. Sprinkle with the sesame seeds, if using. Lay a sheet of oiled aluminum foil on top and let the buns rise at room temperature (75°F to 85°F) until the dough is just below the top of the rings, 20 to 30 minutes, depending on altitude. (Bread rises more quickly at higher altitudes.)

4 Place an oven rack in the middle of the oven. Preheat the oven to 350°F. Bake until the tops are golden brown and firm, 15 to 20 minutes. For a glossier, softer bun top, spray very lightly with cooking spray or brush with melted butter. Cool the buns for 5 minutes on the baking sheet on a wire rack, and then remove the rings and cool the buns completely on the wire rack. To serve, cut the buns in half crosswise and lightly toast the cut side of each bun for a crispier texture.

Hot Dog Buns

Divide the dough evenly among 8 hot dog–shaped foil rings (see How to Make Foil Rings, opposite) or use a specially designed hot dog–bun pan. Bake as directed.

Herbed Buns

Add 1 teaspoon crushed dried rosemary and ½ teaspoon dried Italian seasoning to the dough. Bake as directed.

English Muffins

Toasted English muffins are perfect for breakfast or as the foundation for eggs Benedict, and they are not that hard to make. Make a batch and freeze the extras; they defrost quickly.

2 tablespoons active dry yeast
1 tablespoon sugar
1¼ cups warm (110°F) water
1 tablespoon yellow cornmeal
Cooking spray
2⅓ cups Gluten-Free Flour Blend (page 27)

2 cups tapioca flour
⅔ cup nonfat dry milk powder or Better Than Milk soy powder
3 teaspoons xanthan gum
1 teaspoon salt
¼ cup canola oil
4 large egg whites, at room temperature

V
Makes 12 muffins
Preparation time: 15 minutes
Rising time: 45 to 50 minutes
Baking time: 25 minutes

Per muffin
230 calories;
5g protein;
5g total fat;
2g fiber;
44g carbohydrates;
1mg cholesterol;
218mg sodium

1 Dissolve the yeast and sugar in the warm water. Set aside to let the yeast foam for about 5 minutes. Line a 9x13-inch rimmed baking sheet (not nonstick) with parchment paper, dust with the cornmeal, and arrange 12 store-bought metal English muffin rings or handmade foil rings (see below) on top. Coat the inside of the muffin rings with cooking spray.

2 In the bowl of a heavy-duty stand mixer, combine the flour blend, tapioca flour, dry milk powder, xanthan gum, and salt. Whisk together until well blended, then add the oil, egg whites, and yeast mixture. Beat on low speed until just blended. Increase the speed to medium-low and beat for 1 minute.

3 Divide the dough into 12 equal pieces and press each piece evenly into a muffin ring. Cover with oiled aluminum foil and let rise at room temperature (75°F to 85°F) until not quite level with the top of the ring, 45 to 50 minutes, depending on altitude. (Bread rises more quickly at higher altitudes.)

4 Preheat the oven to 350°F. Bake the muffins until they are lightly browned on top, about 15 minutes. With a spatula, flip the muffins over (rings and all) and bake until lightly browned on top, another 10 minutes.

5 Remove the English muffins (still in the rings) from the baking sheet to cool on a wire rack. When the rings are cool enough to handle, remove the muffins from the rings, and cool completely on the wire rack.

How to Make Foil Rings

If you don't have English muffin rings, make them! Tear off a 12-inch strip of aluminum foil. Fold over and over lengthwise in 1-inch folds. Shape into a circle that is 2½ to 4 inches in diameter for the hamburger bun or a rectangle that is 2x6 inches for the hot dog bun. Secure with masking tape on the outside of the ring. Repeat to make as many as you need.

Desserts 〉

Like many of you, I have a sweet tooth, so having to avoid gluten was a real blow to my lifestyle. A scoop of ice cream or sorbet just doesn't satisfy me when I really want cakes, cookies, and pies. But we can have these treats if we make them with gluten-free ingredients, and making that possible is the goal of this chapter.

I firmly believe in the adage "Eat dessert first; life is uncertain," so my family's desserts were among the first recipes that I converted to be gluten-free. Chocolate cake, oatmeal cookies, vanilla pudding, gingerbread . . . all the basics. Most of these recipes are from my mother's tattered shoe box of scribbled notes on the back of used envelopes, which I now treasure. Then I added a few contemporary treats like Red Velvet Cupcakes, Cherry-Almond Clafouti, Basic Flourless Cake, and Almond Meringue Cookies to round out this otherwise basic set of sweets. So now there is no reason to give up dessert—even if you are brand-new to gluten-free baking.

Q	V
Quick	**Vegetarian**

Cookies and Bars

Cookies
Almond Meringue Cookies
Chocolate Chip Cookies
   Double-Chocolate Cookies
   Refrigerator Cookies
Coconut Macaroons
Oatmeal-Raisin Cookies
Peanut Butter Cookies
Cutout Sugar Cookies
Mexican Wedding Cakes
Gingerbread Cookies
   Gingerbread People
   Whoopies
Spice Drop Cookies

Bars
Crispy Rice–Peanut Butter Bars with
   Chocolate Glaze
Chocolate Brownies
   Double-Chocolate Nut Brownies
Lemon Bars
Seven-Layer Bars

Cakes, Cupcakes, and Frostings

Basic Vanilla Bundt Cake
  Vanilla Layer Cakes
  Rum Bundt Cake
Boston Cream Pie
Carrot Bundt Cake
Chocolate Bundt Cake
  Chocolate Layer Cake
  Chocolate-Raspberry Cake
Basic Flourless Cake
Flourless Chocolate Cake
Gingerbread
Pear-Spice Upside-Down Cake
Pineapple Upside-Down Cake
Spice Bundt Cake
  Spice Layer Cake
  Apple-Spice Cake
Red Velvet Cupcakes with Vanilla Cream Cheese Frosting
Toasted Coconut Cupcakes with Fluffy White
  Frosting

Frostings
  Vanilla Powdered Sugar Frosting
  Chocolate Powdered Sugar Frosting
  Fluffy White Cooked Frosting
  Vanilla Cream Cheese Frosting
  Chocolate Glaze
  Rum Glaze

Pies, Tarts, Cobblers, and Crisps

Pies and Tarts
Basic Piecrust (Double Crust) and Three Pies
  Cherry Pie
  Peach Pie
  Pumpkin Pie
Ice Cream Pie
Pear-Almond Tart
Flourless Piecrusts for No-Bake Pies
  Chocolate–Peanut Butter Crust
  Coconut Crust
  Cookie Crumb Crust

Cobblers, Crisps, and Other Delights
Apple Crisp
Cherry-Almond Clafouti
Cherry Cobbler
  Peach Cobbler
Mini Cream Puffs
Crêpes

Puddings and Cheesecakes

Chocolate Pudding
Chocolate-Cherry Bread Pudding
Chocolate-Cherry Individual Trifles
Vanilla Pudding
Pudding Mix
  Vanilla Pudding from Pudding Mix
  Chocolate Pudding from Pudding Mix
Mini Cheesecakes with Cherries

Almond Meringue Cookies

These pretty little delicacies are often sold in bakeries as a gluten-free option. Amazingly simple to make, they keep well and are perfect for any occasion.

V

Makes 24 cookies
Preparation time: 10 minutes
Baking and cooling time: 3 hours

Per cookie:
15 calories;
1g protein;
0g total fat;
0g fiber;
3g carbohydrates;
0mg cholesterol;
9mg sodium

4   large egg whites, at
       room temperature
¼   teaspoon cream of tartar
½   cup powdered sugar
1   teaspoon almond extract

1 Place a rack in the center of the oven. Preheat the oven to 225°F. Line a 9x13-inch baking sheet (not nonstick) with parchment paper.

2 In a dry, medium bowl, beat the egg whites on low speed until foamy. Add the cream of tartar and beat on medium speed until soft peaks form. Add the powdered sugar gradually— 2 tablespoons at a time—while beating to very stiff peaks (see How to Beat Egg Whites below). Stir in the almond extract.

3 Transfer the batter to a gallon-size, heavy-duty resealable food storage bag, cut off ⅛ inch on one corner, and press the batter onto the baking sheet in 24 rounds, each 1½ inches, leaving 1 inch between cookies.

4 Bake until the cookies are firm and crisp, about 2 hours, turning the baking sheet 180 degrees after 1 hour to assure even baking. Cool the cookies completely on the pan on a wire rack. Or, for maximum crispness, cool in the oven with the door closed. Store the cookies in an airtight container.

Chocolate Meringue Cookies
Replace the almond extract with pure vanilla extract. Replace 1 tablespoon of the powdered sugar with 1 tablespoon Dutch-processed cocoa powder.

How to Beat Egg Whites

The secret to fluffy meringue is correctly beaten egg whites. Make sure the bowl and beaters are squeaky clean and the whites have no yolk residue; either will hamper the incorporation of air, which is what makes meringue so fluffy. Separate the yolks from the whites while cold because they separate more easily that way. But let the egg whites come to room temperature before beating for the best volume. For soft peaks, the peaks curl over slightly when you raise the beaters; for stiff peaks, they stand straight up.

Chocolate Chip Cookies

Chocolate chip cookies are America's favorite cookie. Everyone remembers them from childhood—and wants to continue eating them as adults. Freeze the dough (see Refrigerator Cookies below) and bake as few (or as many) as you like when the urge strikes.

1½ cups Gluten-Free Flour Blend (page 27)	¾ cup packed brown sugar
1 teaspoon xanthan gum	⅓ cup sugar
½ teaspoon baking soda	2 teaspoons pure vanilla extract
¼ teaspoon salt	1 extra-large egg
¼ cup cold butter or buttery spread	1 cup gluten-free chocolate chips
	¼ cup chopped walnuts

1 Place a rack in the center of the oven. Preheat the oven to 350°F. Line a 9x13-inch baking sheet (not nonstick) with parchment paper.

2 In a medium bowl, whisk together the flour blend, xanthan gum, baking soda, and salt.

3 In a large bowl, beat the butter with an electric mixer on low speed until smooth. Add both sugars, the vanilla, and egg and beat until thoroughly blended. Gradually beat in the flour mixture until no visible streaks remain. Stir in the chocolate chips and walnuts. Wrap the dough tightly in plastic wrap and chill for 1 hour.

4 Remove half of the dough and drop 12 tablespoonfuls about 2 inches apart on the baking sheet. (Or, for more uniform cookies, shape the dough into tablespoon-size balls with your hands.) Bake until browned around the edges, 10 to 12 minutes. Cool the cookies for 2 to 3 minutes on the sheet on a wire rack, then use a thin metal spatula to transfer the cookies to the wire rack to cool completely. Repeat with remaining dough.

Double-Chocolate Cookies

Replace 2 tablespoons of the Gluten-Free Flour Blend with 2 tablespoons unsweetened cocoa powder. Bake as directed.

Refrigerator Cookies

Pat the dough into a 1-inch-diameter roll on a cutting board. Cut into 1-inch slices; then lay the slices flat (cut side down) on the cutting board. Wrap the cutting board tightly with foil and freeze. When frozen, remove the cookie slices from the cutting board and put in a resealable plastic freezer bag. To bake, place frozen slices of cookie dough on a baking sheet (not nonstick) and bake as directed above, allowing a little extra time for baking since they are frozen.

V

Makes 24 cookies
Preparation time: 10 minutes
Chilling time: 1 hour
Baking time: about 25 minutes

Per cookie:
125 calories;
1g protein;
5g total fat;
1g fiber;
21g carbohydrates;
13mg cholesterol;
74mg sodium

Coconut Macaroons

Macaroons are so moist, chewy, and delicious—they are simply irresistible! Serve them plain or dipped into melted chocolate for even greater decadence and a professional bakery look.

V

Makes 16 cookies
Preparation time: 10 minutes
Baking time: 15 to 20 minutes

Per macaroon without chocolate dip: 165 calories; 1g protein; 8g total fat; 1g fiber; 23g carbohydrates; 0mg cholesterol; 90mg sodium

Per macaroon with chocolate dip: 240 calories; 3g protein; 16g total fat; 3g fiber; 27g carbohydrates; 1mg cholesterol; 95mg sodium

Macaroons
1   (14-ounce) package sweetened shredded coconut
1   cup powdered sugar
½   cup cornstarch
1   teaspoon xanthan gum
⅛   teaspoon salt
3   large egg whites
1   teaspoon pure vanilla extract

Chocolate Dip
8   ounces bittersweet chocolate chips
1   teaspoon butter or buttery spread

1 Make the macaroons: Place a rack in the center of the oven. Preheat the oven to 350°F. Line a 9x13-inch baking sheet (not nonstick) with parchment paper.

2 In a food processor, process the coconut, powdered sugar, cornstarch, xanthan gum, and salt together just until blended. Add the egg whites and vanilla and pulse just until mixed. The dough will be stiff and somewhat coarse.

3 With wet hands, form 16 balls, about 1¼ inches in diameter. Don't compact the dough too tightly; you want some of the coconut sticking out for the prettiest look. Place at least 1 inch apart on the baking sheet.

4 Bake until the cookies start to brown around the edges, 15 to 20 minutes. Cool the cookies on the baking sheet on a wire rack for 10 minutes. Then transfer the cookies to the wire rack and cool completely.

5 Make the chocolate dip: Place half of the chocolate chips and the butter in a microwave-safe bowl. Heat in the microwave on Medium power until the chocolate starts to melt. Remove from the microwave and stir until smooth, then stir in the remaining chocolate chips until very smooth. If it doesn't all melt together, return to the microwave and cook in 5-second increments until it does.

6 Holding a macaroon with your hands or tongs, dip the bottom or side of the macaroon halfway into the melted chocolate, twist slightly, and then lift it out, letting any excess chocolate drip back into the bowl. Lay the macaroon on an oiled wire rack and repeat with the remaining macaroons. Let stand for 20 to 30 minutes or until the chocolate sets up, and then serve.

Oatmeal-Raisin Cookies

As someone who really missed oatmeal cookies—having grown up eating them—I was overjoyed when several manufacturers began offering gluten-free rolled oats a few years ago. Here, the applesauce lends moisture without adding fat, and soaking the raisins in it further increases the moisture for a soft, chewy cookie—and they stay soft for several days. You can also add ¼ cup finely chopped nuts, your favorite dried fruit, or chocolate chips.

V

Makes 30 cookies
Preparation time: 10 minutes
Baking time: 45 to 60 minutes

Per cookie:
100 calories;
1g protein;
2g total fat;
1g fiber;
20g carbohydrates;
12mg cholesterol;
72mg sodium

❭ *Check with your physician before eating gluten-free oats.

¾ cup raisins
½ cup unsweetened applesauce
1 teaspoon pure vanilla extract
1 large egg
1 cup packed brown sugar
⅓ cup cold butter or buttery spread
2 cups Gluten-Free Flour Blend (page 27)

1 cup gluten-free rolled oats*
1 teaspoon xanthan gum
1 teaspoon ground cinnamon
½ teaspoon salt
¼ teaspoon baking soda

1 Place a rack in the center of the oven. Preheat the oven to 325°F. Line a 9x13-inch baking sheet (not nonstick) with parchment paper.

2 In a medium bowl, stir together the raisins, applesauce, and vanilla and let stand for a few minutes so the raisins soften. With an electric mixer on low speed, beat in the egg, sugar, and butter until the butter is no longer visible. Add the flour blend, oats, xanthan gum, cinnamon, salt, and baking soda and beat on low speed until well blended and the dough holds together when pressed.

3 Drop 10 tablespoonfuls of dough at least 1½ inches apart on the baking sheet. (For thinner cookies, flatten the dough with a wet spatula to a ½-inch thickness.)

4 Bake until the edges of the cookies are firm and lightly browned, 15 to 20 minutes. Cool on the baking sheet on a wire rack for 5 minutes, then use a thin metal spatula to transfer them to the wire rack to cool completely. Repeat with the remaining dough, baking 10 cookies at a time.

Freezing Cookie Dough

This recipe makes 30 cookies; if you don't want to bake that many at one time, simply shape the dough into balls and freeze on a baking sheet. When the balls are frozen, place them in a resealable plastic freezer bag and freeze. When the baking urge strikes, place as many frozen balls as you like on a baking sheet. Let them stand for 15 minutes to thaw slightly, and then bake as directed.

Peanut Butter Cookies

These classic cookies evoke memories of childhood and happy times and were one of the first cookies I learned to make when I was growing up. Back when I didn't have to worry about calories, I could devour a whole batch at a time. But my siblings had other ideas about that, so I had no choice but to make them often.

¾ cup creamy peanut butter
1 cup packed brown sugar
1 teaspoon pure vanilla extract
1 large egg
1¼ cups Gluten-Free Flour Blend
     (page 27)

½ teaspoon xanthan gum
½ teaspoon salt
½ teaspoon baking soda

1 In a medium bowl, beat the peanut butter, sugar, vanilla, and egg together with an electric mixer on low speed until well blended.

2 In a medium bowl, whisk together the flour blend, xanthan gum, salt, and baking soda until well blended and gradually beat into the peanut butter mixture just until blended. Flatten the dough into a disk and refrigerate, tightly wrapped, for 1 hour.

3 Place a rack in the center of the oven. Preheat the oven to 375°F. Line a 9x13-inch baking sheet (not nonstick) with parchment paper.

4 Shape the dough into 20 (1-inch) balls, place on a plate, and freeze for 15 minutes. Place 10 of the balls 2 inches apart on the baking sheet. Flatten slightly with the tines of a fork in a crisscross pattern.

5 Bake until the cookie edges start to set and begin to brown, 7 to 8 minutes. Cool the cookies on the baking sheet on a wire rack for 5 minutes, then use a thin metal spatula to transfer the cookies to the wire rack to cool completely. Repeat with the remaining dough.

V
Makes 20 cookies
Preparation time: 10 minutes
Baking time: about 16 minutes

Per cookie:
130 calories;
3g protein;
5g total fat;
1g fiber;
20g carbohydrates;
9mg cholesterol;
121mg sodium

Cutout Sugar Cookies

Every cook needs a basic sugar cookie to use for cutout cookies at holiday time or other festive occasions. This recipe works best when the dough is made with a food processor because the processor makes quick work of thoroughly blending the ingredients.

V

Makes 16 cookies
Preparation time: 10 minutes
Baking time: about 25 minutes

Per cookie:
115 calories; 1g protein; 4g total fat; 1g fiber; 29g carbohydrates; 24mg cholesterol; 83mg sodium

⅓ cup butter or buttery spread, at room temperature (but not melted)
1 large egg yolk
½ cup sugar
2 teaspoons pure vanilla extract
2 teaspoons grated lemon zest
1½ cups Gluten-Free Flour Blend (page 27)

¼ cup cornstarch
¾ teaspoon xanthan gum
¼ teaspoon salt
⅛ teaspoon baking soda
1 to 2 tablespoons water, if needed
Rice flour (brown or white), for rolling

1 In a food processor, combine the butter, egg yolk, sugar, vanilla, and lemon zest. Process for 1 minute. Add the flour blend, cornstarch, xanthan gum, salt, and baking soda and blend until the mixture forms large clumps or a ball. Scrape down the sides of the bowl with a spatula and blend until the mixture forms large clumps or a ball again. Squeeze a tablespoon of dough between your fingers; it is ready if it holds together without crumbling. Add water—1 tablespoon at a time—only if the dough is crumbly. Shape into two flat disks and wrap tightly. Refrigerate for 2 hours.

2 Place a rack in the center of the oven. Preheat the oven to 375°F. Working with one disk of dough, roll with a rolling pin to ¼ inch thick on a sheet of parchment paper sprinkled with rice flour. Keep the remaining dough chilled until ready to use. Cut into desired shapes (about 2 inches in diameter) and transfer to a 9x13-inch parchment-lined baking sheet (not nonstick). Leave 1 inch between cookies.

3 Bake until the cookies are lightly browned around the edges, 10 to 12 minutes. Cool for 5 minutes on the baking sheet on a wire rack. With a thin metal spatula, gently transfer each cookie to a wire rack to cool completely. Repeat with the remaining dough disk.

Tips for Successful Cutout Cookies

1 To avoid cookies that stick to the baking sheet, use parchment paper or nonstick baking liners (such as Silpat). A very thin metal spatula works best to remove the cookies from the baking sheet without breaking them.

2 Cookies may brown too fast on a nonstick baking sheet. Instead, use a light-colored, shiny aluminum baking sheet. Lining the sheet with parchment paper also helps reduce excessive browning. Insulated baking sheets ensure even baking.

3 Metal cookie cutters work better than plastic cookie cutters because the edges are sharper and cut a cleaner line. Wipe off the cookie cutter occasionally to remove stray bits of dough.

4 If the chilled dough is too stiff, leave it at room temperature (wrapped) for 15 to 20 minutes. Or, knead it with your hands to make it more pliable. If the dough is too soft after rolling, chill or freeze it until firmer, then cut it into desired shapes. Do not roll the dough thinner than ¼ inch or the cookie

Mexican Wedding Cakes

Sometimes called Russian tea cakes or butterballs, these crisp little cookies are typically served at festive occasions such as weddings, Christmas, or Cinco de Mayo. But they are good anytime, so don't wait for a holiday to enjoy them. This is a perfect recipe to get the kids involved: Let them roll the cookies in powdered sugar just before serving.

⅓ cup butter or buttery spread, at room temperature (but not melted)
½ cup sugar
1 tablespoon pure vanilla extract
2 teaspoons grated lemon zest
1½ cups Gluten-Free Flour Blend (page 27)
¼ cup cornstarch
¼ cup nut meal (almond, hazelnut, or pecan)
¾ teaspoon xanthan gum
¼ teaspoon salt
⅛ teaspoon baking soda
1 to 2 tablespoons water, if needed
½ cup powdered sugar

1 In a food processor, combine the butter, sugar, vanilla, and lemon zest. Process for 1 minute. Add the flour blend, cornstarch, nut meal, xanthan gum, salt, and baking soda and blend until the mixture forms large clumps or a ball. Scrape down the sides of the bowl with a spatula and blend until the mixture forms large clumps or a ball again. Squeeze a tablespoon of dough between your fingers; it is ready if it holds together without crumbling. Add water—1 tablespoon at a time—only if the dough is crumbly. Shape into a flat disk; refrigerate for 2 hours.

2 Place a rack in the center of the oven. Preheat the oven to 375°F. Line a 9x13-inch (not nonstick) baking sheet with parchment paper. Shape the chilled dough into 32 (1-inch) balls and place on the baking sheet, about 1 inch apart.

3 Bake until the cookies are lightly browned and set, 10 to 12 minutes. Cool for 5 minutes on the baking sheet on a wire rack, then roll the balls in the powdered sugar while still slightly warm. Transfer to a wire rack to cool completely, then roll in powdered sugar again just before serving.

V
Makes 32 cookies
Preparation time: 10 minutes
Refrigeration time: 2½ hours
Baking time: 10-12 minutes

Per cookie:
60 calories;
1g protein;
2g total fat;
1g fiber;
10g carbohydrates;
5mg cholesterol;
41mg sodium

edges may brown too quickly. Chill the shaped cookies for 30 minutes before baking so they don't brown too much before they are done inside.

5 If you have trouble transferring the shaped cookies to the baking sheet after cutting them out, roll the dough while it is on parchment paper or nonstick liners, cut the desired shapes, remove scraps of dough (leaving cutout cookies on the paper or liner), and transfer the paper or liner (cookies and all) to the baking sheet.

6 Use regular butter or buttery spread, not those labeled "whipped" or "diet" or "spreadable" because these versions contain water, which makes the dough too soft to hold the cookie shape.

Gingerbread Cookies

Due to all of the flavorful spices, these crisp cookies produce a heavenly aroma as they bake. If you don't have time to do cutouts, simply shape them into balls, roll in a little granulated sugar, and bake. Crumbled, these cookies make a great cookie-crumb piecrust (you need about 1½ cups of crumbs for a 9-inch piecrust).

¼ cup butter or buttery spread, at room temperature
3 tablespoons molasses (not blackstrap)
½ cup packed brown sugar
1 teaspoon pure vanilla extract
1 cup Gluten-Free Flour Blend (page 27)
¼ cup cornstarch

1 teaspoon xanthan gum
½ teaspoon salt
1 teaspoon baking soda
1½ teaspoons ground cinnamon
1½ teaspoons ground ginger
¼ teaspoon ground nutmeg
¼ teaspoon ground cloves
2 tablespoons water, if needed

V
Makes 16 cookies
Preparation time: 10 minutes
Baking time: 20 to 25 minutes

Per cookie:
90 calories;
1g protein;
3g total fat;
1g fiber;
16g carbohydrates;
8mg cholesterol;
178mg sodium

1 In a food processor, process the butter, molasses, sugar, and vanilla until thoroughly blended. Add all of the remaining ingredients except the water. Process until the dough forms a ball. (Add water, 1 tablespoon at a time, only if the dough fails to form a large ball—or if using an electric mixer instead of a food processor.) Shape the dough into a 1-inch-thick flat disk, wrap tightly, and refrigerate for 1 hour.

2 Place a rack in the center of the oven. Preheat the oven to 325°F. Line a 9x13-inch rimmed baking sheet (not nonstick) with parchment paper.

3 With your hands, shape the dough into 1-inch balls and place on the baking sheet. Flatten each ball slightly with the bottom of a wet spatula.

4 Bake until the cookies start to brown on the bottom, 20 to 25 minutes. Cool the cookies on the baking sheet for 5 minutes, then use a thin metal spatula to transfer them to the wire rack to cool completely.

Gingerbread People

Make and chill the dough as directed. Working with half of the dough, roll to a ¼-inch thickness between sheets of plastic wrap sprinkled with rice flour to prevent sticking. Keep the remaining dough wrapped and chilled until ready to use. Cut the dough into desired people shapes and transfer to a parchment-lined baking sheet. Bake until the cookies start to brown around the edges, 20 to 25 minutes. Cool cookies on the baking sheet on a wire rack for 10 minutes, then transfer the cookies to the wire rack to cool completely. Repeat with the remaining dough.

Whoopies

Make the Gingerbread Cookies as directed and cool completely. For the filling: In a medium bowl, beat together 1 cup powdered sugar, ¼ cup butter or buttery spread, 1 (3-ounce) package cream cheese or cream cheese alternative, and 2 tablespoons marshmallow crème until very smooth. Spread the filling between 2 cookies of similar size, press gently together, and place on a plate to set up for 10 minutes. This makes 8 Whoopies. Serve immediately.

Whoopies
Per whoopie:
355 calories;
1g protein;
15g total fat;
1g fiber;
49g carbohydrates;
43mg cholesterol;
269mg sodium

Spice Drop Cookies

Drop cookies are free-form cookies that you simply drop onto the baking sheet, rather than shaping or cutting them out. So, they are super easy and quick to make. These spice cookies are perfect for a cold day with a cup of hot tea or coffee.

V

Makes 24 cookies

Preparation time: 10 minutes

Baking time: about 25 minutes

Per cookie:
85 calories;
1g protein;
2g total fat;
1g fiber;
17g carbohydrates;
16mg cholesterol;
74mg sodium

1½ cups Gluten-Free Flour Blend (page 27)
1 teaspoon xanthan gum
½ teaspoon baking soda
¼ teaspoon salt
¼ cup butter or buttery spread, at room temperature
¾ cup packed light brown sugar
⅓ cup granulated sugar
½ teaspoon ground cinnamon
¼ teaspoon ground nutmeg
⅛ teaspoon ground cloves
2 teaspoons pure vanilla extract
1 extra-large egg

1 Place a rack in the center of the oven. Preheat the oven to 350°F. Line a 9x13-inch baking sheet (not nonstick) with parchment paper.

2 In a medium bowl, whisk together the flour blend, xanthan gum, baking soda, and salt until well blended.

3 In a large bowl, beat the butter with an electric mixer on low speed until smooth. Beat in both sugars, the cinnamon, nutmeg, cloves, vanilla, and egg until thoroughly blended. Gradually beat in the flour mixture until no visible streaks remain. Wrap the dough tightly in plastic wrap and chill for 1 hour.

4 Drop 12 tablespoonfuls of dough about 2 inches apart on the baking sheet (or roll into balls with your hands). Bake until firm, 10 to 12 minutes. Cool the cookies for 2 to 3 minutes on the sheet on a wire rack, then use a thin metal spatula to transfer the cookies to the wire rack to cool completely. Repeat with the remaining dough.

Crispy Rice–Peanut Butter Bars with Chocolate Glaze

Until recently, puffed rice cereal was off-limits because of the gluten in barley malt, but now there are several gluten-free brands on the market, so enjoy this childhood favorite often.

⅓ cup butter or buttery spread
⅓ cup creamy peanut butter
1 teaspoon pure vanilla extract
⅛ teaspoon salt
5½ cups miniature marshmallows or
    55 large marshmallows
6 cups gluten-free puffed rice cereal
1 cup gluten-free chocolate chips

Q, V
Makes 24 bars
Preparation time: 10 minutes
Cooling time: 15 minutes

1 Grease a 9x13-inch glass baking dish. In a large saucepan over low heat, stir the butter, peanut butter, vanilla, and salt together until the butters are melted and all the ingredients are well blended. Add the marshmallows and stir until they melt and the mixture is smooth. Remove the saucepan from the heat.

2 Immediately add the cereal to the pan and stir with a spatula or wooden spoon until thoroughly blended together.

3 Press the mixture into the pan so that it is an even thickness. Immediately (while the mixture is hot) sprinkle evenly with the chocolate chips and, using a spatula, spread them evenly across the top as they melt to create the chocolate glaze. Cool completely. With a sharp knife, cut into 24 bars to serve.

Per bar:
125 calories;
2g protein;
7g total fat;
1g fiber;
16g carbohydrates;
7mg cholesterol;
59mg sodium

Chocolate Brownies

These are wickedly decadent—fudgy and chewy. Serve them plain, with a dusting of powdered sugar, or all dressed up with a fudgy frosting. Make sundaes by topping each brownie with vanilla ice cream and chocolate syrup, topped with a maraschino cherry (see photo). If you like nuts and chocolate chips in your brownies, see the variation below.

V

Makes 16 brownies
Preparation time: 10 minutes
Baking time: 20 minutes

Per brownie:
175 calories;
3g protein;
9g total fat;
2g fiber; 24g carbohydrates;
22mg cholesterol;
128mg sodium

Double-Chocolate Nut Brownies
Per brownie:
175 calories;
3g protein;
9g total fat;
2g fiber;
24g carbohydrates;
22mg cholesterol;
128mg sodium

1 cup Gluten-Free Flour Blend (page 27)
½ cup unsweetened natural cocoa powder (not Dutch-processed)
½ teaspoon baking powder
½ teaspoon salt
1 teaspoon xanthan gum

⅓ cup butter or buttery spread, melted and cooled slightly
½ cup sugar
½ cup packed brown sugar
1 large egg, at room temperature
2 teaspoons pure vanilla extract
⅓ cup warm (110°F) water

1 Place a rack in the center of the oven. Preheat the oven to 350°F. Generously grease an 8-inch square nonstick baking pan (gray, not black). In a small bowl, whisk together the flour blend, cocoa, baking powder, salt, and xanthan gum until well blended.

2 In a large bowl, beat the butter and both sugars with an electric mixer on low speed until well combined. Add the egg and vanilla and beat until well combined. With the mixer on low speed, gradually beat in the flour blend mixture and then the warm water, beating until smooth. Spread the batter evenly in the pan.

3 Bake for 20 minutes. Do not overbake, or the brownies won't be fudgy. Cool the brownies in the pan on a wire rack completely before cutting.

Double-Chocolate Nut Brownies
Stir ½ cup chocolate chips and ½ cup chopped walnuts into the batter. Bake as directed.

Lemon Bars

The tart lemon flavor of these scrumptious bars is hard to resist. They are especially pretty with their bright yellow color, topped with the snowy powdered sugar.

Don't use butter, margarine, or buttery spread that is labeled diet, low-calorie, whipped, or spreadable because they have extra water, and that makes the dough too wet for this recipe.

V

Makes 16 bars
Preparation time: 10 minutes
Baking time: 30 to 40 minutes

Crust
- 1 cup Gluten-Free Flour Blend (page 27)
- ¼ cup cold butter or buttery spread
- 1 teaspoon xanthan gum
- ¼ cup powdered sugar
- ⅛ teaspoon salt

Filling
- 1 cup powdered sugar, plus more for dusting
- ½ cup Gluten-Free Flour Blend (page 27)
- 1 whole large egg plus enough yolks to equal ½ cup (about 5 yolks)
- 2 tablespoons lemon juice
- 1 tablespoon grated lemon zest
- ½ teaspoon xanthan gum
- ⅛ teaspoon salt

Per bar:
130 calories;
2g protein;
5g total fat;
1g fiber;
20g carbohydrates;
86mg cholesterol;
73mg sodium

1 Place a rack in the center of the oven. Preheat the oven to 350°F. Grease an 8-inch square nonstick baking pan (gray, not black).

2 Make the crust: In a food processor, process all of the crust ingredients until the texture resembles large peas. Press the crust firmly into the bottom of the pan, placing plastic wrap over it to make it easier to press evenly. Bake until lightly browned, 10 to 15 minutes. Cool slightly on a wire rack.

3 Make the filling: Wipe out the food processor and process all of the filling ingredients until thickened slightly. Spread the filling evenly over the crust. Bake until lightly browned, 20 to 25 minutes. Cool the bars in the pan completely on a wire rack. Dust liberally with powdered sugar just before serving, and then cut into 16 bars.

Seven-Layer Bars

How can we forget this decadent dessert from childhood? We can't . . . but instead of graham crackers (hard to find in gluten-free versions), use crushed gluten-free cookies.

V

Makes 24 bars
**Preparation
time:** 10
minutes
Baking time:
25 to 30
minutes

Per bar:
250 calories;
4g protein;
15g total fat;
2g fiber;
28g
carbohydrates;
17mg
cholesterol;
86mg sodium

½ cup butter or buttery spread, melted
2 cups gluten-free crushed cookie
   crumbs
1 can (14½-ounce) can sweetened
   condensed milk (or see Homemade
   Sweetened Condensed Milk below)
1 cup gluten-free chocolate chips

1 cup gluten-free white chocolate chips
   or butterscotch morsels
1 (7-ounce) package sweetened
   shredded coconut
1 cup chopped walnuts (or your
   favorite nuts)

1 Place a rack in the middle of the oven. Preheat the oven to 350°F. Generously grease a 9x13-inch nonstick baking pan (gray, not black).

2 In a small bowl, stir together the melted butter and crumbs until thoroughly blended. Press the mixture into the bottom of the pan.

3 Spread the sweetened condensed milk evenly over the crumbs. Sprinkle with the chocolate chips, white chocolate chips, coconut, and walnuts. Gently press the mixture down to a uniform thickness with a wet spatula.

4 Bake until the coconut is lightly browned, 25 to 30 minutes. Cool the bars in the pan on a wire rack for 45 minutes. Cut into 24 bars.

Homemade Sweetened Condensed Milk

Some recipes are just better with sweetened condensed milk, but it contains dairy and, sadly, dairy-free versions are not on the market. So, for the dairy intolerant, here is a dairy-free version that makes the equivalent of 1 can. It works best when it is at room temperature.

Makes 15 ounces

½ cup canned coconut milk
1 cup sugar
⅓ cup butter
¼ teaspoon pure vanilla extract

In a small saucepan, combine all of the ingredients and heat over medium heat, stirring constantly, until the butter melts and the sugar dissolves. Refrigerate until ready to use; bring to room temperature before using.

Per 1 ounce:
106 calories; 1g protein; 6g total fat; 0g fiber; 14g carbohydrates; 11mg cholesterol; 43mg sodium

Basic Vanilla Bundt Cake

A basic vanilla cake is an essential in any kitchen, just like the little black dress (LBD) in your closet. Serve it plain or gussied up (see variations below). Bundt pans are especially good for gluten-free cakes because the tube shape allows heat to penetrate more evenly to the center, reducing the risk of falling. Plus, the pan prettily shapes the cake for you. If you like layer cakes, see below. For a lighter-colored cake, use brown rice flour in the Gluten-Free Flour Blend.

½ cup butter or buttery spread, at room temperature
1¼ cups sugar
2 large eggs, at room temperature
2 cups Gluten-Free Flour Blend (page 27)
2 teaspoons baking powder

1 teaspoon xanthan gum
½ teaspoon salt
⅛ teaspoon baking soda
¾ cup water, at room temperature
1 tablespoon grated lemon zest (optional)
2 teaspoons pure vanilla extract

V
Makes 12 slices
Preparation time: 10 minutes
Baking time: 50 to 55 minutes (25 to 30 minutes for 9-inch layer cake)

1 Place a rack in the middle of the oven. Preheat the oven to 350°F. Generously grease a 10-cup nonstick Bundt pan (gray, not black).

2 In a medium bowl, beat the butter and sugar with an electric mixer on medium speed until well blended, about 3 minutes. Beat in the eggs, one at a time, until thick and lemon colored, about 2 minutes.

3 In a separate medium bowl, whisk together the flour blend, baking powder, xanthan gum, salt, and baking soda until well blended. Mix together the water, lemon zest (if using), and vanilla. Gradually beat the flour mixture into the egg mixture on low speed, alternating with the water mixture, beginning and ending with the flour mixture, until the batter thickens slightly, 1 to 2 minutes. Spread the batter evenly in the pan.

4 Bake until the top is golden brown and a toothpick inserted into the center comes out clean, 50 to 55 minutes. Cool the cake in the pan on a wire rack for 5 minutes. Remove the cake from the pan and cool thoroughly on the wire rack.

Vanilla Layer Cakes

Generously grease two 9-inch round nonstick cake pans (gray, not black). Line the bottoms with parchment paper and grease again. Prepare the batter as directed and spread evenly in the pans (a scant 2 cups batter per pan). Bake until the cakes start to pull away from the edges of the pan and a toothpick inserted in the center comes out clean, 25 to 30 minutes. Cool the cakes in the pans for 15 minutes on a wire rack. Gently run a knife around the edge of the pan to loosen the cakes. Invert the cakes onto serving plates, discard the paper, and cool the cakes completely.

Rum Bundt Cake

Reduce the water to ½ cup; add ¼ cup light rum to the water and add following the recipe directions. When baked and cooled, brush the cake with Rum Glaze (page 207) and then drizzle with Vanilla Powdered Sugar Frosting (page 207), using light rum rather than milk as the liquid to prepare the frosting.

Per slice:
250 calories;
2g protein;
9g total fat;
1g fiber; 40g carbohydrates;
52mg cholesterol;
271mg sodium

Rum Bundt Cake
Per slice:
355 calories;
2g protein;
12g total fat;
1g fiber;
60g carbohydrates;
62mg cholesterol;
333mg sodium

Boston Cream Pie

Despite its name, this is not a pie but a double-layer cake with a vanilla custard filling and chocolate frosting on top. If you slightly warm the frosting in the microwave oven, it will drip down the sides as you frost it and look like a professionally baked cake.

V

Makes 12 slices

Preparation time: 10 minutes

Baking time: 30 to 35 minutes

Per slice:
335 calories;
4g protein;
13g total fat;
1g fiber;
54g carbohydrates;
33mg cholesterol;
289mg sodium

1 batch batter from Basic Vanilla Bundt Cake (page 193)
1 cup store-bought vanilla pudding or Vanilla Pudding (page 222)
½ cup Chocolate Powdered Sugar Frosting (page 207), or more if you like lots of frosting

1 Place a rack in the middle of the oven. Preheat the oven to 350°F. Generously grease two 8-inch nonstick round pans (gray, not black) and line the bottoms with parchment paper and grease again.

2 Spread the cake batter evenly in the pans.

3 Bake until the tops of the cakes are golden brown and a toothpick inserted into the center comes out clean, 30 to 35 minutes. Cool the cakes in the pans for 10 minutes. Gently run a knife around the edge of the pan to loosen the cakes. Invert the cakes onto plates, discard the paper, and cool the cakes completely.

4 Spread one cake layer with the pudding. Place the remaining cake layer on top. Gently spread the chocolate frosting on the top cake layer. Cut into 12 slices and serve immediately. Refrigerate leftovers.

Carrot Bundt Cake

This very moist and dense cake is usually served with cream cheese frosting, my favorite way. It makes a big cake, so invite guests to share it with you. To save time, buy the carrots already shredded. For best results, have all the ingredients—especially the butter, eggs, carrots, and milk—at room temperature.

V

Makes 12 slices
Preparation time: 15 minutes
Baking time: 55 to 60 minutes

2½ cups Gluten-Free Flour Blend (page 27), plus more for dusting the pan
2 teaspoons xanthan gum
1½ teaspoons baking soda
1½ teaspoons baking powder
2 teaspoons ground cinnamon
1 teaspoon salt
½ teaspoon ground ginger
3 large eggs, at room temperature
2 cups sugar

⅓ cup canola oil
¾ cup buttermilk or buttermilk substitute, at room temperature (see Buttermilk Substitutes, page 148)
1 tablespoon pure vanilla extract
3 cups finely shredded carrots
1 cup sweetened shredded coconut
1 cup chopped walnuts
1 batch Vanilla Cream Cheese Frosting (page 207)

Per slice:
495 calories;
7g protein;
16g total fat;
4g fiber;
84g carbohydrates;
48mg cholesterol;
418mg sodium

1 Place a rack in the middle of the oven. Preheat the oven to 350°F. Generously grease a 10-cup nonstick Bundt pan (gray, not black). Lightly dust with a little flour blend to prevent sticking and shake out any excess. In a medium bowl, whisk together the first 7 ingredients (flour blend through ginger) until well blended.

2 In a large bowl, beat together the eggs, sugar, oil, buttermilk, and vanilla with an electric mixer on low speed until well blended, about 1 minute. Add the flour mixture gradually until just blended. Stir in the carrots, coconut, and nuts. Spread the batter evenly in the prepared pan.

3 Bake until a toothpick inserted in the center comes out clean, 55 to 60 minutes. Cool the cake in the pan on a wire rack for 15 minutes. Loosen the cake around the edges with a sharp knife and then invert the cake onto the wire rack to cool for 20 minutes. Transfer the cake to a serving plate and cool completely. Frost the cake, then cut into 12 slices and serve. Refrigerate leftovers.

Chocolate Bundt Cake

This is the chocolate cake I grew up with; it was my mother's standby and the first dessert recipe I converted to be gluten-free, so it is near and dear to my heart. Every kitchen needs a good, versatile chocolate cake. Use this one as the base for a variety of chocolate treats—cupcakes, layer cakes, and more. For best results, have all the ingredients—especially the butter, eggs, and milk—at room temperature.

⅔ cup butter or buttery spread, at room temperature
1½ cups packed brown sugar
2 large eggs, at room temperature
2 teaspoons pure vanilla extract
½ cup milk of choice
2⅔ cups Gluten-Free Flour Blend (page 27)

⅔ cup unsweetened natural cocoa powder (not Dutch-processed)
1½ teaspoons xanthan gum
1 teaspoon baking soda
½ teaspoon salt
1 cup hot (120°F) brewed coffee

V
Makes 12 slices
Preparation time: 10 minutes
Baking time: 50 to 55 minutes

Per slice:
295 calories; 4g protein; 12g total fat; 3g fiber; 46g carbohydrates; 61mg cholesterol; 516mg sodium

Chocolate Raspberry Cake
Per slice:
300 calories; 4g protein; 12g total fat; 3g fiber; 47g carbohydrates; 61mg cholesterol; 516mg sodium

1 Preheat the oven to 350°F. Generously grease a 10-cup nonstick Bundt pan (gray, not black).

2 In a large bowl, beat the butter and sugar with an electric mixer on low speed for 2 minutes. Beat in the eggs, vanilla, and milk until well blended.

3 In a medium bowl, whisk the dry ingredients together (flour blend through salt) until well blended. Add the dry ingredients alternately with the hot coffee until the batter is thoroughly blended and slightly thickened. Spread the batter evenly in the pan.

4 Bake until a toothpick inserted into the center comes out clean, 50 to 55 minutes. Cool the cake in the pan on a wire rack for 15 minutes. Loosen the cake around the edges with a sharp knife and then invert the cake onto the wire rack to cool completely.

Chocolate Layer Cakes

Generously grease two 8-inch round nonstick cake pans (gray, not black). Line with parchment paper and grease again. Prepare the batter as directed and divide evenly between the pans. Bake until the cakes start to pull away from the edges of the pan and a toothpick inserted into the center of the cakes comes out clean, 30 to 35 minutes. Cool the pans on a wire rack for 15 minutes. Gently run a knife around the edge of the pan to loosen the cakes. Invert the cakes onto a serving plate, discard the paper, and cool the cakes completely.

Chocolate-Raspberry Cake

Reduce the coffee to ¼ cup. Add 1 cup thoroughly crushed raspberries (frozen or fresh) before spreading the batter in the pan. Bake as directed for Chocolate Bundt Cake.

Basic Flourless Cake

Flourless cakes are my go-to desserts for dinner parties (my chocolate version follows this recipe). They are super simple and taste great no matter how high they rise. This particular cake rises and then falls somewhat for a dense delight. For a lighter texture, separate the eggs and beat the egg whites to soft peaks with an electric mixer. Blend the remaining ingredients (including the yolks) together; then fold the egg whites in by hand. Serve this cake with a dusting of powdered sugar, your favorite frosting, or glazed with melted apricot preserves or orange marmalade.

V

Makes 10 slices
Preparation time: 10 minutes
Baking time: 40 to 45 minutes

Per slice:
355 calories;
8g protein;
26g total fat;
3g fiber;
26g carbohydrates;
100mg cholesterol;
119mg sodium

2 cups whole or slivered almonds or 2¼ cups almond flour/meal
1 cup sugar
½ cup butter or buttery spread, melted, or canola oil
Grated zest of 1 lemon

4 large eggs, at room temperature
1 teaspoon almond extract
¼ teaspoon salt (or ½ teaspoon if using canola oil)

1 Place a rack in the middle of the oven. Preheat the oven to 350°F. Grease a 9-inch nonstick springform pan (gray, not black) and line the bottom with parchment paper.

2 In a food processor, grind the almonds to the consistency of almond flour (or use store-bought almond flour). Add all of the remaining ingredients and blend for 30 to 40 seconds. Stop the machine, scrape down sides of the bowl with a spatula, and blend again for 30 to 40 seconds or until the batter is smooth. Spread the batter evenly in the pan.

3 Bake until a toothpick inserted in the center of the cake comes out clean, 40 to 45 minutes. Cool the cake in the pan on a wire rack for 5 to 10 minutes. Gently run a knife around the edge of the pan to loosen the cake. Remove the outer rim. Cool the cake completely on the wire rack. Gently run a knife around the edge of the pan to loosen the cake. Invert the cake onto a serving plate, discard the paper, and cool the cake completely.

Almond Flour/Meal
Almond flour is sometimes called almond meal, although the two are usually used interchangeably. In my mind, almond flour is ground from slivered or blanched almonds, which produces light-colored flour. Almond meal is ground from the whole almond, so the skins make the flour a darker color. Other experts may disagree on this differentiation, but it works for me. Regardless, both taste about the same. If you can't find almond flour/meal, grind whole nuts in your food processor to as fine a texture as possible without turning them into almond butter.

Flourless Chocolate Cake

Lots of restaurants now serve a flourless chocolate cake, in a variety of versions—some incredibly dense, others a bit lighter. If you like a lighter texture, separate the eggs and beat the egg whites to soft peaks with your electric mixer. Blend the remaining ingredients together, then fold the egg whites in by hand. The cake rises as it bakes, then falls slightly as it cools. Serve it plain or gussied up with powdered sugar and fresh fruit.

2 cups pecans
1 cup packed brown sugar
1 cup large eggs (4 or 5), at room
   temperature
½ cup canola oil
5 tablespoons unsweetened cocoa
   powder (either natural or Dutch-
   process will work)

1 teaspoon pure vanilla extract
⅛ teaspoon salt
   Powdered sugar, for garnish
   Garnishes of your choice: raspberries,
   strawberries, and/or mint sprigs

V
Makes 10 slices
Preparation time: 10 minutes
Baking time: 40 to 45 minutes

Per slice:
340 calories;
5g protein;
28g total fat;
3g fiber;
20g carbohydrates;
103mg cholesterol;
64mg sodium

1 Place a rack in the middle of the oven. Preheat the oven to 350°F. Grease a 9-inch nonstick springform pan (gray, not black) and line the bottom with parchment paper.

2 In a food processor, grind the pecans to the consistency of pecan meal. Add all of the remaining ingredients (except the garnishes) and blend for 30 to 40 seconds. Stop the machine, scrape down sides of the bowl with a spatula, and blend again for 30 to 40 seconds or until the batter is smooth. Spread the batter evenly in the pan.

3 Bake until a toothpick inserted in the center of the cake comes out clean, 40 to 45 minutes. Cool the cake in the pan on a wire rack for 5 to 10 minutes. Gently run a knife around the edge of the pan to loosen the cake. Remove the outer rim. Cool the cake completely on the wire rack. Gently run a knife between pan bottom and cake to loosen. Invert onto a serving plate and remove the parchment paper. Slice and serve with a dusting of powdered sugar plus garnishes of fresh fruit and/or mint sprigs.

Types of Cocoa Powder

Cocoa powder comes in two different forms. One is natural; the other is Dutch-process (sometimes called alkali or European). Cocoa is naturally acidic, so Dutch-process cocoa is simply natural cocoa that has been treated with alkali to reduce the acidity and make the cocoa more alkaline. This increased alkalinity mellows the chocolate flavor but also has important consequences for whether the recipe uses baking powder, baking soda, or both. Baking powder is acidic and baking soda is alkaline, so the cocoa has to balance properly with the other ingredients in your recipe. That's why it is so important to use the type of leavening specified in the recipe or else the baked item might not rise properly. Since my Flourless Chocolate Cake doesn't use baking powder or baking soda, you can use either type of cocoa powder. Natural cocoa will produce a more intense flavor compared to the subtler, mellower flavor from the Dutch-processed cocoa.

Gingerbread

The spices in gingerbread are so flavorful, and the lemon sauce accentuates these flavors. It is the perfect dessert for a crisp autumn day. The aroma of this gingerbread while it bakes is just heavenly, and it keeps nicely on the countertop (tightly covered) for a couple of days, so you can cut off a slice for an anytime snack.

V

Makes 12 slices
Preparation time: 10 minutes
Baking time: 25 to 30 minutes

Per slice:
200 calories;
2g protein;
6g total fat;
1g fiber;
35g carbohydrates;
16mg cholesterol;
260mg sodium

Cake
- ¼ cup canola oil
- ½ cup packed brown sugar
- 1 large egg, at room temperature
- ½ cup molasses
- 1 teaspoon pure vanilla extract
- 1½ cups Gluten-Free Flour Blend (page 27)
- 1 teaspoon baking soda
- 1½ teaspoons ground ginger
- ¾ teaspoon ground cinnamon
- ½ teaspoon ground cloves
- ½ teaspoon salt
- ½ teaspoon xanthan gum
- ½ cup buttermilk or buttermilk substitute (see Buttermilk Substitutes, page 148)

Lemon Sauce
- ¼ cup sugar
- 1 tablespoon cornstarch
- ⅛ teaspoon salt
- ½ cup water
- 2 teaspoons grated lemon zest
- 1 tablespoon lemon juice
- 1 teaspoon canola oil

1 Make the cake: Place a rack in the middle of the oven. Preheat the oven to 350°F. Grease a 9-inch nonstick square pan (gray, not black).

2 In a large bowl with an electric mixer on low speed, beat the oil and brown sugar just until well blended. Beat in the egg, molasses, and vanilla until well blended, about 30 seconds.

3 In a medium bowl, whisk together the flour blend, baking soda, ginger, cinnamon, cloves, salt, and xanthan gum until well blended. Add the flour mixture to the egg mixture alternately with the buttermilk, beginning and ending with the flour mixture. Spread evenly in the prepared pan.

4 Bake until a toothpick inserted into the center of the gingerbread comes out clean, 25 to 30 minutes. Cool the gingerbread in the pan on a wire rack.

5 Make the sauce: In a small pan, whisk together the sugar, cornstarch, and salt until well blended. Gradually stir in the water. Cook, stirring constantly, over medium heat until the mixture thickens. Remove from the heat and stir in the lemon zest, lemon juice, and oil. Cut the gingerbread into 12 pieces, and serve slightly warm, drizzled with the lemon sauce.

Pear-Spice Upside-Down Cake

This comfort food dessert is similar to Pineapple Upside-Down Cake (page 202), but this version uses pears and gingerbread to make a fabulous fall dessert. It is best when fresh pears (especially Bosc) are in season, but you can also use canned pears any time of the year.

½ cup packed brown sugar
1 firm, ripe Bosc pear, peeled, cored, and cut into 16 thin wedges
1 batch batter from Gingerbread recipe (opposite)

1 Place a rack in the middle of the oven. Preheat the oven to 350°F. Generously grease a 10-inch nonstick pie pan (gray, not black). Sprinkle the bottom evenly with the sugar and layer the pear slices evenly over the sugar in a decorative pinwheel design.

2 Spread the batter evenly over the pears in the pan.

3 Bake until the top of the cake is firm and a toothpick inserted into the center comes out clean, 35 to 40 minutes. Cool the cake in the pan for 10 minutes. Invert the pan onto a serving plate, remove the pan, and cool the cake thoroughly before cutting into 10 slices.

V

Makes 10 slices
Preparation time: 10 minutes
Baking time: 35 to 40 minutes

Per serving:
250 calories;
2g protein;
6g total fat;
1g fiber;
50g carbohydrates;
19mg cholesterol;
263mg sodium

Pineapple Upside-Down Cake

This cake is as down-home as they come, but it never fails to please with its simple yet straightforward flavors. If you're not a fan of maraschino cherries, add fresh raspberries to the center of each pineapple ring after the cake is baked and cooled, just before serving.

V

Makes 2 (10-inch) cakes (16 slices)

Preparation time: 10 minutes

Baking time: 35 to 40 minutes

Per serving:
455 calories;
2g protein;
8g total fat;
3g fiber;
98g carbohydrates;
23mg cholesterol;
226mg sodium

1½ cups packed brown sugar
10 pineapple slices (from a 20-ounce can), well drained
10 maraschino cherries
1 batch batter from Basic Vanilla Bundt Cake (page 193)

1 Place a rack in the middle of the oven. Preheat the oven to 350°F. Generously grease two 9-inch nonstick (gray, not black) round pans. Sprinkle the bottom of each of the pans with ¾ cup of the brown sugar. Arrange 5 pineapple slices on the sugar in each pan and place a cherry in the center of each slice.

2 Spread the batter evenly over the pineapple slices in the pans.

3 Bake until the tops of the cakes are golden brown and a toothpick inserted into the center comes out clean, 35 to 40 minutes. Cool the cakes in the pans for 10 minutes. Invert the pans onto serving plates, remove the pans, and cool the cakes thoroughly before cutting into slices.

❨ This recipe makes two cakes. If you don't need two cakes, halve the brown sugar and pineapple and bake half the batter (about 2 cups) as Pineapple Upside-Down Cake. Bake the remaining half of the batter for 25 to 30 minutes in a 9-inch round nonstick pan (gray, not black) that has been greased, lined with parchment paper, and greased again. Cool the cake in the pan for 10 minutes. Gently run a knife around the edge of the pan to loosen the cake. Invert the cake onto a plate, and cool the cake thoroughly. Freeze the cooled cake (tightly wrapped). Thaw in the refrigerator or on the countertop and serve as you would any single-layer cake.

Spice Bundt Cake

This intensely flavored spice cake continues to be one of my most popular recipes. I serve it in the fall and winter, when the lovely spice aromas waft through the house and seem just right for the season, but you can make it anytime. For best results, have all the ingredients—especially the milk, butter, and eggs—at room temperature.

3 cups Gluten-Free Flour Blend (page 27), plus more for dusting the pan	1½ cups milk of choice, at room temperature
1½ teaspoons xanthan gum	2 cups packed brown sugar
1½ teaspoons baking soda	¾ cup butter or buttery spread, at room temperature
1 teaspoon salt	½ cup molasses (not blackstrap)
1½ tablespoons ground ginger	1½ teaspoons pure vanilla extract
1 tablespoon ground cinnamon	2 large eggs, at room temperature
½ teaspoon ground nutmeg	
¼ teaspoon ground cloves	

1 Place a rack in the middle of the oven. Preheat the oven to 325°F. Generously grease a 10-cup nonstick Bundt pan (gray, not black) and dust lightly with the flour blend.

2 In a large bowl, whisk together the flour blend, xanthan gum, baking soda, salt, ginger, cinnamon, nutmeg, and cloves until well blended.

3 In a medium heavy saucepan over medium heat, bring the milk and sugar just to a boil. Remove from the heat and stir in the butter, molasses, and vanilla until the butter is melted.

4 With an electric mixer on low speed, beat the butter-sugar mixture into the flour mixture until thoroughly blended, about 30 seconds. Beat in the eggs until well blended and the mixture thickens slightly, about 30 seconds. Spread the batter evenly in the pan.

5 Bake until a toothpick inserted in the center of the cake comes out clean, 55 to 60 minutes. Cool the cake in the pan on a wire rack for 5 minutes. Loosen the cake around the edges with a sharp knife and then invert the cake onto the wire rack to cool completely.

Spice Layer Cake
Generously grease two 8-inch round nonstick cake pans (gray, not black). Line the bottoms with parchment paper and grease again. Prepare the batter as directed and divide evenly in the pans. Bake until the cakes start to pull away from the edges of the pans and a toothpick inserted into the center of the cakes comes out clean, 30 to 35 minutes. Cool the pans on a wire rack for 15 minutes. Gently run a knife around the edge of the pans to loosen the cakes. Invert the cakes onto serving plates, discard the paper, and cool the cakes completely.

Apple-Spice Cake
Stir 1 cup peeled, grated Granny Smith apples and ½ cup chopped walnuts into the batter before spreading it in the pan. Bake as directed.

V

Makes 12 slices
Preparation time: 10 minutes
Baking time: 55 to 60 minutes

Per slice:
325 calories;
3g protein;
13g total fat;
1g fiber; 51g carbohydrates;
63mg cholesterol;
490mg sodium

Apple-Spice Cake
Per slice:
360 calories;
4g protein;
16g total fat;
2g fiber;
53g carbohydrates;
63mg cholesterol;
490mg sodium

Red Velvet Cupcakes with Vanilla Cream Cheese Frosting

Now you can enjoy this wildly popular treat, just like everybody else. This recipe makes dainty little cupcakes with flat tops (easier to frost), and their brilliant red color is so inviting. Arrange them on a pedestal cake stand for maximum effect when serving your guests. If you like, feel free to vary the frosting.

1 cup Gluten-Free Flour Blend (page 27)

2 tablespoons unsweetened cocoa powder

¾ teaspoon xanthan gum

¼ teaspoon baking soda

¼ teaspoon salt

¾ cup sugar

½ cup butter or buttery spread, melted and cooled slightly

2 large whole eggs, at room temperature

1 teaspoon pure vanilla extract

1 tablespoon red food coloring

½ cup water, at room temperature

1 batch Vanilla Cream Cheese Frosting (page 207)

V
Makes 12 cupcakes
Preparation time: 10 minutes
Baking time: 25 to 30 minutes

1 Preheat the oven to 350°F. Grease a 12-cup standard nonstick muffin pan (gray, not black) or line with paper liners.

2 In a small mixing bowl, whisk together the flour blend, cocoa, xanthan gum, baking soda, and salt until well blended.

3 In a medium bowl, beat the sugar and butter with an electric mixer on low speed until well blended. Beat in the eggs, one at a time, until well blended. Add the vanilla and food coloring to the water. With the mixer on low speed, beat in one-third of the flour mixture at a time alternating with the water, beginning and ending with the flour mixture. Spoon ¼ cup of the batter into each liner.

4 Bake until the cupcakes are firm and a toothpick inserted into the center comes out clean, 25 to 30 minutes. Cool the cupcakes in the pan on a wire rack for 10 minutes. Transfer the cupcakes to the wire rack to cool completely. Frost and serve.

Per frosted cupcake:
325 calories;
3g protein;
16g total fat;
1g fiber;
43g carbohydrates;
37mg cholesterol;
135mg sodium

Toasted Coconut Cupcakes with Fluffy White Frosting

Coconut lovers will adore this decadent little cupcake, piled high with fluffy white frosting and crunchy toasted coconut. They are best served on the same day they're made, while the frosting remains soft. You can also offer visual variety by using other frostings or glazes.

V

Makes 24 cupcakes
Preparation time: 10 minutes
Baking time: 50 to 60 minutes

Per frosted cupcake:
200 calories;
2g protein;
8g total fat;
1g fiber;
31g carbohydrates;
26mg cholesterol;
134mg sodium

½ cup butter or buttery spread, at room temperature
1¼ cups sugar
2 large eggs, at room temperature
2 cups Gluten-Free Flour Blend (page 27)
1 teaspoon xanthan gum
½ teaspoon baking powder
½ teaspoon baking soda

½ teaspoon salt
1 tablespoon lemon juice
1 teaspoon coconut extract
1¼ cups canned coconut milk (may use light version)
1 batch Fluffy White Frosting (opposite)
¾ cup sweetened shredded coconut, toasted, for topping

1 Place a rack in the middle of the oven. Preheat the oven to 325°F. Line a 12-cup standard nonstick muffin pan (gray, not black) with paper liners. (Plan to repeat this step for the second batch of 12 cupcakes or use two muffin pans.)

2 In a large bowl, beat together the butter and sugar for 2 minutes with an electric mixer on medium speed. Reduce the speed to low and beat in the eggs, one at a time, until well blended.

3 In a medium bowl, whisk together the flour blend, xanthan gum, baking powder, baking soda, and salt until well blended. Add the lemon juice and coconut extract to the coconut milk. With the mixer on low speed, beat in the flour mixture alternately with the coconut milk mixture, beginning and ending with the flour mixture. Beat just until the batter thickens slightly. Spoon ¼ cup of the batter into each liner.

4 Bake until the cupcakes are golden brown and a toothpick inserted into the center comes out clean, 25 to 30 minutes. Cool the cupcakes in the pan on a wire rack for 10 minutes. Transfer the cupcakes to the wire rack to cool completely. Repeat with the remaining batter. Frost the cupcakes and immediately sprinkle each cupcake with 1½ teaspoons toasted coconut before the frosting sets up. Serve on the same day.

Frostings

A dinner guest once watched me make a basic powdered sugar frosting and remarked, "Why aren't you measuring the ingredients?" I had always made frosting this way, just like my mother did. Here, I have measured everything for you so that you can make your own frostings without the guessing game.

Vanilla Powdered Sugar Frosting

In a medium bowl, mix 2 cups powdered sugar, ½ teaspoon pure vanilla extract, and ⅛ teaspoon salt. Add ¼ cup softened butter or buttery spread and 2 tablespoons milk or water and stir with a spatula until smooth. For a stiffer frosting, add powdered sugar, 1 tablespoon at a time. For a softer frosting, add milk or water, 1 tablespoon at a time. For a shinier frosting, replace 2 teaspoons of milk with 1 teaspoon corn syrup and 1 teaspoon canola oil.

Frosting for an 8- or 9-inch single-layer cake (divide by your number of servings) or 12 cupcakes (divide by 12): 1365 calories; 1g protein; 47g total fat; 0g fiber; 48g carbohydrates; 128mg cholesterol; 752mg sodium

Chocolate Powdered Sugar Frosting

Add 2 tablespoons unsweetened cocoa powder to the Vanilla Powdered Sugar Frosting. For a shinier frosting, replace 2 teaspoons of milk with 1 teaspoon corn syrup and 1 teaspoon canola oil.

Frosting for an 8- or 9-inch single-layer cake (divide by your number of servings) or 12 cupcakes (divide by 12): 1405 calories; 4g protein; 48g total fat; 3g fiber; 246g carbohydrates; 128mg cholesterol; 757mg sodium

Fluffy White Frosting

In a double boiler over simmering water, combine 3 large egg whites, 1¼ cups sugar, ¼ teaspoon cream of tartar, and 3 tablespoons cold water. Beat with a handheld electric mixer for 7 minutes, or until glossy and smooth. Remove from the heat, and stir in 1 teaspoon pure vanilla extract. Use immediately, before the frosting starts to set.

Frosting for an 8- or 9-inch 2-layer cake (divide by your number of servings): 1020 calories; 11g protein; 0g total fat; 0g fiber; 251g carbohydrates; 0mg cholesterol; 169mg sodium

Vanilla Cream Cheese Frosting

In a medium bowl with an electric mixer on low speed, beat 3 ounces softened, reduced-fat cream cheese or cream cheese alternative, 2 cups powdered sugar, 2 tablespoons milk or water, and 1 teaspoon pure vanilla extract together until well blended and smooth.

Frosting for an 8- or 9-inch single-layer cake (divide by your number of servings) or 12 cupcakes (divide by 12): 1586 calories; 10g protein; 67g total fat; 0g fiber; 243g carbohydrates; 193mg cholesterol; 1092mg sodium

Chocolate Glaze

In a 2-cup glass measuring cup, stir together 3 tablespoons unsweetened cocoa powder, 1 tablespoon butter or buttery spread, and ⅓ cup corn syrup. Microwave on High power until smooth, 1½ to 2 minutes, stirring twice during cooking. Immediately pour over cooled cake, allowing glaze to run down sides. Cool cake for 30 minutes before serving.

Glaze for a Bundt cake (divide by your number of servings): 470 calories; 4g protein; 13g total fat; 5g fiber; 92g carbohydrates; 31mg cholesterol; 257mg sodium

Rum Glaze

In a 1-quart glass measuring cup, microwave ¼ cup packed light brown sugar and 3 tablespoons butter or buttery spread on High power until bubbly (check after 1 minute). Stir twice during cooking. Whisk in 1 tablespoon light rum or lemon juice and ⅓ cup powdered sugar until smooth. Immediately pour over cake. Cool cake for 30 minutes before serving.

Glaze for a Bundt cake (divide by your number of servings): 700 calories; 0g protein; 35g total fat; 0g fiber; 93g carbohydrates; 93mg cholesterol; 373mg sodium

Basic Piecrust (Double Crust) and Three Pies

Gluten-free piecrusts may seem challenging to beginners, but they are not impossible. This one rolls out beautifully and is very pliable. With a little practice, you'll make pies like a professional baker. The double-crust version works best with stone fruit fillings like cherries, peaches, or apricots. If you only need a single crust, freeze the remaining half (tightly wrapped) for another pie. Following this, see all of the different pies you can make with this basic piecrust recipe.

V

Makes 1 (9-inch) pie (6 slices)
Preparation time: 15 to 20 minutes
Chilling time: 1 hour
Baking time: 40 to 45 minutes

Per slice of basic pie crust, no filling:
390 calories;
3g protein;
22g total fat;
2g fiber;
48g carbohydrates;
26mg cholesterol;
226mg sodium

1 cup Gluten-Free Flour Blend (page 27)
⅔ cup tapioca flour
½ cup sweet rice flour
1 tablespoon sugar
¾ teaspoon xanthan gum
½ teaspoon salt
½ cup shortening
2 tablespoons butter or buttery spread, at room temperature
¼ cup milk of choice
1 large egg, beaten with 1 tablespoon water, for egg wash

1 Place the dry ingredients (flour blend through salt), shortening, and butter in a food processor. Process until the mixture resembles large peas. With the motor running, add the milk and process until the dough forms a ball (or large clumps). Remove the lid, break up the clumps with a spatula, and process until a ball forms again. If it doesn't form a ball, add a tablespoon of water and process again.

2 Flatten the dough to two 1-inch disks, wrap tightly in plastic wrap, and chill for 1 hour so the liquids are well distributed throughout the dough. When ready to bake, arrange oven racks in the bottom and middle positions of the oven. Preheat the oven to 375°F.

3 Massage one of the disks of dough between your hands until it feels the same temperature as your skin and is pliable, which makes it easier to handle. (Keep remaining dough wrapped tightly to avoid drying out.) Roll the dough to a 10-inch circle between two pieces of heavy-duty plastic wrap. (Use a damp paper towel between the countertop and the plastic wrap to prevent slipping.) Move the rolling pin from the center of the dough toward the outer edge, moving around the circle clockwise, to ensure uniform thickness of the piecrust.

4 Remove the top plastic wrap and invert the crust, centering it over a 9-inch nonstick pie pan (gray, not black). Remove the remaining plastic wrap and press the dough into place. If the dough is hard to handle or breaks, press the entire bottom crust in place with your fingers, leaving a 1-inch overhang of dough all the way around the pie pan. For a single-crust pie, proceed to Step 5. For a double-crust pie, add the filling and proceed to Step 6.

5 For a single-crust pie with a no-bake filling: Flute the edges of the dough decoratively. Use fork tines to gently prick a few holes in the bottom of the crust so it bakes evenly. Bake for 15 minutes on the lower oven rack so the bottom of the crust browns. Move the pie to the next highest oven rack and bake for another 10 to 15 minutes, or until the crust is nicely browned. Cover the crust loosely with aluminum foil if the edges brown too much. Cool the crust completely on a wire rack before adding the filling.

6 For a double-crust pie with a baked filling: Massage the remaining disk of dough between your hands until it feels the same temperature as your skin and is pliable. Roll the dough out as directed in Step 3. Invert and center the dough on the filled bottom crust. Don't remove the top plastic wrap until the piecrust is centered. Shape a decorative edge around the rim of the pie pan (see Tips for Gluten-Free Piecrust below). Brush the crust with beaten egg for a glossier crust. Prick the top crust several times with a fork to allow steam to escape. Sprinkle with sugar. Place on a nonstick baking sheet. Bake for 15 minutes on the lower oven rack so the bottom crust browns. Move the pie to the next highest oven rack and bake for another 25 to 35 minutes—or until the crust is nicely browned and the filling is bubbling. Cover the pie loosely with aluminum foil if the edges brown too much. Cool the pie completely on a wire rack before cutting.

Cherry Pie

In a large bowl, stir together 2 (14½-ounce) cans (about 3 cups) well-drained tart red cherries, ⅔ cup sugar, 1 tablespoon quick-cooking tapioca, and 1 teaspoon almond extract. Let stand to thicken while preparing the piecrust. Place the cherry filling in the prepared crust. Proceed as directed in Step 6.

Per slice: 525 calories; 4g protein; 22g total fat; 3g fiber; 82g carbohydrates; 26mg cholesterol; 231mg sodium

Peach Pie

In a large bowl, stir together 3 cups sliced peeled fresh peaches (about 3 large), ½ cup sugar, 2 tablespoons potato starch, 1 teaspoon almond extract, and ¼ teaspoon salt. Just before placing the peaches in the prepared piecrust, drain all but 2 tablespoons juice. Place the peaches in the prepared crust. Proceed as directed in Step 6.

Per slice: 550 calories; 4g protein; 22g total fat; 4g fiber; 88g carbohydrates; 26mg cholesterol; 231mg sodium

Pumpkin Pie

Arrange oven racks in the bottom and middle positions of the oven. Preheat the oven to 425°F. In a large bowl, stir together 1 (15-ounce) can pumpkin puree (not pumpkin pie filling), ¾ cup sugar, 2 teaspoons pumpkin pie spice, 1 teaspoon ground cinnamon, ¾ teaspoon salt, 2 large eggs, and 1 cup milk of choice. Pour into a prepared bottom piecrust that has been chilled for 15 minutes. Bake for 15 minutes on the lowest oven rack. Move the pie to the middle rack; reduce the heat to 350°F and bake until a knife inserted at the center comes out clean, 40 to 50 minutes. Cover the edges of the crust with aluminum foil if it starts to brown too much. Cool the pie for 2 hours on a wire rack. Serve immediately or refrigerate.

Per slice: 355 calories; 5g protein; 13g total fat; 3g fiber; 58g carbohydrates; 69mg cholesterol; 421mg sodium

Tips for Gluten-Free Piecrust

The method for making gluten-free piecrusts differs in many ways from gluten-containing piecrusts—primarily because handling our dough does not make it tougher, because there is no gluten.

1 Room temperature—rather than cold—butter makes the crust easier to handle and prevents breakage.

2 Breaks and tears can be patched with scraps of dough, or simply press the tear together with your fingers to seal it.

3 Roll the dough to a uniform thickness so that it cooks and browns evenly. This is especially important on the bottom crust and around the rim of the piecrust. Thinner dough heats up and then browns more quickly than thicker dough, so take the time to make the dough uniformly thick throughout the pie. (To see piecrust being made, see Pie Crust 101 under Videos at www.glutenfree101.com, and see How to Flute a Piecrust on page 210.)

4 Keep a few piecrusts in the freezer for those days when you are in a hurry. Make an extra batch of dough, shape two piecrusts into pie pans, and freeze, tightly covered. Then you have your own—much less expensive—piecrusts that are ready for filling at a moment's notice.

Ice Cream Pie

Perhaps one of the simplest pies to make—all you need is a crust and a carton of ice cream, which makes it perfect for beginners. Try different combinations, such as a chocolate crust with chocolate ice cream; or a vanilla cookie crust with strawberry or peach ice cream; or a ginger cookie crust with lemon sorbet. My son's favorite is a chocolate crust with mint chocolate chip ice cream (drizzled with chocolate sauce) to make our own version of grasshopper pie. The options are endless, so use your imagination. Try different store-bought gluten-free sauces and sprinkle with chopped nuts or whipped topping.

V

Makes 10 slices
Preparation time: 10 minutes
Freezing time: 6 hours

Per slice:
220 calories;
3g protein;
13g total fat;
1g fiber;
25g carbohydrates;
24mg cholesterol;
192mg sodium

1 quart ice cream of choice, softened but not melted
1 (9-inch) cookie crumb crust (see Flourless Piecrusts for No-Bake Pies, page 212), frozen
Toppings: chocolate syrup, caramel sauce, or sliced fresh fruit such as strawberries (optional)

1 With a spatula, gently press the ice cream into the frozen piecrust in an even layer. Freeze the pie for at least 6 hours.

2 Let the pie stand at room temperature for 10 minutes before cutting into slices. Serve plain or topped with your choice of toppings.

How to Flute a Piecrust

Shaping the edges of a piecrust in a decorative design is called "fluting," and there are many ways to do it. My favorite way is to place my thumb and index finger on one side of the ridge of dough and my index finger on the other side, pressing them together to form a "U" shape and then continuing around the whole rim of the pie to form multiple "U" shapes.

Pear-Almond Tart

Tart pans with removable sides do the work for you; their fluted border makes a lovely decorative edge for a professional look with no extra effort on your part. Look for them in kitchen stores or online, then make this scrumptious tart that will look like it was made by a professional baker.

Crust
- ½ cup Gluten-Free Flour Blend (page 27)
- ½ cup gluten-free yellow cornmeal
- 5 tablespoons sliced almonds
- 2 tablespoons sugar
- ½ teaspoon xanthan gum
- ¼ teaspoon ground cinnamon
- ¼ teaspoon salt
- ¼ cup butter or buttery spread
- ¼ cup milk of choice

Filling
- 2 medium Bosc or Anjou pears, peeled, cored, and halved lengthwise
- 2 large eggs, at room temperature
- ½ cup plus 2 tablespoons sugar
- ⅓ cup Gluten-Free Flour Blend (page 27)
- ¼ cup milk of choice
- 1 tablespoon butter or buttery spread, melted
- 1 teaspoon almond extract
- ⅛ teaspoon salt
  Whipped topping or vanilla ice cream (optional)

V

Makes 10 slices

Preparation time: 20 minutes

Baking time: 35 to 40 minutes

Per slice:
255 calories; 4g protein; 11g total fat; 2g fiber; 37g carbohydrates; 53mg cholesterol; 164mg sodium

1 Make the crust: Place racks in the bottom and next-to-bottom positions of the oven. Preheat the oven to 400°F. In a food processor, process the flour blend, cornmeal, 4 tablespoons of the almonds, sugar, xanthan gum, cinnamon, and salt until the nuts are finely ground. Add the butter and pulse until pea-size balls form. With the motor running, add the milk and process until a soft dough forms. Press the dough evenly into the bottom and one inch up the sides of a 9-inch springform pan or a tart pan (with a fluted, removable side). Place the pan on a 9x13-inch rimmed baking sheet.

2 Make the filling: Cut each pear half into ¼-inch wedges and arrange attractively in a concentric circle on the crust. In a medium bowl, beat the eggs, ½ cup of the sugar, the flour blend, milk, butter, almond extract, and salt until well blended, then pour evenly over the pears. Sprinkle with the remaining 1 tablespoon almonds and the remaining 2 tablespoons sugar.

3 Bake for 15 minutes on the bottom rack of the oven, then move the tart to the next-to-bottom rack, reduce the heat to 350°F, and bake until the top is golden brown and set, 20 to 25 minutes. Cool the tart on a wire rack, then remove the side and cut into slices. Serve with whipped topping or ice cream, if you wish.

Flourless Piecrusts for No-Bake Pies

Sometimes you don't want or need a flaky pastry crust for your pie, so use the following crusts for wonderful variety, texture, and taste. We typically use these crusts for single-crust pies filled with no-bake puddings, custards, or fruit. Some of these crusts require no prebaking, while others do. But, once baked, the crust should not be baked again because it will likely burn. The nutritional information for each crust is based on the pie being cut into 6 slices. Each crust is vegetarian.

Chocolate–Peanut Butter Crust

Grease a 9-inch pie pan. In a small heavy saucepan, stir together ¾ cup chocolate chips and 2 tablespoons peanut butter over low heat until melted. Remove from the heat and stir in 1 cup gluten-free crisp brown rice cereal until well blended. With a wet spatula, spread the crust in the prepared pie pan. Chill until firm. Add a no-bake filling of choice, such as a custard or pudding, and chill until set. Bring to room temperature before serving for easier cutting.

Per slice of crust: 175 calories; 3g protein; 11g total fat; 2g fiber; 21g carbohydrates; 0mg cholesterol; 28mg sodium

Coconut Crust

Grease a 9-inch pie pan. In a medium bowl, stir together 1½ cups shredded coconut, 2 tablespoons soft butter or buttery spread, 1 tablespoon cornstarch, 1 teaspoon pure vanilla extract, and ¼ teaspoon salt until thoroughly blended. With a wet spatula, press the mixture onto the bottom and up the sides of the prepared pie pan. Bake on the middle rack of a preheated 325°F oven until lightly toasted, 10 to 15 minutes. Watch carefully to avoid burning. Cool thoroughly on a wire rack, then add a no-bake filling of choice, such as a custard or pudding, and chill until set.

Per slice of crust: 112 calories; 1g protein; 11g total fat; 2g fiber; 4g carbohydrates; 10mg cholesterol; 132mg sodium

Cookie Crumb Crust

Grease a 9-inch microwaveable pie pan. In a food processor, process 1½ cups finely crushed gluten-free cookie crumbs, ¼ cup butter or buttery spread at room temperature, ¼ cup finely ground nuts of choice, and 2 tablespoons sugar. Press into the prepared pie pan. Microwave on High power until the crust looks firm, 2 to 3 minutes. Add a no-bake filling of choice, such as a custard, pudding, or fresh fruit, and chill until ready to serve. You may use chocolate, vanilla, or lemon cookies to make this crust.

Per slice of crust: 200 calories; 3g protein; 13g total fat; 1g fiber; 20g carbohydrates; 21mg cholesterol; 140mg sodium

Apple Crisp

This crisp is especially wonderful in autumn, when apples are at their best. You can substitute pears or peaches in this easy home-style dessert. My version is sweetened with fruit juice and maple syrup, which is a very healthy, delicious choice. I peeled the apples for this version, but when I make it for my family I usually leave the peels on to retain their nutrients and fiber.

Filling

- 3 cups peeled, sliced apples (Gala, Granny Smith, Red Delicious, or a mixture)
- ¼ cup maple syrup (or more if apples are tart)
- 1 tablespoon lemon juice
- ½ teaspoon cornstarch
- 1 teaspoon pure vanilla extract
- ¼ teaspoon ground cinnamon
- ¼ teaspoon salt

Topping

- ¼ cup gluten-free rolled oats*
- ¼ cup Gluten-Free Flour Blend (page 27)
- ¼ cup finely chopped nuts of choice
- ¼ teaspoon ground cinnamon
- ¼ teaspoon salt
- 2 tablespoons maple syrup
- 2 tablespoons butter or buttery spread, melted
- 1 teaspoon pure vanilla extract
  Whipped topping or ice cream (optional)

1 Place a rack in the middle of the oven. Preheat the oven to 375°F. Grease an 8-inch square nonstick baking pan (gray, not black).

2 Make the filling: In a large bowl, stir together all of the filling ingredients until well blended. Spread evenly in the pan.

3 Make the topping: In a small bowl, stir together the oats, flour blend, nuts, cinnamon, and salt until well blended. With a spatula, stir in the maple syrup, butter, and vanilla until the dry ingredients are thoroughly coated, then sprinkle this mixture evenly over the apples. Cover with aluminum foil.

4 Bake for 25 minutes. Uncover; bake until the topping is crisp and browned, about 15 minutes longer. Cool the crisp in the pan on a wire rack for 15 minutes. Serve warm, topped with whipped topping or vanilla ice cream, if desired.

V
Makes 6 servings
Preparation time: 15 minutes
Baking time: 40 minutes

Per serving:
190 calories;
2g protein;
8g total fat;
2g fiber;
31g carbohydrates;
10mg cholesterol;
131mg sodium

❨ *Check with your physician before eating gluten-free oats.

Cherry-Almond Clafouti

Clafouti is a French dessert consisting of fruit baked in a creamy custard. It is perfect for beginning cooks because it is extremely easy to prepare and delicious to eat, no matter how it turns out. It can be made at any time of the year, varying the fruit to match the season and adjusting the amount of sugar up or down depending on the fruit's sweetness. And it is a great way to try out different gluten-free flours (see Clafouti: The Perfect Dessert for Experimenting below). Dusted with a little powdered sugar, it looks like a professional dessert . . . making you look like a star!

V
Makes 4 servings
Preparation time: 10 minutes
Baking time: 25 to 35 minutes

Per serving:
290 calories;
5g protein;
10g total fat;
2g fiber;
48g carbohydrates;
186mg cholesterol;
110mg sodium

1 (15-ounce) can tart red cherries, well drained
2 large eggs, at room temperature
⅓ cup milk of choice, at room temperature
2 tablespoons butter or buttery spread, melted and cooled
1 teaspoon almond extract
⅓ cup almond flour/meal or Gluten-Free Flour Blend (page 27)
½ cup plus 1 tablespoon sugar
¼ teaspoon salt
1 tablespoon sliced almonds
2 tablespoons powdered sugar

1 Place a rack in the middle of the oven. Preheat the oven to 375°F. Grease an 8-inch baking dish with 2-inch sides. Spread the cherries evenly on the bottom.

2 In a blender, process the eggs, milk, butter, and almond extract until very smooth. With the blender running, gradually add the almond flour/meal, ½ cup of the sugar, and the salt and process until very smooth, about 1 minute. Pour the batter over the cherries and sprinkle with the almonds and remaining 1 tablespoon sugar.

3 Bake until the top is puffy and the nuts are golden brown, 25 to 35 minutes. Remove from the oven and dust with the powdered sugar. Serve immediately.

Clafouti: The Perfect Dessert for Experimenting

Clafouti is the perfect dessert to try various gluten-free flours. Instead of almond flour/meal or Gluten-Free Flour Blend, use the same amount of flour made from millet, buckwheat, or gluten-free oats.

This dessert is also easily baked and served in individual (3- or 4-ounce) ramekins. Assemble the clafouti ahead and refrigerate, and then bake it while you eat dinner. The lovely aroma from your kitchen will tantalize your guests, and it is so easy to just place each warm ramekin on a small plate and serve (without going through the last-minute process of cutting and plating).

Cherry Cobbler

Cobblers are very simple to make, so that may be the reason my mother served them often—filled with fresh seasonal fruit. In fact, at least one of those cobblers was always made after our yearly trek to the cherry tree of a generous neighbor. The catch was that we had to pick the cherries ourselves. Then, after we got home, we had to pit the cherries (by hand, of course). But all that work was worth it, and we looked forward to those cobblers. Substitute your own seasonal fruit—perhaps fresh apricots or peaches—in this family favorite.

Filling
- 2 (14½-ounce) cans tart red cherries, well drained (reserve ¼ cup juice)
- ⅔ cup sugar
- 1 tablespoon quick-cooking tapioca
- 1 teaspoon almond extract

Topping
- 1 cup Gluten-Free Flour Blend (page 27)
- ½ cup plus 1 tablespoon sugar
- 1 teaspoon baking powder
- ½ teaspoon xanthan gum
- ¼ teaspoon salt
- ¼ cup cold butter or buttery spread
- 1 large egg
- 1 teaspoon grated lemon zest
- ⅓ cup buttermilk or buttermilk substitute (see Buttermilk Substitutes, page 148)
- 1 teaspoon pure vanilla extract

V

Makes 6 servings
Preparation time: 15 minutes
Baking time: 35 to 40 minutes

1 Place a rack in the middle of the oven. Preheat the oven to 375°F. Grease an 8-inch square nonstick baking pan (gray, not black).

2 Make the filling: In a medium bowl, stir together the cherries, reserved cherry juice, sugar, tapioca, and almond extract. Spread evenly in the prepared pan and let stand while preparing the topping.

3 Make the topping: In a medium bowl, whisk together the flour blend, ½ cup of the sugar, baking powder, xanthan gum, and salt until well blended. With a pastry cutter or fork, mash the butter into the dry ingredients until the texture resembles green peas. In a small bowl, whisk together the egg, lemon zest, buttermilk, and vanilla until smooth, and then stir it into the dry ingredients until just mixed. Drop by tablespoonfuls onto the filling; the topping will spread out as it bakes. Sprinkle the topping with the remaining 1 tablespoon sugar.

4 Bake until the topping is browned, 35 to 40 minutes. Cool the cobbler in the pan on a wire rack for 15 minutes. Serve warm.

Peach Cobbler

Grease a 7x11-inch nonstick baking pan (gray, not black). In a large bowl, stir together 3 cups peeled sliced fresh peaches (about 3 large) and 1 tablespoon sugar. Let stand for 30 minutes. Drain. Combine ½ cup sugar, 2 tablespoons potato starch, and ¼ teaspoon each cinnamon, nutmeg, and salt, and toss with the drained peaches until well blended. Stir in 1 teaspoon almond extract. Spread evenly in the prepared pan. Prepare the topping as directed, and bake as directed.

Per serving:
365 calories;
4g protein;
9g total fat;
3g fiber;
77g carbohydrates;
52mg cholesterol;
274mg sodium

Peach Cobbler
Per serving:
355 calories;
3g protein;
9g total fat;
3g fiber;
70g carbohydrates;
52mg cholesterol;
361mg sodium

Mini Cream Puffs

Cream puffs may look hard to make, but in reality, they are really quite simple. Serve these dainty little gems filled with whipped topping and dusted with powdered sugar. Or drizzle with chocolate for a French touch. Stir cocoa powder into the whipped topping for a chocolate filling. Larger cream puffs (made with a larger ice cream scoop or spoon) make great sandwiches with savory fillings such as chicken salad, egg salad, or ham salad. Drop a dozen 2-inch mounds of dough on the baking sheet and bake as directed in Step 5, then slice in half just like a hamburger bun.

V

Makes 24 cream puffs

Preparation time: 15 minutes

Baking time: 25 to 35 minutes

Per cream puff:
75 calories;
1g protein;
4g total fat;
1g fiber;
9g carbohydrates;
30mg cholesterol;
58mg sodium

½ cup white or brown rice flour
¼ cup potato starch
¾ cup water
5 tablespoons butter or buttery spread
2 teaspoons sugar

¼ teaspoon salt
3 large eggs, at room temperature
1 cup whipped cream or whipped topping
½ cup gluten-free chocolate syrup
   Powdered sugar, for garnish (optional)

1 Preheat the oven to 450°F. Line a 9x13-inch baking sheet (not nonstick) with parchment paper. Whisk together the rice flour and potato starch and have it ready by the stovetop.

2 In a medium heavy saucepan, bring the water, butter, sugar, and salt to a boil over medium-high heat. Immediately remove the pan from the heat and add the flour mixture all at once, stirring with a wooden spoon until the flour is no longer visible. Return the pan to the heat and continue stirring until the mixture pulls away from the sides of the pan and a film forms on the bottom of the pan.

3 Remove the pan from the heat and let cool for 5 minutes. Transfer the mixture to a medium bowl. Beat in the eggs with an electric mixer on medium speed, one at a time, mixing well after each addition until smooth before adding the next egg. (Or, use a food processor to blend everything together.)

4 Using a 1¼-inch-diameter spring-action metal ice cream scoop or a small spoon, drop 24 mounds of dough (1¼ inches each) onto the baking sheet at least 1 inch apart. With a wet finger, press in protruding bits of dough so the top is smooth and the puffs will brown more evenly.

5 Bake for 15 minutes (20 minutes for large cream puffs), then reduce the oven temperature to 350°F and continue baking until the cream puffs are deep golden brown, about another 10 minutes (another 15 minutes for large cream puffs). Remove the cream puffs from the oven. Immediately cut a 1-inch horizontal slit in the side of each cream puff, right where you will eventually cut them completely in half. Cool the cream puffs on the baking sheet on the wire rack. When completely cool, cut in half horizontally along the slit and fill with whipped cream or topping, about 2 teaspoons per cream puff. Drizzle with 1 teaspoon chocolate syrup and dust with powdered sugar, if desired. Serve immediately.

Crêpes

Despite their association with fancy desserts, crêpes are actually quite easy to make and not all that much different from making pancakes—they're just a little thinner. Crêpes are often folded or rolled, making them a very pretty and elegant dessert. But they can also be filled with scrambled eggs for breakfast or with creamed chicken or turkey for dinner.

V

Makes 12 small crepes (6 servings)

Preparation time: 10 minutes

Cooking time: 35 to 45 minutes

Per serving:
105 calories;
4g protein;
3g total fat;
1g fiber;
16g carbohydrates;
64mg cholesterol;
78mg sodium

⅔ cup Gluten-Free Flour Blend (page 27)
2 teaspoons sugar
⅛ teaspoon xanthan gum
⅛ teaspoon salt
¾ cup milk of choice
2 large eggs
2 teaspoons butter or buttery spread, melted and cooled

1 In a blender, combine all of the ingredients and process until very smooth, about 30 seconds. Let the batter stand for at least 15 minutes at room temperature (or refrigerate in an airtight container for up to 1 day; bring to room temperature and whisk before cooking the crêpes).

2 Heat an 8-inch nonstick skillet (gray, not black) or a skillet specially designed for crêpes over medium heat and lightly coat with butter. Add 2 to 3 tablespoons batter and quickly swirl the skillet so that the batter completely covers the bottom. Cook until the underside of the crêpe is golden brown, 2 to 3 minutes.

3 Loosen the edge of the crêpe with a rubber spatula, then with the spatula or your fingertips, quickly flip the crêpe. Cook for 1 minute more. Slide the crêpe out of the skillet onto a sheet of parchment paper and repeat with the remaining batter, stacking the crêpes between sheets of parchment paper to prevent sticking. The first crepe may not turn out as well if the skillet is too hot—or not hot enough—so some adjustment may be needed. Coat the pan with additional butter as needed. Use these crêpes in any recipe calling for crêpes.

Chocolate Pudding

I grew up on chocolate pudding. It was quick and inexpensive, and everyone in the family liked it, so it was served often. I prepare it often when we want a smooth and creamy comfort food dessert. I like to eat it while it's still warm; my husband prefers it chilled. Either way, it's delicious.

½ cup packed brown sugar
⅓ cup unsweetened cocoa powder
   (either natural or Dutch-process
   will work)
3 tablespoons cornstarch*
⅛ teaspoon salt
2 cups milk of choice
1 tablespoon butter or buttery spread
1 teaspoon pure vanilla extract

1 In a medium heavy saucepan, whisk together the sugar, cocoa, cornstarch, and salt until well blended. Gradually whisk in the milk until well blended and cook over medium heat, stirring constantly with a heatproof spatula, until the mixture starts to boil. Cook for 30 seconds, stirring constantly as it thickens.

2 Remove from the heat; stir in the butter and vanilla until thoroughly blended. Pour into a serving bowl or 4 individual dessert bowls and press a sheet of plastic wrap on the top to prevent a skin from forming. Chill until firm, about 2 hours, then serve.

Q, V
Makes 4 servings (about ½ cup each)
Preparation time: 5 minutes
Chilling time: 2 hours

Per serving: 235 calories; 6g protein; 5g total fat; 2g fiber; 42g carbohydrates; 13mg cholesterol; 239mg sodium

❨ *Use ¼ cup cornstarch if using rice milk or coconut milk or any low-protein milk substitute.

Chocolate-Cherry Bread Pudding

Bread pudding is the quintessential down-home dessert, probably developed by thrifty grandmothers to use up stale bread. But today it has become quite trendy in upscale restaurants, with a wide variety of different approaches. My modern version contains dark chocolate and dried cherries. Serve it slightly warm while the chocolate chips are mouthwateringly soft. You can use store-bought bread or your own homemade bread for this old-fashioned dessert, but white bread works best.

V

Makes 12 servings

Preparation time: 15 minutes

Baking time: 45 to 55 minutes

Per serving:
530 calories;
14g protein;
11g total fat;
4g fiber;
98g carbohydrates;
65mg cholesterol;
780mg sodium

6 cups gluten-free bread cut into 1-inch cubes (no need to trim crusts)
1 cup gluten-free dark chocolate chips
½ cup dried cherries or cranberries
½ cup chopped walnuts, almonds, or pecans
2 cups milk of choice (the richer the better), at room temperature
½ cup sugar
½ teaspoon ground cinnamon
½ teaspoon salt
4 large eggs, at room temperature
2 teaspoons pure vanilla extract
1 cup gluten-free chocolate syrup or fudge sauce

1 Place a rack in the middle of the oven. Preheat the oven to 325°F. Grease an 8-inch square glass baking dish. Spread half of the bread cubes evenly in the dish. Scatter half of the chocolate chips on top, followed by all of the cherries and nuts.

2 In a medium bowl, whisk together the milk, sugar, cinnamon, salt, eggs, and vanilla until well blended. Pour half of the milk mixture evenly on top of the bread. Add the remaining bread cubes, sprinkle with the remaining chocolate chips, and then pour the remaining milk mixture on top. Let stand for 15 minutes, occasionally pressing down on the bread with a wide spatula to make sure all of the bread cubes are moistened.

3 Bake until the top is nicely browned, 45 to 55 minutes. Lay a sheet of aluminum foil on top for the first 30 minutes, then remove it to let the top brown during the last 15 minutes of baking. Cool the bread pudding in the pan for 15 minutes. To serve, cut the bread pudding into 9 slices and serve warm, drizzled with the chocolate syrup.

Chocolate-Cherry Individual Trifles

Trifles are like parfaits; they are simply layered desserts, served in glass goblets to show off the pretty ingredients—such as the layers of bright red cherry pie filling in this version—nestled inside. If you have leftover chocolate cake or brownies, crumble it and use instead of chocolate cookies.

¼ teaspoon almond extract
2 cups store-bought vanilla pudding or Vanilla Pudding (page 222), chilled
1½ cups cherry pie filling
8 gluten-free chocolate cookies, coarsely crushed
Shaved chocolate, for garnish

Stir the almond extract into the pudding until well blended. Place ¼ cup pudding in each of 4 glass parfait glasses or wineglasses. Top each with 3 tablespoons of the cherry pie filling, then a crushed cookie, then ¼ cup of the pudding. Top each with another crushed cookie, then another 3 tablespoons of the cherry pie filling. Refrigerate for at least 2 hours. Serve cold, garnished with a shaving of chocolate.

V

Makes 4 individual trifles
Preparation time: 10 minutes
Chilling time: 2 hours

Per trifle:
355 calories;
6g protein;
9g total fat;
1g fiber;
63g carbohydrates;
224mg cholesterol;
92mg sodium

Vanilla Pudding

Silky smooth and creamy, this simple pudding is perfect with a dollop of whipped topping. It is creamiest and richest when made with whole milk (or half-and-half), but it is delicious when made with whatever milk substitute you choose, including coconut milk.

V

Makes 4 servings (about ½ cup each)
Preparation time: 10 minutes
Chilling time: 2 hours

Per serving:
250 calories;
6g protein;
9g total fat;
1g fiber;
36g carbohydrates;
224mg cholesterol;
83mg sodium

❱ *Use ¼ cup cornstarch if using rice milk or coconut milk or any low-protein milk substitute.

- 4 large egg yolks, at room temperature
- 1½ cups whole milk or milk of choice
- ½ cup sugar
- 3 tablespoons cornstarch*
- 1 tablespoon butter or buttery spread
- 2 teaspoons pure vanilla extract

1 In a medium heavy saucepan, beat the egg yolks with an electric mixer on medium speed until thick and lemon-colored, 30 to 40 seconds, and then beat in the milk until well blended.

2 In a small bowl, whisk together the sugar and cornstarch until well blended. Slowly beat the sugar-cornstarch mixture into the egg yolk mixture on low speed until very smooth.

3 Place the saucepan over medium heat and cook, whisking constantly, until the pudding thickens, 5 to 7 minutes (depending on the type of milk used).

4 Remove the pudding from the heat and stir in the butter and vanilla until smooth. Pour into a serving bowl or 4 individual dessert bowls and press a sheet of plastic wrap on the top to prevent a skin from forming. Chill for 2 hours before serving.

Pudding Mix

Making pudding is even easier when you keep this easy dry mix in your pantry. It makes five batches of pudding (2 cups each), and each batch serves four people.

8 cups nonfat dry milk powder (not Carnation) or Better Than Milk soy powder
2 cups sugar
1 cup cornstarch
1 teaspoon salt

Q, V
Makes 20 servings (about ½ cup each)
Preparation time: 5 minutes
Chilling time: 2 hours

Whisk all of the ingredients together until thoroughly combined and store, tightly covered, in a dark, dry place.

Vanilla Pudding from Pudding Mix

In a heavy saucepan, whisk together 2 cups water and 4 egg yolks until very smooth. Whisk in 2 cups Pudding Mix. Cook the mixture over medium-high heat, whisking constantly, until the pudding thickens. Remove from the heat and stir in 1 teaspoon pure vanilla extract. Pour into a serving bowl or 4 individual dessert bowls and press a sheet of plastic wrap on the top to prevent a skin from forming. Chill for 2 hours before serving.

Per serving (½ cup): 310 calories; 15g protein; 5g total fat; 1g fiber; 50g carbohydrates; 219mg cholesterol; 331mg sodium

Chocolate Pudding from Pudding Mix

In a heavy saucepan, whisk together 2 cups water, 2 cups Pudding Mix, and ¼ cup unsweetened cocoa until very smooth. Cook the mixture over medium-high heat, whisking constantly, until the pudding thickens. Remove from the heat and stir in 1 teaspoon pure vanilla extract. Pour into a serving bowl or 4 individual dessert bowls and press a sheet of plastic wrap on the top to prevent a skin from forming. Chill for 2 hours before serving.

Per serving (½ cup): 270 calories; 13g protein; 1g total fat; 2g fiber; 53g carbohydrates; 6mg cholesterol; 327mg sodium

Replacing Nonfat Dry Milk Powder

If you're dairy sensitive, use soy-based or rice-based nondairy milk powders such as Better Than Milk. They are available in natural foods stores or online. Carnation, the brand that many people have in their pantries, is not nonfat dry milk powder. Instead, it is granular rather than powdered and is not as concentrated in sugar and protein, hence it doesn't enhance desserts as well as nonfat dry milk powder.

Mini Cheesecakes with Cherries

There's something about the creamy, rich texture of cheesecake that lures me in—and everyone I know, too. One way to make cheesecake more fun when entertaining is with these pretty little mini cheesecakes, made in small, ready-to-serve portions that eliminate the last-minute fuss of plating. I use reduced-fat cream cheese in this version, but you can use full-fat cream cheese if you prefer.

 6 gluten-free vanilla or lemon cookies
16 ounces reduced-fat cream cheese or
      cream cheese alternative
 ½ cup sugar
 1 teaspoon pure vanilla extract
 2 large eggs, at room temperature
 ¾ cup cherry pie filling

1 Preheat the oven to 325°F. Place a paper or foil cupcake liner in each cup of a standard 12-cup nonstick muffin pan (gray, not black). Crumble half of a cookie into the bottom of each liner.

2 In a large bowl, beat the cream cheese, sugar, and vanilla with an electric mixer on medium speed until well blended, then add the eggs and mix just until they are incorporated. Divide the filling among the liners.

3 Bake until the tops are dry and just start to crack, 30 to 35 minutes. Remove the pan from the oven and cool the cupcakes in the pan for 15 minutes. They may fall slightly; but the cherry topping will fill the indentation. Remove the mini cheesecakes from the pan and refrigerate for 2 hours.

4 At serving time, remove the cheesecakes from the liners (discard the liners), place each cheesecake on a dessert plate, and serve, topped with 2 tablespoons of cherry pie filling.

V

Makes 12 mini cheesecakes
Preparation time: 10 minutes
Baking time: 30 to 35 minutes
Chilling time: 2 hours

Per cheesecake: 160 calories; 5g protein; 10g total fat; 1g fiber; 14g carbohydrates; 60mg cholesterol; 162mg sodium

Menus ❯

Winter Supper
Meat Loaf (page 104)
Scalloped Potatoes (without ham)
    (page 101)
steamed broccoli
Cherry-Almond Clafouti (page 214)

Sunday Dinner with the Family
Roasted Chicken with Gravy (page 116)
mashed potatoes
steamed carrots and peas
Dinner Rolls (page 170)
Toasted Coconut Cupcakes with Fluffy
    White Frosting (page 206)

Diner Dinner
Chicken-Fried Steak with Gravy (page 99)
mashed potatoes
steamed green beans
Cherry Cobbler (page 215)

Small Dinner Party
Pan-Roasted Pork Tenderloin with
    Honey-Mustard Pan Sauce (page 107)
brown rice
steamed broccolini
French Baguettes (page 156)
Flourless Chocolate Cake (page 199)

Weekend Brunch
Quiche Lorraine (page 62)
Cranberry-Orange Muffins (page 136)
fresh fruit salad

Comfort Food Supper for Autumn
Swiss Steak (page 113)
basmati rice
steamed green beans
Apple-Spice Cake (page 203)

Too-Tired-to-Cook Supper
Black Bean Soup (page 84)
vegetable sticks
Vanilla Pudding from Pudding
    Mix (page 223)

Winter Supper
Six-Layer Casserole (page 108)
mixed green salad
"Cracked Wheat" Bread (page 152)
Gingerbread (page 200)

Tailgate Party
Marinated Flank Steak with
    Herbs (page 102)
Pasta Salad with Italian
    Dressing (page 94)
Focaccia Bread (page 171)
Double-Chocolate Cookies (page 177)

For Kids Young and Old
Chicken Fingers (page 122)
Macaroni & Cheese (page 133)
vegetable sticks
Chocolate Pudding (page 219)

Italian Dinner
Spaghetti & Meatballs (page 110)
Focaccia Flatbread (page 171)
mixed green salad
Almond Meringue Cookies (page 176)

Southwest Supper
One-Skillet Tortilla Casserole (page 103)
mixed green salad
corn tortillas
Lemon Bars (page 190)

**Cool-as-a-Cucumber Vegetarian
Light Supper**
Whole-Grain Sorghum Salad (page 97)
Breadsticks (page 168)
Ice Cream Pie (page 210)

Make Mine Vegetarian, Please
Hash Brown Casserole (page 132)
White Bean Salad with Peppers and
    Olives (page 93)
Popovers (page 154)
Carrot Bundt Cake (page 196)

One-Pot-Wonder Meal
One-Pot Roasted Salmon on Mediterranean
    Vegetables and Rice (page 125)
Breadsticks (page 168)
Coconut Macaroons (page 178)

**South-of-the-Border Slow Cooker
Meal**
Slow Cooker Pork Shoulder
    Roast (page 109)
baked sweet potatoes
pinto beans
Corn Bread (page 144)
Mexican Wedding Cakes (page 183)

Friday Night Pizza with the Guys
Veggie Pizza (page 128)
vegetable tray
Chocolate Brownies (page 188)
gluten-free beer

Brands Used in Developing Recipes ❱

This list of ingredients is not an endorsement of these companies but a list of the brands used in developing the recipes in this book (so you know they work). These brands were gluten-free at the time, but always read labels before buying any food or ingredient to make sure it is gluten-free. Manufacturers can change ingredients or manufacturing practices, making a formerly gluten-free product no longer safe. Also, some manufacturers use similar packages for their gluten-containing and gluten-free products, so reading the labels is imperative to distinguish between the two.

Baking and Cooking Aids
Apple pectin: Now
Butterscotch morsels: HyVee, Safeway, Shurfine
Chocolate chips: Sunspire, Enjoy Life Foods, Ghirardelli
Chocolate cookies: Pamela's Dark Chocolate Chocolate Chunk
Cookie crumbs: Pamela's
Dry milk powder (nonfat): Organic Valley
Dry milk powder substitute: Better Than Milk soy milk powder
Guar gum: Bob's Red Mill
Shortening (non-hydrogenated): Spectrum, Earth Balance, Crisco
White chocolate chips: Sunspire
Xanthan gum: Bob's Red Mill

Beverages and Drinks
Coffee creamer (plain): Silk, So Delicious
Milk of choice:
  almond: Silk
  coconut: So Delicious
  flax: Flax USA, Good Karma
  hazelnut: Pacific Natural Foods
  hemp: Living Harvest
  rice: Rice Dream
  soy: Silk
  sunflower: SOL, Sunsational

Bread, Tortillas, and Crackers
Corn tortillas: Mission
Crackers: Edward & Sons, Mary's Gone Crackers, Flackers, Crunchmasters
Flour tortillas: Food for Life, La Tortilla Factory, Rudi's
Graham crackers: Kinnikinnick
Italian breadsticks (grissini): Dr. Schär
Polenta tube: Food Merchants
Rice bran crackers: Health Valley
Sandwich bread: Rudi's, Udi's, Whole Foods, Canyon Bakehouse

Candy, Desserts, Toppings, and Sauces
Chocolate syrup: Hershey's
Marshmallows: Kraft Jet-Puffed
Vanilla pudding: Kozy Shack, Better Bowls
Whipped cream or topping: Lucerne, Soyatoo

Cereal
Brown rice crisps: Erewhon, Barbara's
Corn flakes: Nature's Path, Erewhon
Puffed rice cereal: Erewhon, Kellogg's

Condiments
Beau monde seasoning: Spice Islands
Fish sauce: Taste of Thai, Thai Kitchen
Hoisin sauce: Premier Japan
Mexican salsa: Mission, Tostito
Soy Parmesan: Galaxy
Soy sauce: San-J, Kikkoman
Worcestershire sauce: French's (also Lea & Perrins in the United States, but not in Canada)

Dairy and Cheese
Cheese alternative: Vegan Gourmet, Daiya
Cream cheese alternative: Tofutti, Vegan Gourmet
Cultured coconut milk (also known as kefir): So Delicious
Dry milk powder (nonfat): Organic Valley
Dry milk powder substitute: Better Than Milk soy powder
Mozzarella or cheddar cheese alternative wedges: Daiya

Parmesan cheese, Galaxy
Sour cream alternative: Tofutti, Vegan Gourmet

Flours and Grains
Almond flour/meal: Bob's Red Mill, Honeyville Farms
Amaranth (flour and whole grain): Bob's Red Mill
Brown rice: Bob's Red Mill
Buckwheat flour: Bob's Red Mill (or grind Bob's Red Mill
	Creamy Buckwheat Hot Cereal into flour with a small
	coffee grinder)
Buckwheat groats: Bob's Red Mill
Corn grits (polenta): Bob's Red Mill
Cornmeal (yellow): Bob's Red Mill
Kañiwa (baby quinoa): Roland
Millet (flour and whole grain): Bob's Red Mill
Millet grits/meal: Bob's Red Mill
Oat bran: Bob's Red Mill
Oat groats: Bob's Red Mill
Oats (steel-cut): Bob's Red Mill
Quinoa: Bob's Red Mill
Rice bran: Bob's Red Mill
Sorghum (flour and whole grain): Bob's Red Mill
Sweet rice: Bob's Red Mill
Teff: Bob's Red Mill, Teff Company
Wild rice: Lundberg

Meats
Deli meat: Boar's Head
Ham: Boar's Head
Italian sausage: Applegate
Pepperoni slices: Hormel
Pork sausage: Jimmy Dean

Pasta
Elbow macaroni: Tinkyada
Penne or spiral pasta: Tinkyada
Spaghetti pasta: Tinkyada

Soups
Beef broth: Swanson's
Bouillon powder or cubes: Ener-G, Herb-Ox, Lee Kum Kee
Chicken broth: Swanson Natural Goodness
Creamy mushroom soup: Imagine, Progresso
Tomato soup: Imagine

Vegetables (Canned)
Mexican-style tomatoes: Ro-Tel

Miscellaneous
Plastic wrap (must be heavy-duty or premium): Saran

Index❯

Page numbers in *italics* indicate illustrations